His Art

God's Messages of Truth to Us Through the Elements & Principles of Design

Paula L. Moore

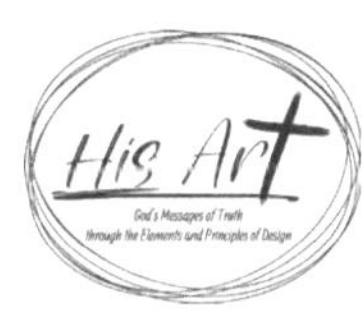

Nixa, MO

HIS ART: GOD'S MESSAGES OF TRUTH TO US THROUGH THE ELEMENTS & PRINCIPLES OF DESIGN

Paperback ISBN: 979-8-9923911-0-7

 Published by His Art, contact paula@paulamooreart.com.

For more information on Paula L. Moore, visit https://www.PaulaMooreArt.com

Cover and interior design by Debra L. Butterfield, Butterfield Editorial Services

Printed in the United States

Foreword

Paula is a caring, gifted artist and teacher. When she took my first *en plein aire* painting workshop, I realized she was very hungry for knowledge and soaked it up like a sponge. She has been able to use this knowledge in her own unique way, translating it to her students.

She has a beautiful philosophy of life and art. Paula has incorporated the Scriptures with the language of art using the fifteen words of design. She has broken it down into simple terms, using the elements and principles in an easily understood manner.

Her vision of how she created the two forms of art through God's teaching is a testament to her creativity and faith. You will be impressed with her easily understood language of art, her self-critique kaleidoscope guide for painting, and her journey into His Art.

~ Jane E. Jones, award-winning artist and instructor, co-author of *Creativity Through Design*

Paula, what a delight and blessing to be included in your work "His Art" endeavor! In the very beginning, I was caught up in your vision and how hearing from God can be blurred by the busyness of life. Deeper still, I am so happy that I reread this work after my return from our trip to Alaska. The scenes of God's glorious creation are still fresh in my mind's eye. Although I am art-challenged, I found myself applying these ideas to both the study of God's word and approaching a new piece of instrumental music. Your dedication and heart in teaching not only art but the truth of The Lord's gospel is a blessing to those kids and to the work of Canaan Church. Thank you for your kind words.

~ Brother Mike Rowan, Deacon, Adult Sunday School Instructor, Musician,
Canaan, Missionary Baptist Church, Springfield, MO

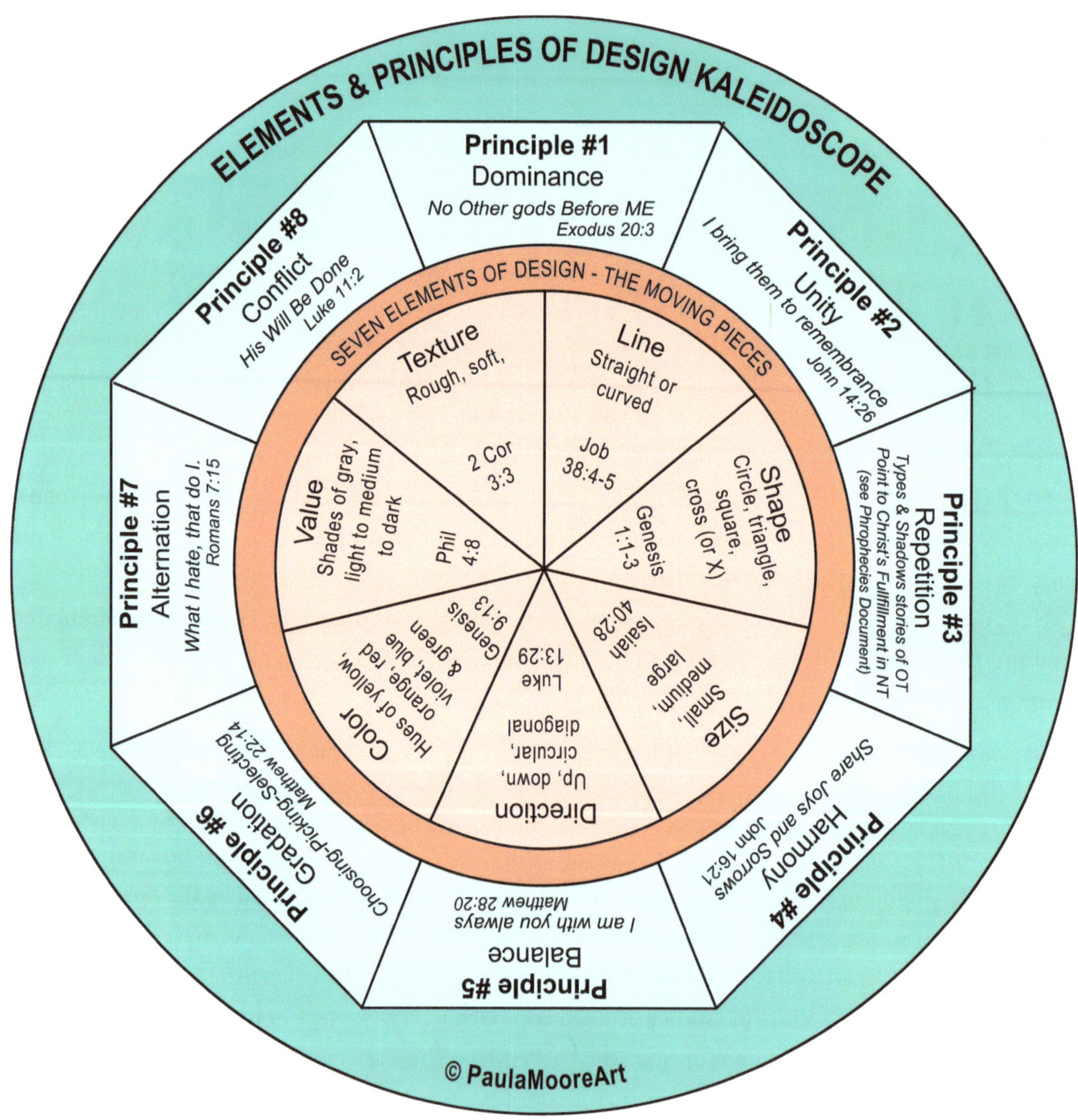
ELEMENTS & PRINCIPLES OF DESIGN KALEIDOSCOPE
Principle #1
Dominance
No Other gods Before ME
Exodus 20:3
Principle #2
Unity
I bring them to remembrance
John 14:26
Principle #3
Repetition
Types & Shadows stories of OT
Point to Christ's Fulfillment in NT
(see Phrophecies Document)
Principle #4
Harmony
Share Joys and Sorrows
John 16:21
Principle #5
Balance
I am with you always
Matthew 28:20
Principle #6
Gradation
Choosing-Picking-Selecting
Matthew 22:14
Principle #7
Alternation
What I hate, that do I.
Romans 7:15
Principle #8
Conflict
His Will Be Done
Luke 11:2
SEVEN ELEMENTS OF DESIGN - THE MOVING PIECES
Line
Straight or curved
Job 38:4-5
Shape
Circle, triangle, square, cross (or X)
Genesis 1:1-3
Size
Small, medium, large
Isaiah 40:28
Direction
Up, down, circular, diagonal
Luke 13:29
Color
Hues of yellow, orange, red violet, blue & green
Genesis 9:13
Value
Shades of gray, light to medium to dark
Phil 4:8
Texture
Rough, soft,
2 Cor 3:3
© PaulaMooreArt

Contents

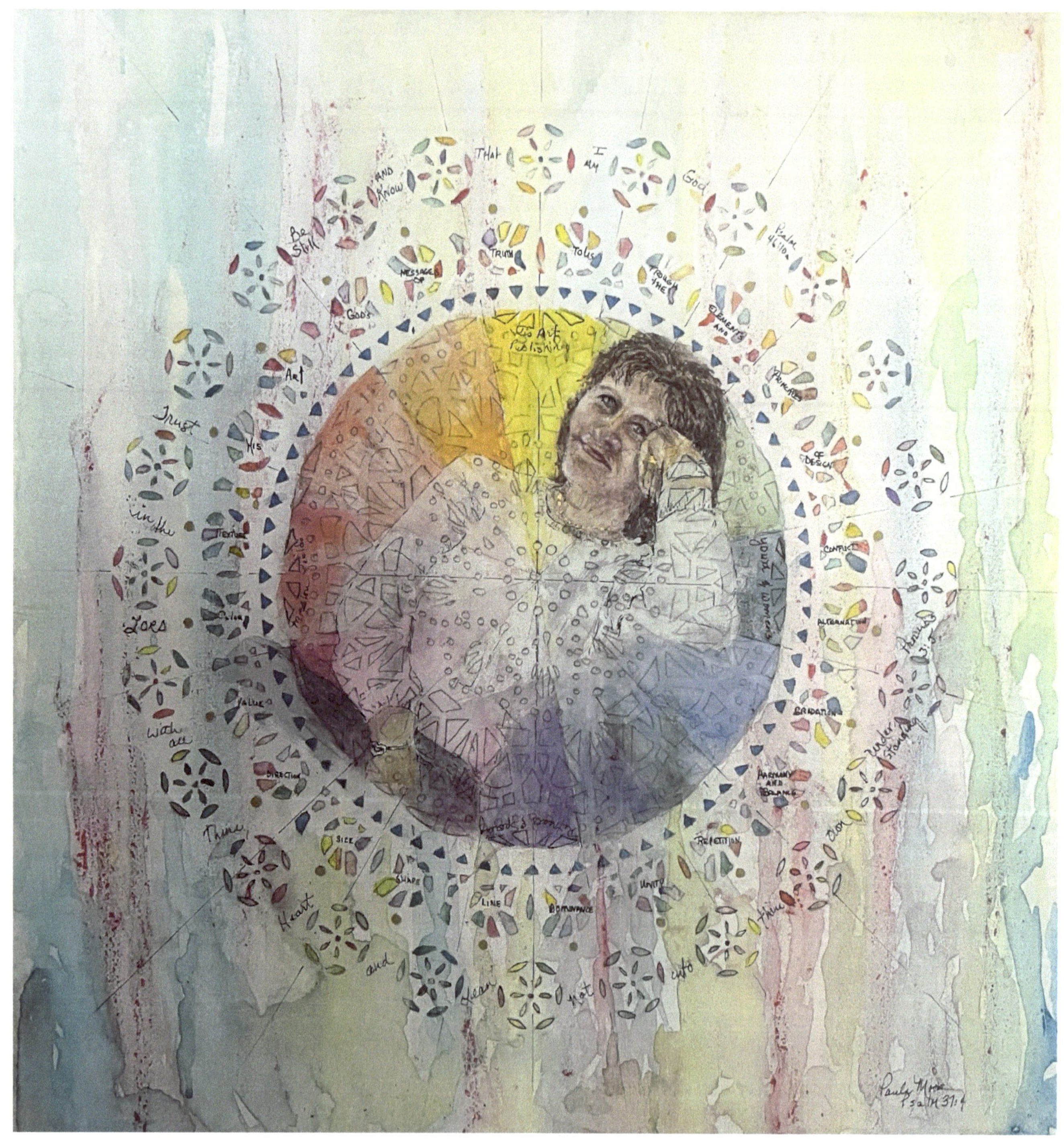

Be Still and Know That I am God Psalm 46:10a
God's Messages of Truth To us Trough the Elements and Principles of Design
Art
Texture
Color
Value
Direction
Size
Shape
Line
Dominance
Unity
Repetition
Harmony and Balance
Gradation
Alternation
Conflict
Trust His in the Lors with all Thine Heart and lean not unto thine own understanding

Why This Book

"How Great Thou Art!" — I recall listening to my father's clear tenor voice leading the congregation in this song of praise to the Creator. Even as a child, I could close my eyes and envision every scene each verse presented. I now realize why this favorite hymn has always resonated with me and stayed with me throughout my life. It was a seed planted for the dream purpose offered to me.

Years later, a friend mentioned a poem that deeply touched my soul again. Suddenly, I considered that beloved hymn differently! Through these words, I envisioned God, with his holy paintbrush, painting the scenes each verse sang out. How Great Thou ART was not only from the old English language expressing an action verb. Instead, it was the subject. As in, "O God, How Great is YOUR ART!"

The Great Artist

Robert Boggs

Minute crystals of beauty lay sparkling on the ground

From the freshly fallen snow which came without a sound.

This cover of splendor is more beautiful than any artist could ever paint, For God the Great Artist did it without restraint.

Only God could bring about such a great work of art, And cause His creation to respond, O God, how great Thou Art.

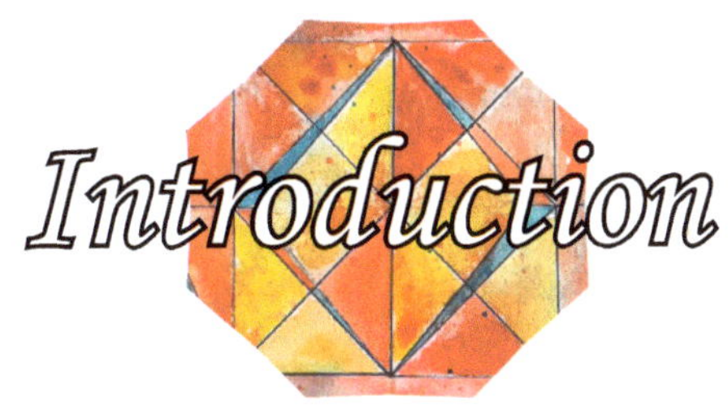

Introduction

Whispers of My Soul's Dream Purpose

I truly believe that God gives each soul a dream purpose before they are even born. This dream purpose, when carried out, gives glory and honor to him. Certainly, he does not need us to do anything. God is all-knowing, all-seeing, all-in control. His desire is for our obedience. He invites each of us to pursue the unique dream purpose which he bestows to us individually, and it is an invitation to come dream and plan with him! Ponder these two verses and see if they do not complement each other!

"Delight thyself also in the Lord; and he shall give thee the desires of thine heart" (Psalms 37:4).

"And we know that all things work together for good to them that love God, to them who are the called according to HIS purpose" (Romans 8:28).

I have also concluded that each of us must search for our Dream Purpose. He knows our talents and strengths and desires us to give them back to him. Additionally, it is not revealed to us all in one finished work. More importantly, it is our choice to accept it since he will not force it upon us. It is a journey of walking and communicating with the Holy Spirit. He whispers to us in a still, small voice.

I have known for some time that my dream purpose was to blend somehow my love of God and my love of art. The plan did not come to me until I was ready and willing to hear it, when I became earnest in discovering how to accomplish my quest; that still, small voice began pouring out ideas and methods for organizing and painting it out.

The song and the poem were the first two whispers I was ready to hear. Then, there was a third whisper and a fourth.

The Third Whisper

My desire to improve as an artist probably started in a small town called Lake City in the southwest corner of Colorado. What good comes from a little place with a total population of approximately 400 residents? An old town that has no stoplights and more dirt roads than paved? Surprising events are born out of obscure locations. In scripture, there is a short conversation between Philip and Nathanael about this man called Jesus. His hometown was a little village of no importance, perhaps no more than 300 Jews simply living their day-to-day lives. Nathanael asks Philip, "Can any good thing come out of Nazareth? Philip saith unto him, come and see" (John 1:46).

Majestic 14,000-ft. elevation mountains surround Lake City, Colorado; it is home to the second largest lake in the state, Lake San Cristobal. The thriving art community is inspired by the beauty all around them. Each summer, we drove close to 1,000 miles to experience life in the mountains again. I always bring my watercolors and supplies with the intent of capturing nature's surrounding essence. One year, I visited the new Lake City Gallery, which features the watercolor renditions of Jane E. Jones. Can you imagine my excitement when I learned Jane resides in Lake City and is teaching a workshop that week? I took a chance to call her studio in the hope of meeting and learning from her. After that session of painting outside and meeting new artists, I was hooked. I have found my mentor friend, who can lead me to another level of creating art. We begin planning our vacations around Jane's workshop. I also find an art tribe as some of those original painters continue to be dear friends.

Starting in 2004, I signed up every year for Jane's yearly Summer Workshop, en plein Aire, a French phrase meaning painting a landscape scene outdoors. Painting outside sounds easy and fun, doesn't it? It is enjoyable, although not for the faint of heart. Wind, rain, bugs, moose, and the light and colors change. Packing all your art supplies, easels, and other necessary gear sometimes makes it challenging, and you learn to pack just the essentials. However, you are thoroughly enjoying the fresh mountain air of God's colorful Colorado! Jane shared with us the following year that she was offering a Color Theory Workshop and a Design Principles Workshop in Dallas, Texas. "I think I'm interested in registering for them, Jane." To my surprise, Jane replied, "You aren't ready to learn the more difficult concepts yet. Just keep learning and stay with it. You'll be ready soon." Her wise advice was taken to heart; I did what she instructed and increased my painting efforts and understanding. The following summer, I studied under Jane again. With a smile at the end of the week-long workshop, she leaned in close and said quietly, "You're ready for both my Color Theory and Language of Design studies." I realize now that it would have been too much to grasp this art language when I first approached Jane. In her wisdom, she knew I would be overwhelmed with the concepts. I wasn't ready then. With my efforts to study and practice, I felt the thrill of comprehending something greater. Apparently, Jane thought I was on the brink of more, and I was encouraged by her extending the invitation! Undoubtedly, I had a heart of willingness. Remember this little story, as there will be more on this concept in a spiritual sense.

A few months later, I flew to Dallas and was privileged to stay at the home of Jane and her dear husband, Elwyn. I will never forget how welcoming I felt and how strangely confident! I had the overwhelming willingness to take a step toward understanding this next step as an artist. I would be a student in the "Color Theory Workshop." Before I took the study, I assumed I had a fair understanding of color theory. On the contrary, I actually understood very little. I absorbed so much from this intensive study. It was the beginning of a foundation of understanding.

Then, I was able to take the Language of Design Workshop in the spring. I had no idea what I would learn, only the earnest awareness that if I was to become a better artist, I needed this course. I trusted Jane in her encouragement that I needed a stronger grasp of the elements and principles of design language and how intricately they work together. There were only fifteen conceptual words we were going to explore in this so-called language. How hard can it be?

It was absolutely the most challenging class I have ever attempted, and that includes even looking back on my college courses. I desired this art knowledge so much, and I pressed towards the mark, determined to understand the language. I remember something Jane stated in the middle of teaching. She said, "These elements and principles of design are nothing new! I didn't think this up! It is in God's Nature—everywhere you look! Everything you are learning can be observed!" Really? I would have to start looking more closely. Each exercise was exciting, thrilling, and scary all at the same time. I would take my work up for Jane to review, and she would always have a change for me to make. What was I not understanding? What was the missing key I needed to unlock this door of design? Then, in an instant, that last afternoon session, I found it. I got it. I understood. There must be the principle of dominance within every element. This mysterious art language kaleidoscope was coming into focus, one click at a time. More on this thought later as well.

I flew back home exhausted but hopeful. I clutch my jumbo three-ring binder, plastic-sleeved protected Elements and Principles of Design written course, including photos, original drawings, and forty-plus pages of handwritten notes. I was ready now to conquer the art world with my newly acquired head-knowledge manual of how-tos. I knew it on paper. However, not by heart, and that fact was uncomfortable. What if I lost this information or forgot all I had learned! "It is everywhere you look," Jane had said. In God's ART, I wondered?

The Fourth Whisper

I am quite aware that I will not be able to describe what I experienced next. Hopefully, by sharing my Dream Purpose, I will be able to paint a picture for you of all the components. It is essential for me to share with you the touch points of how this writing all came about. My hope is that you, too, will find God's messages of truth through the elements and principles of design.

I returned home from my design workshop with all the concepts and design language swirling through my head like turning clicks of a kaleidoscope. How could I ever organize and understand how to translate all I had learned through my art? It was daunting to think I would ever see things with clarity.

The following Sunday morning, we participated in our Sunday school class, taught by Mike Rowan. His many hours of studying biblical topics confirm his gift as a deep thinker and teacher of the Word. That particular day, he was starting a new series on the book of Revelation. As you may know already, this last book of the Bible is a mystery to many and difficult to understand. On this side of eternity, I believe we are unable to comprehend all that is relayed to us from John on the Isle of Patmos. He was envisioning so many events all at once and tried his best to describe what he was experiencing.

Mike began by comparing the book of Revelation to a painting of Christ and God's plan coming to fruition. That perked up my artist's ears. "What? A painting?"– (remember, I had just returned from an intensive study of art theory.) He described the book as watching a movie. You are watching one particular scene in its totality; however, there are many camera perspectives from which you are observing the scene. One camera lines up to show how it looks from the left, another one directs your focus to the right, and then another one will show the very same shot from above. There might be a close-up to see the texture of white flowing robes. You'll watch the same view several times, going back and forth in repetition. Some cameras record speeding up, and others bring you around again to where he leads you to observe. Revelation is a recording of John visualizing everything at once!

Literally, I was trembling. As Mike introduced us to this study, he echoed the very same language of design I had just studied the week before! Could it be that I was being offered the answer to my imploring soul search to the question: How Great is HIS ART? Could his creation and his message to us in the scriptures hold the original kaleidoscope blueprint of the very same elements and principles of design?

I meekly thought to myself, Have I perhaps just been given a key to open the door to a deeper understanding? I began my discovery quest that very morning and shared it with Mike, after the lesson, I knew he was aware something was happening to me because a few soul tears welled up in my eyes. I wanted to filter all I had learned through God's Word. Would I find truth? The Whisper was gently leading me to search it out. Reading, praying, listening, drawing, painting, and observing have brought me to this point.

Jane was correct. Everything you're learning can be observed in God's creation!

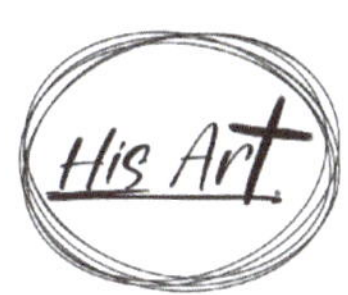

"They said unto him, Lord, that our eyes may be opened. So, Jesus had compassion on them and touched their eyes; and immediately their eyes received sight and they followed him" (Matthew 20:33–34).

After each chapter, there will be one or more Scripture selections inspired by the story. Please take a moment to reflect upon how the story relates to the Word.

Additionally, I have a section entitled "Kaleidoscope Click" at the end of each chapter. I have called it this as a comparison to every turn of the kaleidoscope; you discover something new and interesting. It is my challenge for you to search out the elements and principles of design of his art in nature and life. Please keep your eyes of faith wide open so you won't miss them. (Here's a clue – his ART is everywhere!) I suggest keeping a sketch journal using your chosen art medium, whether pencils or paints, to jot down some notes and capture your discoveries on paper. Even if you have ten or fifteen minutes a day, you can create a special time to do this or merely incorporate the practice into your day. I would love to hear about your "aha" moments! By all means, sketch, paint, and be creatively inspired by your deeper understanding!

"These elements and principles of design are nothing new! I didn't think this up! It's in God's Nature — everywhere you look! ~Jane E. Jones

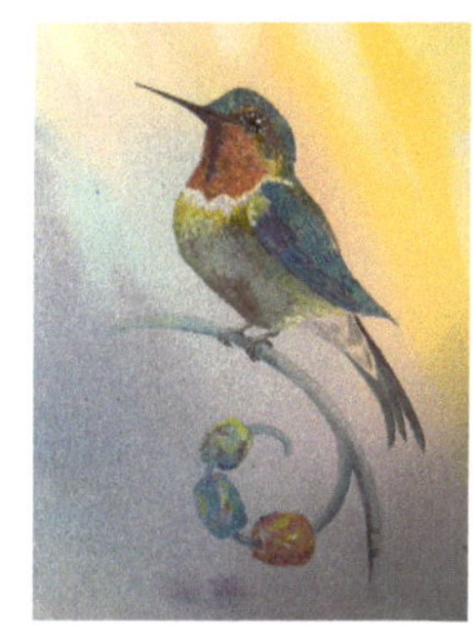

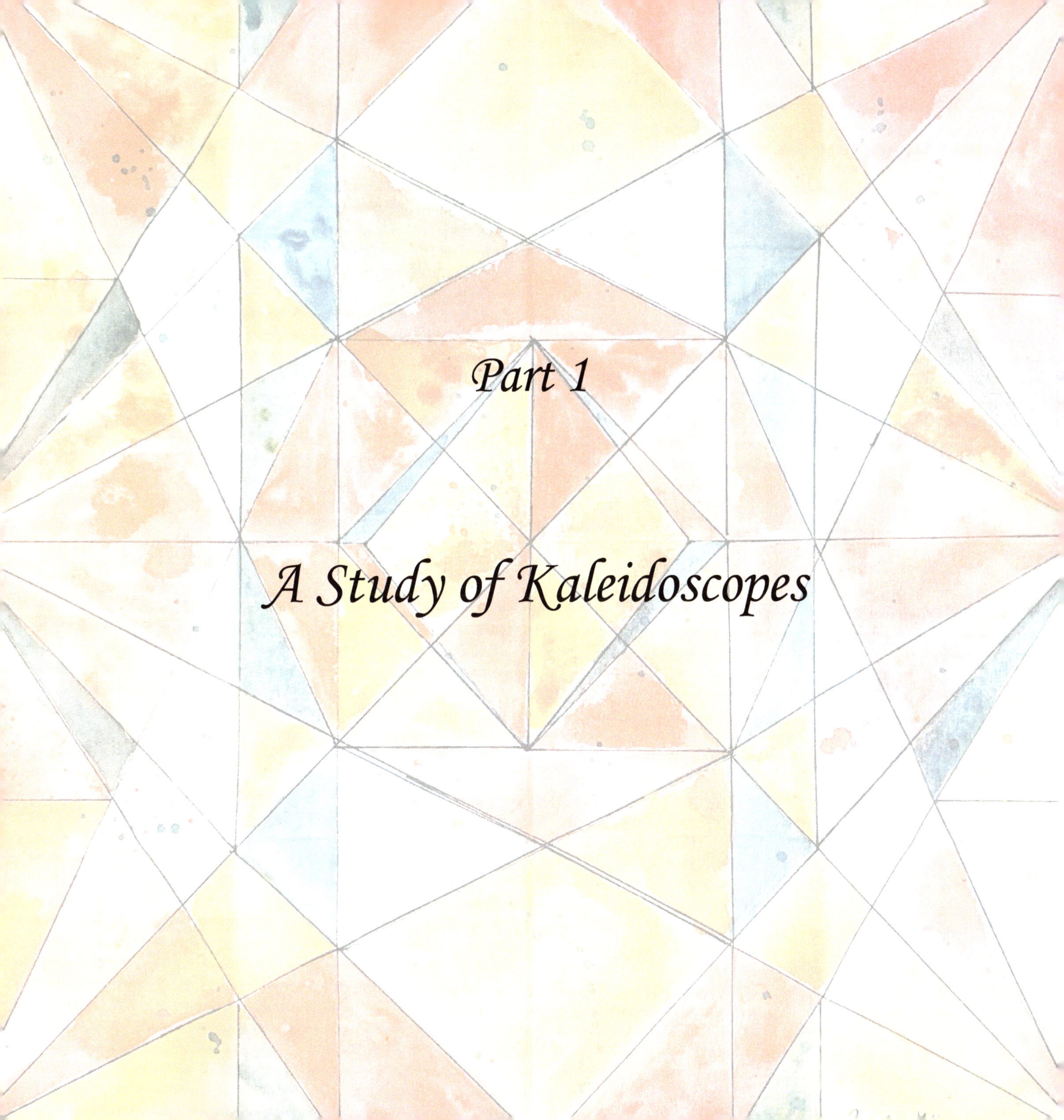

Part 1

A Study of Kaleidoscopes

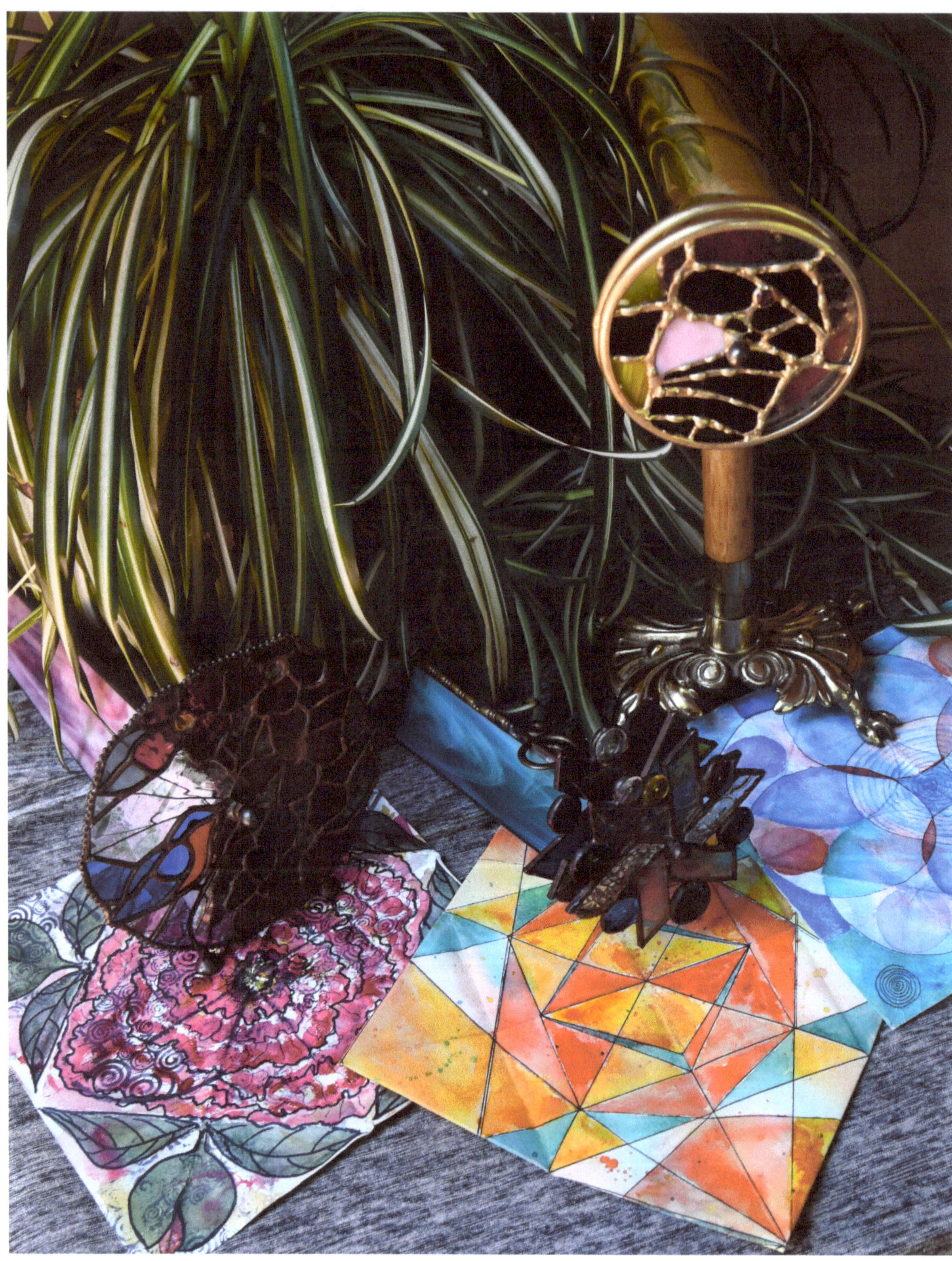

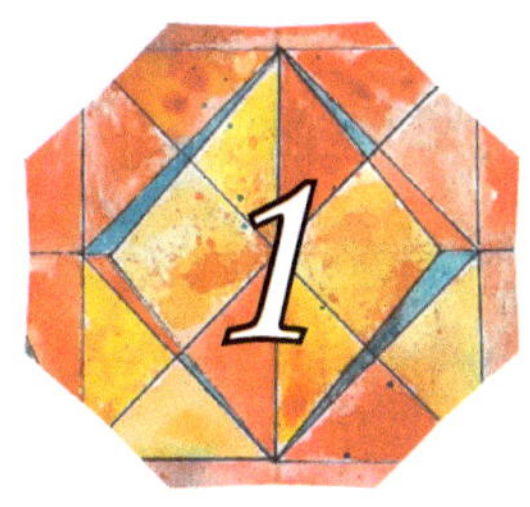

Kaleidoscope: History of this Invention

In 1816, Scientist, Sir David Brewster, invented the first kaleidoscope in Edinburgh, Scotland.

The simplistic design consisted of a long, cylinder tube containing at least three angled lengths of reflective mirrors. At the end of the tube, a small glassed container held loose bits of glass beads and small-shaped items. When the cylinder was held towards the light and turned, stunning designs of colorful patterns resulted because of the reflective mirrors.

The meaning of the word kaleidoscope has its root beginning in the ancient Greek καλός (kalos), "beautiful, beauty," + εἶδος (eidos), "that which is seen: form, shape" and σκοπέω (skopeō), "to look to, to examine." Thus, the meaning, to see beautiful forms and shapes.

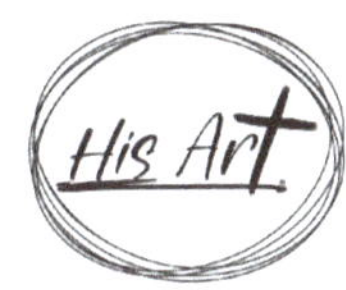

"For now we see through a glass, darkly; but then face to face: now I know in part; but then shall I know even as also I am known"
(1 Corinthians 13:12).

Since the beginning of time, when the Creator began the universe's precise spin on its axle, every living creature has depended on this configuration for its very existence. We have two choices: float aimlessly, in freefall, tumbling in our belief system, or be tethered securely, aligning our soul's purpose as part of his glorious design.

Kaleidoscope Click

Go with me here on this virtual quest. Close your eyes, take a deep, cleansing breath of God's Grace, then exhale anxiety. Repeat at least two or three times until you sense quietness. Imagine yourself as one of the kaleidoscope's tiny glass beads or shapes. Are you stuck? Spiraling out of control? What would it feel like to trust and know you are being held? What peace to know you are not falling apart. You are falling into place.

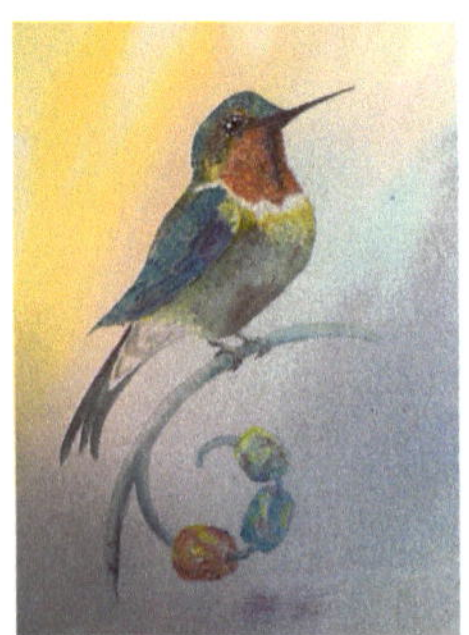

All scriptures paint the portrait of Christ.~ Mike Rowan

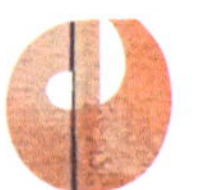
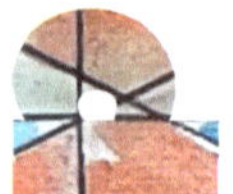
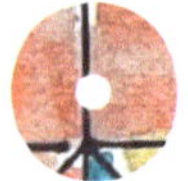
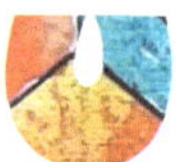
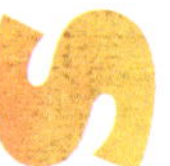
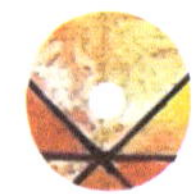
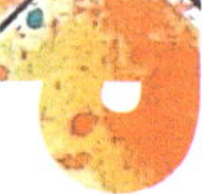

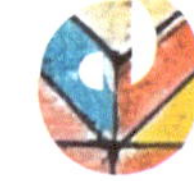
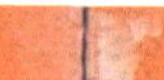
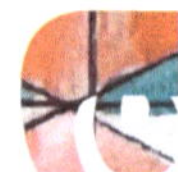
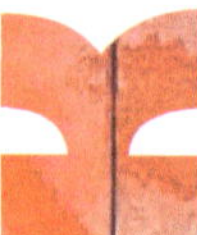

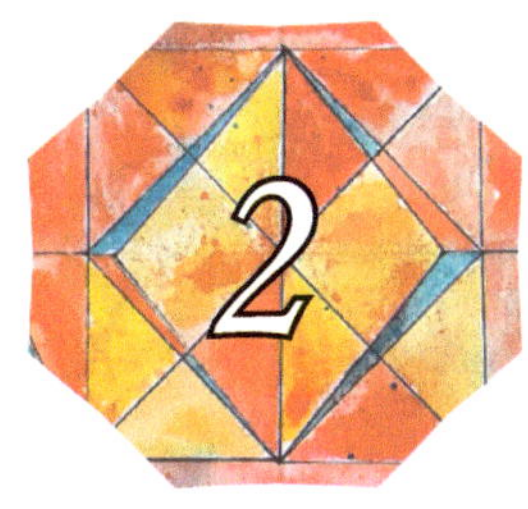

Remembering My First Kaleidoscope

Early Christmas mornings were always exciting and happy in our household. Wearing new flannel pajamas, I would noisily fidget in the narrow staircase with my little sister and brother, waiting for Mother and Daddy to open the door so we could scamper over to the tinseled cedar tree we had chopped down from our grandparents' farm.

One year, there were three brightly wrapped tube-shaped presents for each of us. This odd gift rattled when I shook mine, but I could not guess what it was! When I tore off the paper, I was still confused—what was this cardboard thing with a little peephole on one end? Mother told me it was a kaleidoscope! She showed me how to lift it to the light and take a look through the narrow opening. The thrill of simultaneously seeing all those lines, colors, shapes, and sizes! Wait! There was more! One slight turn exploded into one art design after another! It was a very simple gift, yet within it, it contained a complexity of mesmerizing scenes with each pivotal turn.

Decades later, I have come full circle to understand that all art elements and principles of design in nature work together as a kaleidoscope. His fundamental promises are fixed for eternity. The artful masterpiece of his art bursts into everlasting manifestations of his divinity. His perfect plan reflects his love for us when we lift it to the Light, his only son, Jesus Christ. All we are to do is trust, believe, and see with eyes of faith as we turn to him.

All we are to do is Trust—Believe—See with eyes of faith as we turn to him.

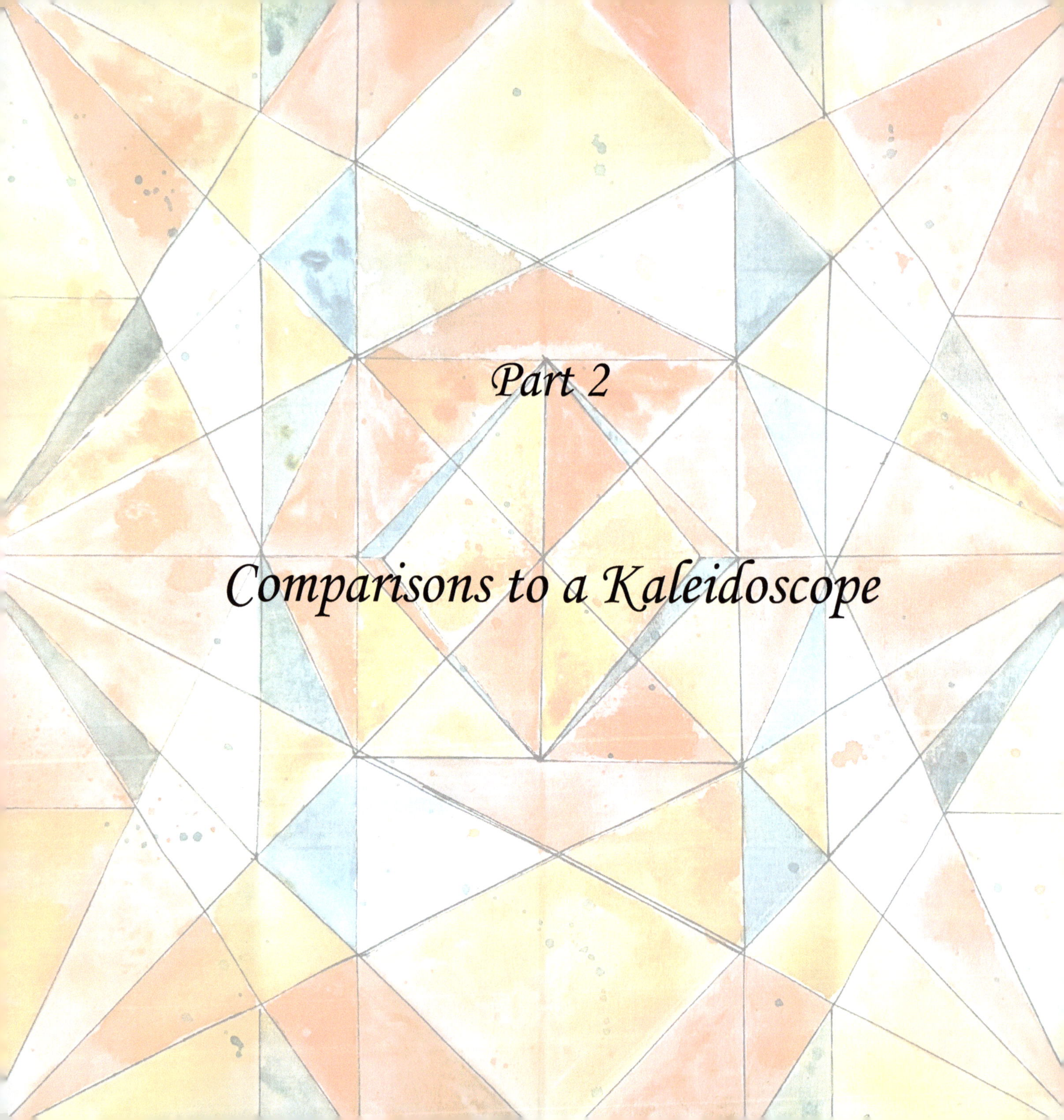

Part 2

Comparisons to a Kaleidoscope

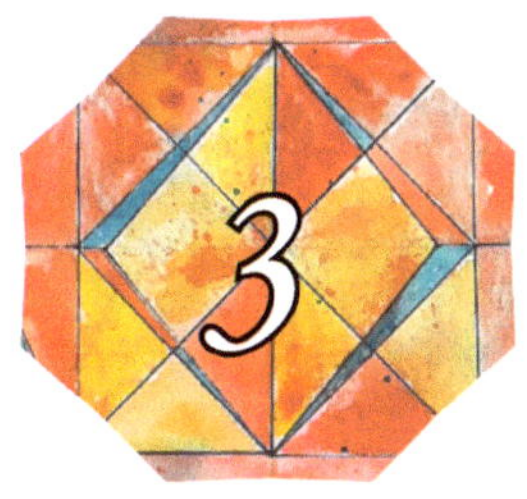

In the Beginning…

"When I was a child, I spake as a child, I understood as a child, I thought as a child: but when I became a man, I put away childish things: (1 Corinthians 13:1).

Watch a child with a new box of crayons and a piece of white paper. There is no inhibition, no preconceived notion of what "correct" color to use, no rigid rules to follow, as in, "stay within the lines!"

He or she is merely enjoying the pure bliss of creating and the joy of freely trusting. Their knowledge grows; however, they often become self-conscious of their colorful masterpiece, comparing the work to their peers. Without encouragement and further training, perhaps they might stop creating altogether! Likewise, they can become overconfident. "This is the only way we can do this! I'll do it myself!" "I don't need any help!" "I know everything there is to know!" All too often, as adults, we let our creativity be buried in the busyness of life. Our inner child only listens to those voices who might have, even unknowingly, criticized our art talents. How sad to lose that pleasure of creating!

I remember an impromptu coloring page contest in the living room of my childhood friend, Judy. My little sister and I deliberated on selecting the perfect page out of the coloring book. We carefully selected each crayon hue to complete our contest entry. We tore them out of the book and leaned them up side by side on the brown sofa cushions, waiting for the one Judge and Juror to give out the award. I was so nervous. In my heart, I knew Judy's entry was the best… after all, she had two more years of practice than my eight-year-old tenure. My six-year-old little sister, Krista, had done her very best, too. I can still envision her concentrating so hard with the tip of her little pink tongue held tightly between her sweetheart-shaped lips. Looking at our offerings, even I could distinguish the skill levels. My heart sank as I just knew I was unworthy of any prize. That torn piece of colored paper represented all of who I was. I was anxious about the final results as Judy's big teenage brother, Johnny, lumbered in the living room turned art gallery. I can even remember what Judge Johnny was wearing: a white t-shirt, blue jeans, and high-top tennis shoes. Would he be fair? Would he show favorites and pick his own sister's entry? I knew who Johnny was; however, I had never really talked to him….and now he was my Judge and Juror! All I could do was stand there helplessly, awaiting his word and authority. Looking back, I know now that he had fun making a big production out of our art contest. He examined each page carefully and thoughtfully. With his fingers over his mouth, he considered what seemed like an eternity. Finally, he announced, "This one is awarded the Most Colorful!! This one is awarded the Most Use of Shading! This one is awarded the Most Creative!" We were all happily satisfied and encouraged to continue our coloring career. Judge Johnny had accepted us each as individuals, just who we were. From that day forward, I wasn't afraid to talk to that big, kind teenage boy anymore.

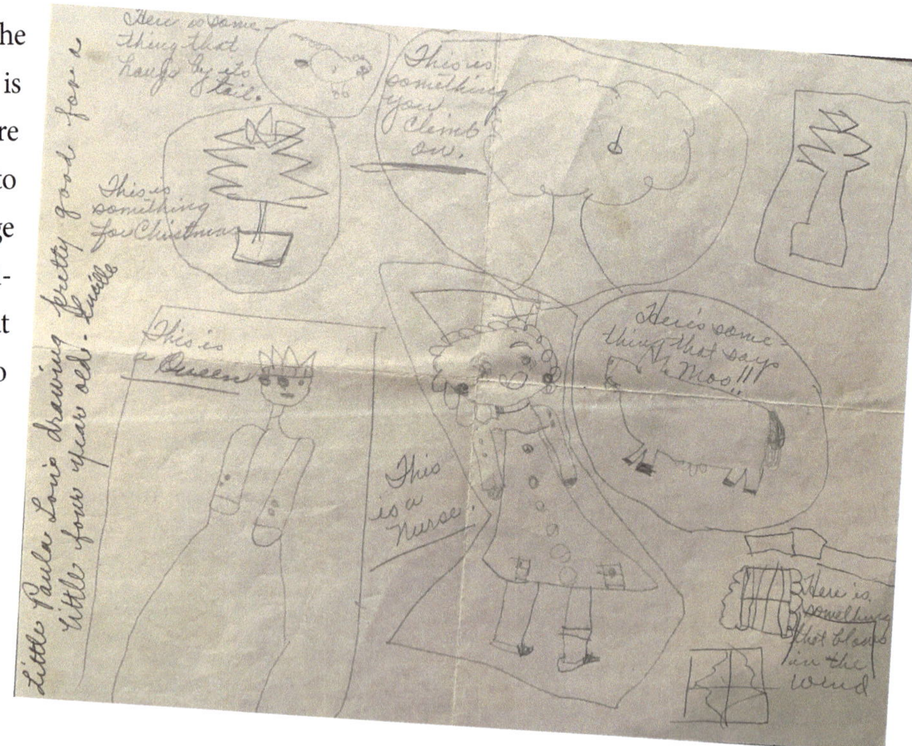

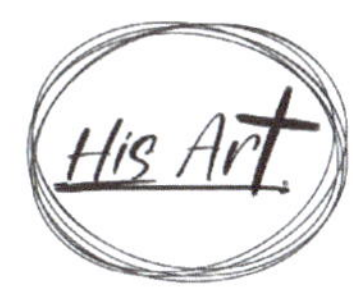

"Draw nigh to God and He will
draw nigh to you" (James 4:8).
"But continue thou in these things which
thou had learned and hast been assured of
knowing of whom thou hast learned them;
and that from a child thou hast known the
holy scriptures, which are able to make thee
wise unto salvation through faith which is
in Christ Jesus" (2 Timothy 3:14–15).

Now, looking back on that little living room scene, I see a sweet comparison to our adopted Big Brother, Jesus Christ. We must come fully believing that he is our Judge and is all authority. Laying our unworthiness before him and trusting fully that he will judge our willing hearts individually with all fairness and love. He seeks a personal relationship with us. A relationship where we can commune with him always.

Decades later, I still am fond of Johnny and for the Christ-like attitude he demonstrated to those three little artists that afternoon. He had all power to squelch our creative spirit or give us hope. He chose hope. True colors show.

We must come fully believing that he is our Judge and has all authority.

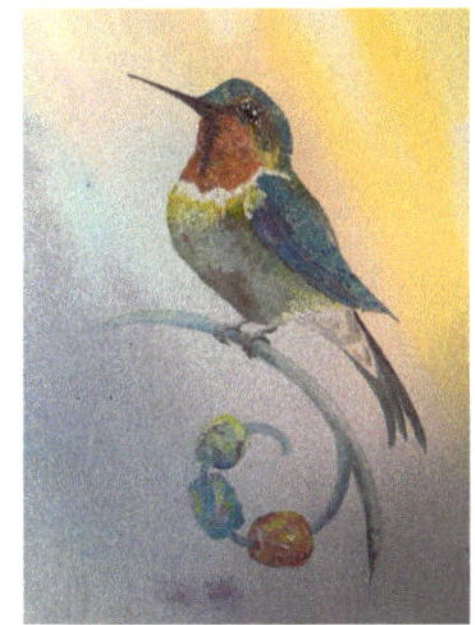

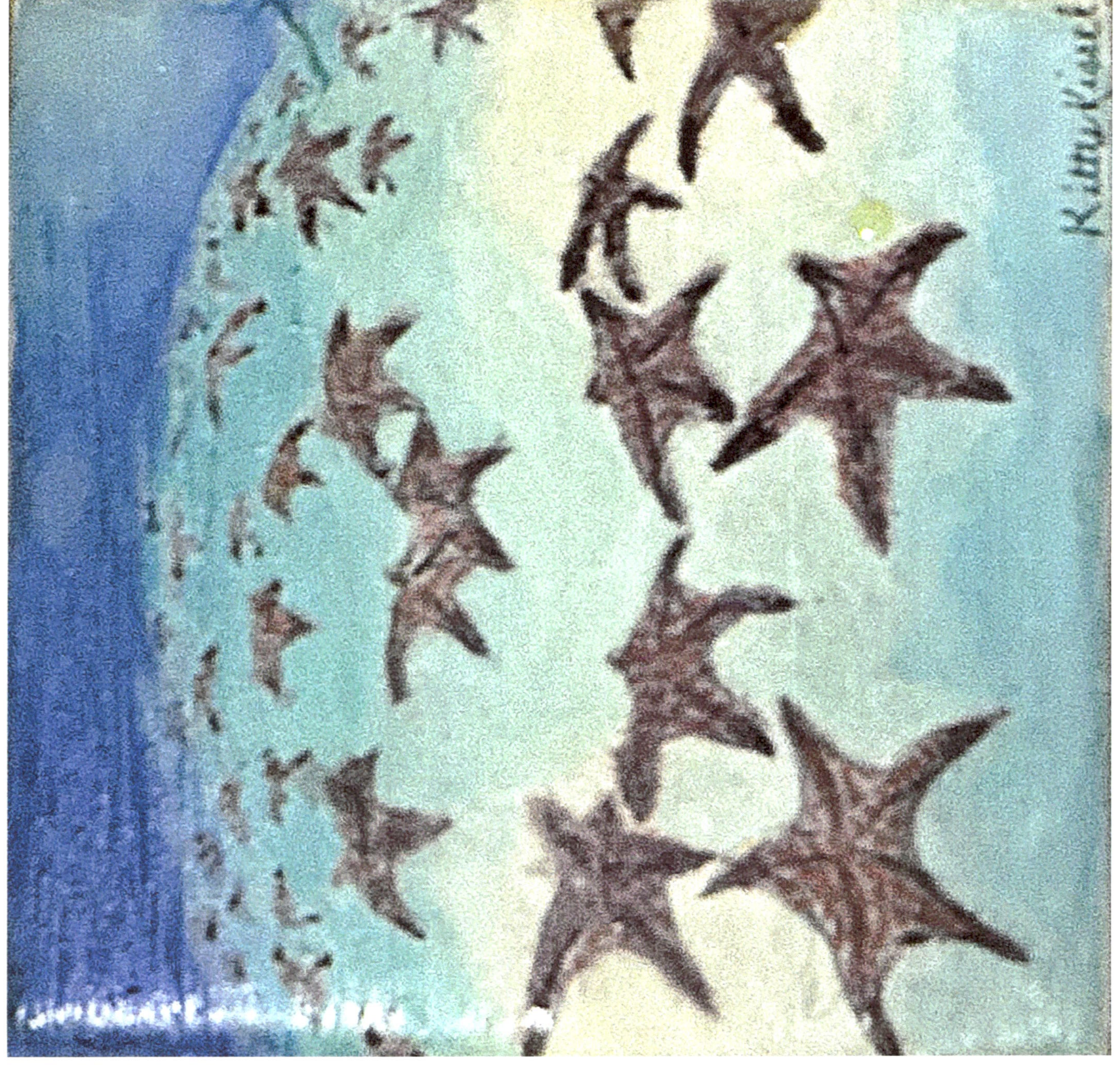

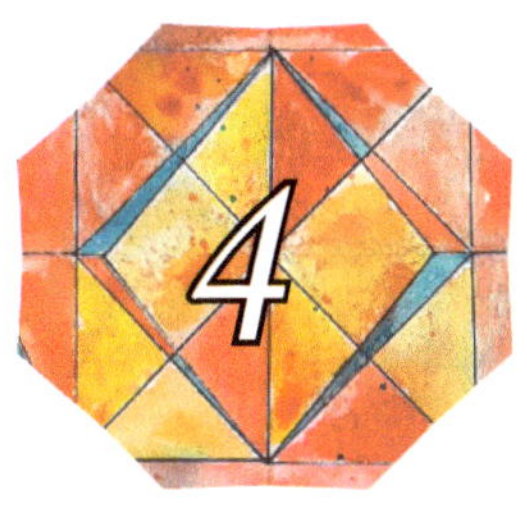

Deeper Still – Searching for the Elements and Principles of Design

An appreciation of art is innate, a natural path for a child or any beginning art student for that matter. (Why are we surprised at this? We are made in the image of the great Creator himself!) Naturally, we learn colors, shapes, and symbols. He or she may like the colors or the subject matter; however, he or she may be unable to articulate and express the "Why and How." At this point, we are not ready for structure and challenging things. Be mindful not to be too critical of your talent, artistically tearing your efforts into pieces. Additionally, it is not the time to consider criticizing questions and comments.

Is it good art or bad art?

I can't even draw a stick person.

Is there hope for me to improve?

In the process, there will be a pivotal point where you know you have gone as far as you can with your art. To develop new skills, you need to practice proven techniques and methods, invest in better equipment and supplies, and, most importantly, learn from a master.

Over time, exploring new mediums, practicing, and sharing with like-minded people motivates us to learn even more. These experiences become ingrained in our artistic being. We are eager to learn more techniques and art theory. We begin discerning what works and what doesn't. In other words, we begin to trust the elements and principles to create successful art.

In art, it is very easy to mix all the paint hues without thought, creating luscious shades of gray. Think about a time you observed a little child enthralled in the messy joy of finger painting.

Bright colors smushed together and suddenly turned into shades of gray. Two sections are devoted to the Elements of Color and Value, however for now, knowing that mixing equal parts of the colors that are directly across the color wheel from each other will always make shades of grey: Red and Green, Blue and Orange, Yellow and Purple to name a few complements.

In fact, greyed values actually hold a painting structure together. The wisdom is in developing an awareness of how, when, where, and why to include them in a painting. Early in my painting studies with Jane, I had a similar realization. After a full day of painting outside, we would set all of our works together, anticipating Jane's critique of each one. We all gained a wealth of knowledge from her suggestions and expertise as she observed all our efforts; I have kept all my photos and notebook of these sessions as references. (Jane has her own dedicated shelf in my art studio.) That particular afternoon, I noticed that my works were muted shades of greys and, frankly, quite dull compared to the other artists' vibrant, exciting paintings. I asked Jane for her counsel about this phenomenon. The source revealed itself, and I had eyes to see what I was doing wrong. A sloppy habit had crept into my routine of not cleaning my paint pallet and water container often enough. Keeping the water clear and applying uncompromised fresh paint pigments while taking into account the Elements of Color and Values dramatically improves the work. Trusting made all the difference.

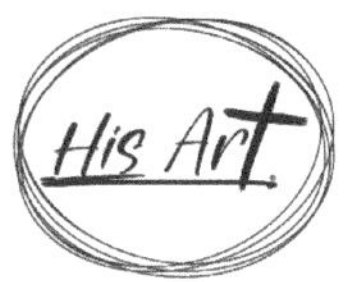

"I can do all things through Christ, which strengtheneth me" (Philippians 4:13).

I remember the lullabies, Bible stories, and Sunday School songs. Repeating these lessons begins the building of the foundation of faith. Studies show that childhood experiences are carried throughout an individual's life. We are scripted, hotwired, if you will, how we perceive the world around us.

Broadly considering, other religious systems worldwide will have their core values tied to an original document or individual leader. I know very little of other belief structures.

Followers of Jesus Christ believe that the 66 books of the bible are writings by several authors over 4,000 years, all inspired by God. There are mysterious shadows of harmony played from the Old Testament, repeated in clear fulfillment melodies in the New Testament. In the back of this book, I am sharing with you just a few of the over 1,000 prophecies scriptures mentioned in the Old Testament and where the fulfillment is revealed in the New Testament. Personally, I am in awe of the concept that a man or a woman can be inspired by God. As I pen this book to you, my inspiration is also Spirit-led! To teach truths is crucial and that which is false cannot become truth. That which is true cannot become false, which is why spiritual truths are described as pillars of faith. The original scriptures were written in languages of ancient Hebrew, Greek, and Aramaic. The Old Testaments are said to have been translated into approximately 700 languages. The New Testament has now been translated into over 1,500 different dialects. Humanity, through the centuries, has tweaked and interpreted scriptures. Knowingly or unknowingly, there have been additions and subtractions for a variety of reasons, including greed, power, and self-interests. God's sovereignty cannot be contained in a box, nor can his truth be watered down and muddied up into shades of gray. More often than not, that dusty, unopened box is being placed on the top shelf, unreachable to the ones who need its contents most. Each of us should check our understanding and perhaps ask ourselves, "Just where did I put that God box?"

Be careful when reading only one translation; without mindful study, the word translation may change. For example, this reading in Mark 10:14: "But when Jesus saw it, he was much displeased, and said unto them, Suffer the little children to come unto me, and forbid them not: for of such is the kingdom of God."

The word suffer in today's language is interpreted as "hurting." The original book of Mark was written in Greek in approximately 60–70 CE. One definition of the ancient Greek word Pathos is compassion.

In this above-mentioned Scripture passage, suffer meant be patient and compassionate and allow the little children to come close!

One Scripture encourages you not to lean on your own ideas and comprehension. Instead, be curious and research for a clearer understanding. This will help you become more acquainted with the Bible. I encourage you to discover the actual word meanings in the original languages and explore Bible archeology history as well, as this will enhance your understanding greatly.

Indeed, reading Bible passages can be confusing at first. However, please be aware that the opposite is also true. Some translation versions may be so watered down and easy to read that the original message may be diluted, so be mindful and filter out the questionable. With that said, find a Bible that speaks to you and start there!

Did you realize that there are no specific religions mentioned in the holy scriptures? There is only one truth.

With maturity, each of us begins to take into account the principles upon which we have been raised. We begin to discern whether those principles are authentic and worthy to hold. Our narrow viewpoint of the world is limited within our life span. Our families, cultures, and experiences influence us. If situations were not the best, hopefully, some individuals came to our aid. Many opportunities are often presented to make changes in one's life. A few examples are an elementary teacher's reports after recognizing that a child is suffering from mental or physical abuse from a family member or being bullied by a classmate. Perhaps a high school instructor senses a hidden talent for writing and says one encouraging statement that sends the student on a confident path of journalism. A Sunday School teacher who loves her students unconditionally as she points them to where they can find answers to life's struggles. We are blessed to live in an age where counseling services are readily available and mental health stigmas are met with more proactive awareness methods. Terrible life events need not define who you are now. Individuals have a choice to become bitter and continue the cruel, negative cycles to the next generation. We also possess within our psychic the ability to respond. That is the very definition of the word Responsibility: The ability to respond.

Can you change the past? Of course not. What you can change is how you use those experiences. Each of us can encourage others by sharing, teaching, and being a role model as we live our lives in truth.

In Hebrews 5:11, Paul said, "I have so much to tell you, but I don't think you can hear it." He was speaking to the new believers about a shallow relationship with Christ. There is a huge difference between knowing about Jesus and actually knowing him. Truth will have all the elements demonstrated and evident.

Are you ready to dive deeper still? Both wells of art and of God's messages are very deep; the bottom has yet to be found. This writing does not even touch the surface of all there is to understand of either topic.

The following chapters will compare the seven elements and eight principles of art design to the foundational truths of God. With his help, I hope I can paint the masterpiece so that you might see how I envision it: a multifaceted, turning kaleidoscope.

The elements and principles of design are the building blocks of all art. Likewise, God's messages can be the precious underpinnings of your life. Here's a thought to ponder…the life principles you live by influence those around you.

> "Then open he up their understanding that they might understand the scriptures" (Luke 14:45).

In the creative process, there will be a pivotal point. You know you have gone as far as you can with your own ability.

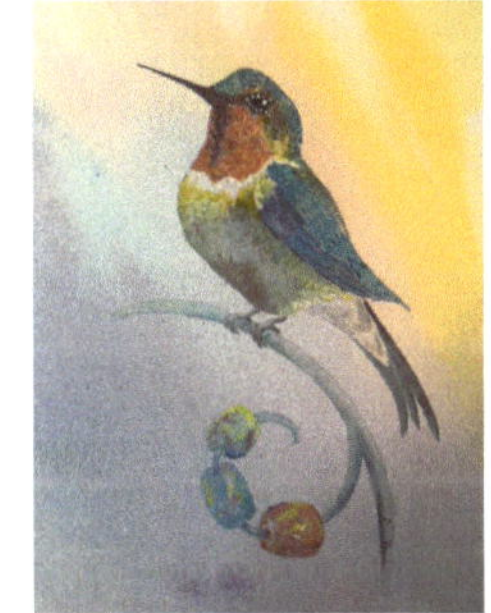

To develop new skills, you need to practice proven techniques and methods, invest in better equipment and supplies, and most importantly, learn from a master.

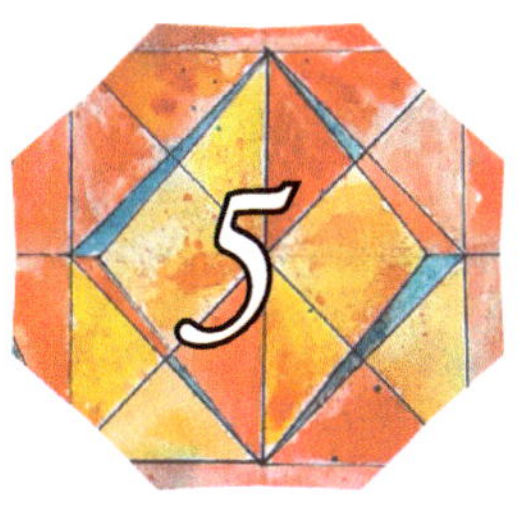

Fear of the White Piece of Paper

It is close to scary looking at that white, clean paper. Who wants to make any mistakes?! One of my watercolor students, Debra, once told me, "When I thought I'd try watercolor, I said to myself, "How hard can this be? Throw some paint and water on paper. I don't want to "Think" – I want to paint! Boy, was I ever wrong!" You should see her lovely work now after practicing and trusting the bite-size pieces of art theory introduced in my classes. Her work is stunning. It is quite evident how she is mastering the techniques. Debra realized that the elements and principles of design are tried and true. They do not change. They are consistent.

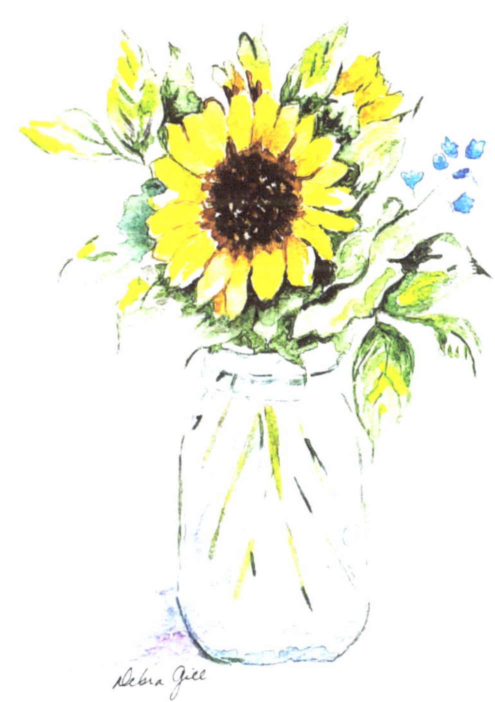

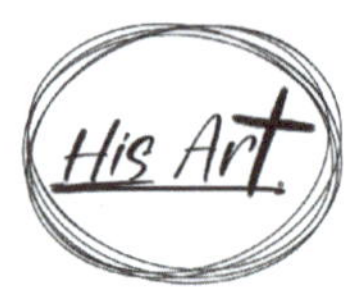

"Be strong and of a good courage, fear not, nor be afraid of them; for the LORD thy God, he (it is) that doth go with thee; he will not fail thee, nor forsake thee" (Deuteronomy 31:6).

Kaleidoscope Click

Is there an area in your life where you hesitate to take the next step forward?

If you start moving closer to your dream purpose, are you afraid you might fail?

Then Don't!

Don't move closer to your dream purpose?! No, my dear reader.

Don't Fail.

Take one baby step at a time. This book is living proof a dream purpose can be accomplished.

The Elements and Principles of Design are tried and true. They do not change. They remain consistent.

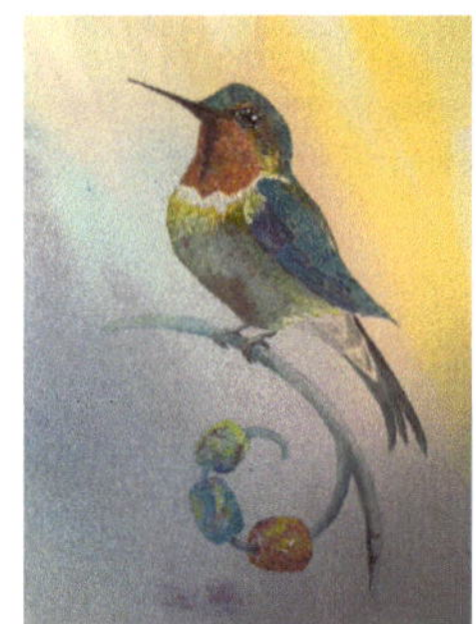

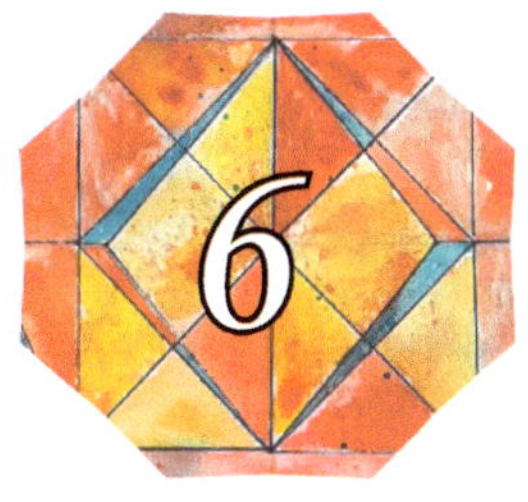

Planning to Plan

Before you begin splashing paint onto paper, it is best to take a little time to make some decisions and develop a plan. Otherwise, there is a good chance you will be disappointed with your art. Lean on those practices that are proven to create a better experience. Whether painting outside or in your studio, here are a few steps to benefit your success greatly before you begin to paint. The process should take less than 15 minutes.

1). Quiet yourself. Observe the scene you want to capture in your painting. Something will inspire you to paint. What story do you want to convey to your viewers? Jot down a few ideas to remind you using descriptive art words or short phrases such as rough textured tree bark, lacy leaves, smooth mist, spiky weeds, bright red poppies on a summer day, etc.

2). Decide upon a composition. Portrait or landscape orientation? High or low horizon line?

3). Determine your light, medium and dark values. Take photos!

This is a crucial part of the process that most casual artists do not do. Weather and light change so quickly, so capturing the essence of what you see at the beginning is best practice.

4). Color scheme and painting a few quick thumb-nail sketches._Taking time to decide on your chosen colors and painting a small color study is so important! Not only for the reasons mentioned but also to determine what colors will relay your story to the viewer.

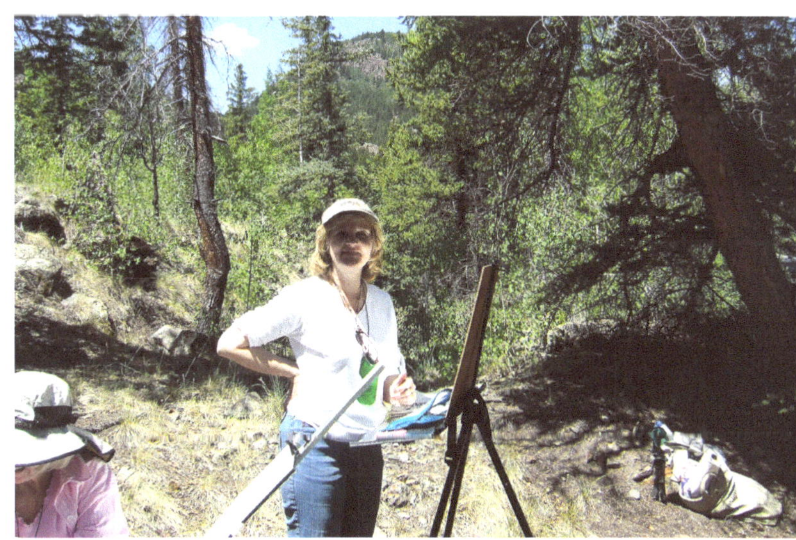

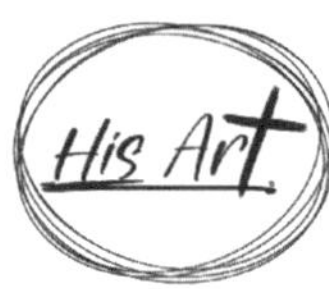

Before the world began, God envisioned a painting of a beautiful creation. They had a plan thought out from beginning to completion. (Yes, I did type "They" as the Holy Trinity were there from the beginning: God the Father, God the Son, and God the Holy Spirit. You can find where God speaks to them!). Consider all the planning God took to create his masterpiece from a fresh, white piece of nothingness! Here are his inspired thoughts from the book of Genesis. Please take a few minutes to read the Trinity's conversation passage mindfully.

"In the beginning God created the heaven and the earth. And the earth was without form, and void; upon the face of the water. And the Spirit of God moved. And God said, Let there be light: and there was light. And God saw the light, and it was good: and God divided the light from the darkness. And God called the light Day, and the darkness he called Night. And the evening and morning were the first day.

"And God said, let there be a firmament in the midst of the waters, and let it divide the waters from the waters. And God called the firmament Heaven. And the evening and the morning were the second day.

"And God said, Let the waters under the heaven be gathered together unto one place, and let the dry land appear: and it was so. And God called the dry land Earth, and the gathering together of the waters called he Seas: and God saw that it was good.

"And God said, Let the earth bring forth grass, the herb yielding seed, and the fruit tree yielding fruit after his kind, whose seed is in itself, upon the earth: and it was so. And the earth brought forth grass, and herb yielding seed after his kind, and the tree yielding fruit, whose seed was in itself, after his kind: and God saw that it was good.

"And the evening and the morning were the third day.

"And God said, Let there be lights in the firmament of the heaven to divide the day from the night; and let them be for signs, and for seasons, and for days, and years: and let them be for lights in the firmament of the heaven to give light upon the earth: and it was so.

"And God made two great lights; the greater light to rule the day, and the lesser light to rule the night: he made the stars also.

"And God set them in the firmament of the heaven to give light upon the earth. And to rule over the day and over the night, and to divide the light from the darkness: and God saw that it was good. And the evening and the morning were the fourth day.

"And God said, Let the waters bring forth abundantly the moving creature that hath life, and fowl that may fly above the earth in the open firmament of heaven.

"And God created great whales, and every living creature that moveth, which the waters brought forth abundantly, after their kind, and every winged fowl and after his kind: and God saw that it was good.

"And God blessed them, saying, Be fruitful, and multiply, and fill the waters in the seas, and let fowl multiply in the earth. And the evening and the morning were the fifth day. And God said, Let the earth bring forth the living creature after his kind, cattle, and creeping thing, and beast of the earth after his kind: and it was so.

"And God said, Let us make man in our image, after our likeness: and let them have dominion over the fish of the sea, and over the fowl of the air, and over the cattle, and over all the earth, and over every creeping thing that creepeth upon the earth. So God created man in his own image, in the image of God created he him; male and female created he them" (Genesis 1:1–27).

Kaleidoscope Click

Is there a new creative project you are considering? There are many ways to organize your ideas and projects on our cell phones and online. I am rather old school; therefore, for the creative gatherers, here is one of my best practice tips for you to collect ideas and materials. When something catches my eye, I will take a photo, press the flower, tear out the picture, pick up the found single butterfly wing or remains of the beautiful, perfect dragonfly. I'll draw out a sketch or make a color swatch when I have another few minutes. I carefully store these tiny steps in a single plastic sleeve. Before long, I have a plan for a painting. Instead of the bits of ideas scattered everywhere, they are all in one place, just waiting for me to begin. The sleeves are kept in a hanging file, or when a theme develops, such as "Pet Portraits," the sleeves are stored neatly in three-ring binders.

I'll give you one guess who shared this concept with me. Jane. Once, when I stayed a few days with her, I mentioned that I would like to get into her head. She gave me a puzzled look, so I explained further that I wanted to see how she organized supplies, projects, paper, everything! She welcomed me into the inner art studio sanctuary and gave me a guided tour of closets, drawers, paint storage and her plastic sleeve storage secrets. Everything was findable and available. I also remember another pearl of wisdom she shared that afternoon. You can be too organized. The goal is to have a place for everything so you can go right to your project without spending time searching. This method is much preferred than frittering away time you could be creating. I'm not quite to Jane's level yet, but I have claimed the value of plastic sleeves!

Lean on those practices and habits that are proven to create a better experience.

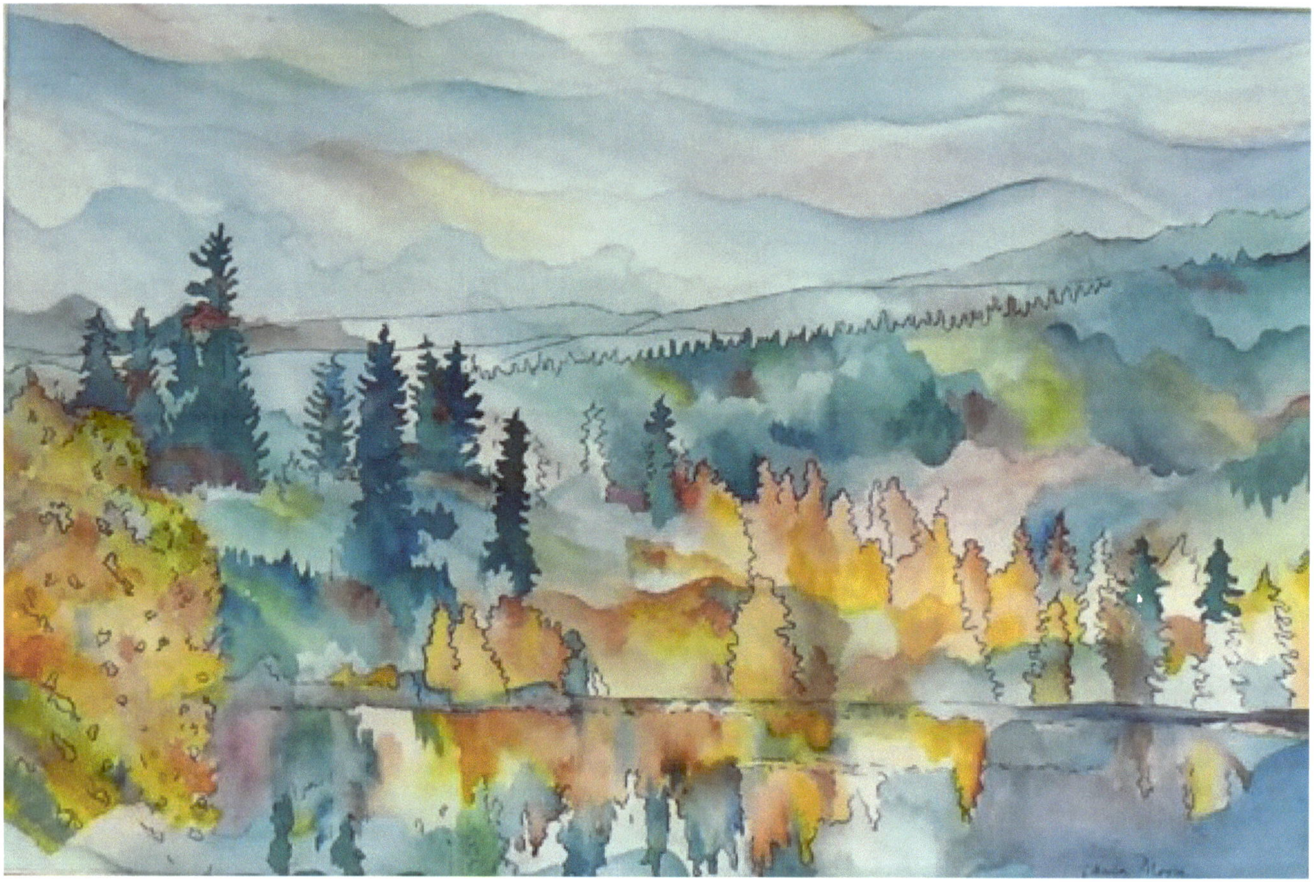

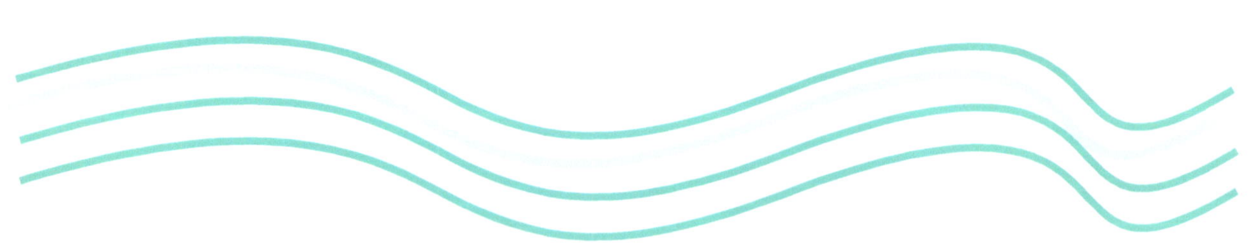

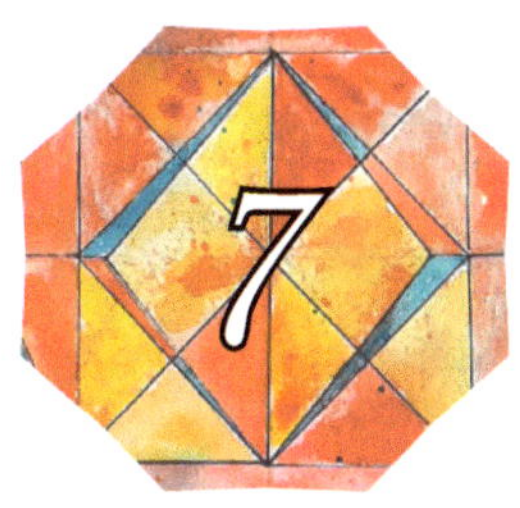

Seeing Things Differently

Earlier, I shared some of my childhood love of art and faith. I realized a weaving of the two; however, I couldn't see the entire plan. I did not yet comprehend how he was teaching me to see his principles through art.

I've always, even now, felt the need to create something; I'm busy with my hands and always thinking up a new project. My mother told me she would get me involved in dolls or toys, keeping me occupied for a few minutes. Then I'd have other plans, ready to start something else. My dad called me "Polly Wolly," as in the tune lyrics, "Polly Wolly doodles all the day!" How true that turned out to be! This trait is my greatest strength and greatest weakness! (But it is also how God wired me, and he does not make mistakes.) I will continue to methodically doodle with the Holy Spirit all the day. I have a little plaque in my art studio that serves as a mantra. It reads: "Find Faith in Everything You Do."

Perhaps a little warning is appropriate here. My students tell me that after they start my watercolor classes, they start to see the world differently. I hope you say the very same after reading my book!

This story illustrates the difference I want you to experience. My artist friend, Audrey, is a beautiful and accomplished pastel portrait artist. She told me of a moment while flying 30,000 feet over Colorado. She peered out the plane's little porthole, looking down at the Rocky Mountains, and spoke quietly to herself, "Just look at all those purples!" Her friend sitting next to her said, "Where?" Audrey explained, "Down there! All those purples, greens, oranges, and reds! What do you see?" As the seatmate looked out the window, she said, "Hmmmm, all I see is dirt!!" Obviously, the lesson of this little story is that her friend did not yet have the "eyes" to see.

The rest of the story is about her intrigued friend, who soon begins taking art lessons from Audrey, learning the techniques of distinguishing those colors. She now creates some lovely paintings, and I am confident she can discern those purple hues the next time she takes flight.

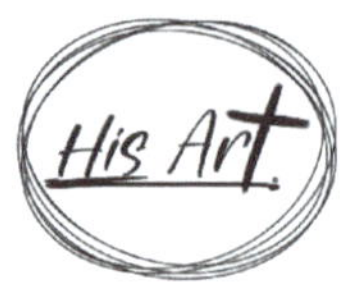

"Hear now this, O foolish people, and without understanding: Which have eyes and see not; which have ears and hear not" (Jeremiah 5:21).

The very fact that you are reading this book tells me that you are interested in seeing how I see. Are you ready to ponder the comparisons I envision between art's elements and principles of design and the principles of God's doctrines? An in-depth understanding of God's Elements insists our eyes of faith to see…our soul to decode.

I hope you take the time to consider the parallels. First, I will outline the individual Elements of Design and their purpose. In my comparison, these elements are the small, crystal glass shapes contained inside a kaleidoscope. The explanations will be followed by a "His Art" discussion, pointing you to how they compare to God's Elements of Design found in scripture.

The following section will outline the eight Principles of Art Design. These principles are similar to the solid kaleidoscope mirrored walls, which reflect how the pieces, i.e., the elements of design, move beautifully together. In the "His Art" section, I will lead you through the comparison of God's Principles of Design.

As I often tell my students, you can't eat an elephant all at once. You must take bite-sized pieces and chew each one slowly. The same applies to the study of the comparison of elements and principles of design. Each concept must be digested and absorbed, nourishing you and helping you grow into a more confident artist. Each component is the building block for the next. Please keep an open mind and an open heart as I share the mysteries of design in these very simplistic explanations.

"But Mary kept all these things, and pondered them in her heart" (Luke 2:19).

Kaleidoscope Click

Undoubtedly, you will soon have an opportunity when a question comes to mind, whether it be a new painting idea or a different life situation. Instead of making a quick judgment and decision, consider other possibilities, perspectives, understanding, and looking beyond the first impression. There is a difference between being closed-minded and single-minded. It is called Empathy.

Find Faith in Everything You Do

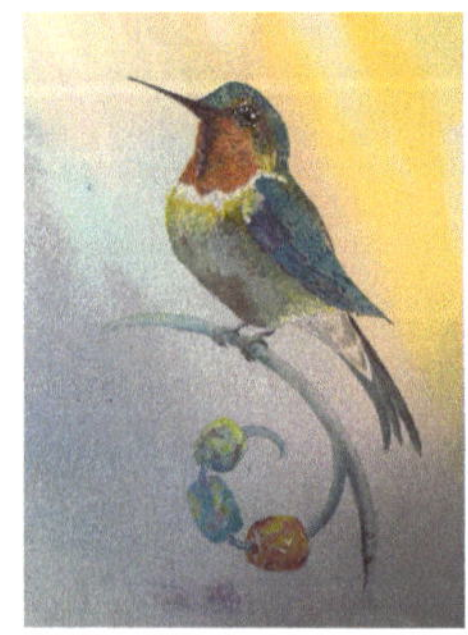

Part 3

The Seven Elements of Design Comparisons to God's Messages of Truth

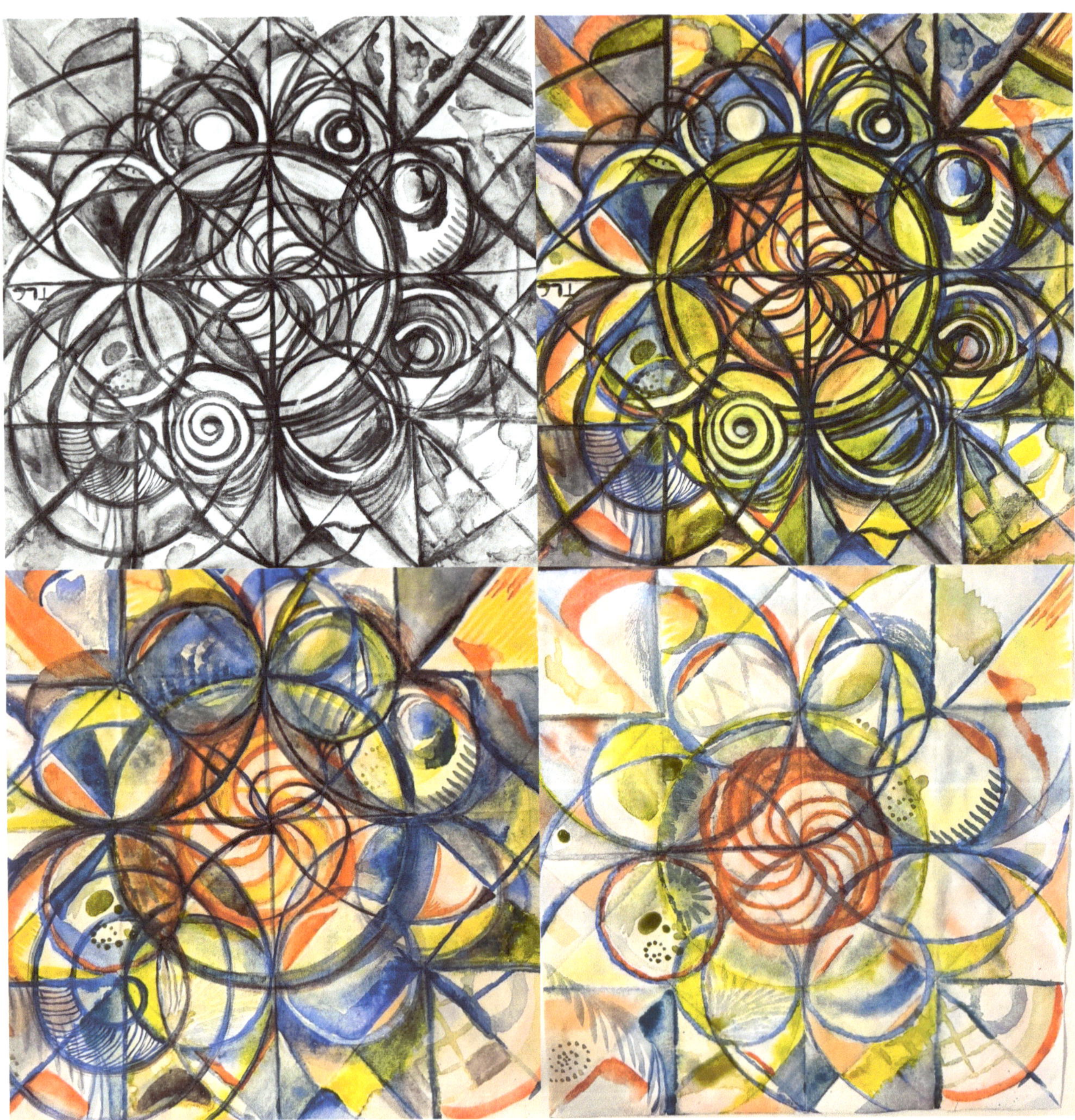

A Closer Look, a Deeper Understanding

First, please note that the elements and principles of design are complete. Nothing needs to be added, and nothing new will ever be required or manufactured by man.

When a painting is almost finished, it is placed on the mantle, and I walk by and look at the work, sometimes leaving it there for several days, to "see" where an area might need to be adjusted and strengthened. Turning it upside down or looking at it backward in a mirror helps! Art instructors had told me I had a pretty good eye; however, my efforts did not meet my expectations. Before being introduced to the design language, I strived to move from being a reasonably good artist to more mastery. I knew there was room for improvement in my paintings.

When the principles are understood, the artist develops a mental checklist of design questions she can ask herself to determine what might make this particular painting successful. The painting will provide clues about where an area might be improved. Once you are familiar with the principles, there is no guessing. The power is in remembering to use the checklist. I have developed a method to test your painting to see where it might become more successful. (Of course, I will share it with you in the latter section of this book!!)

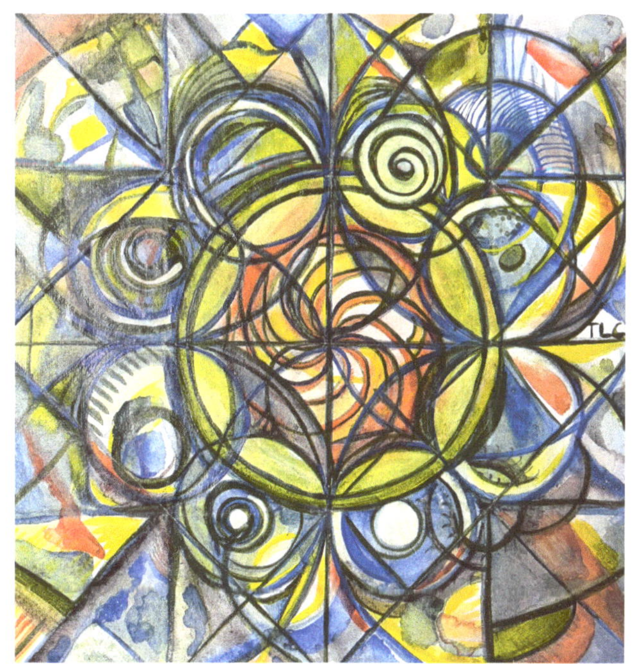

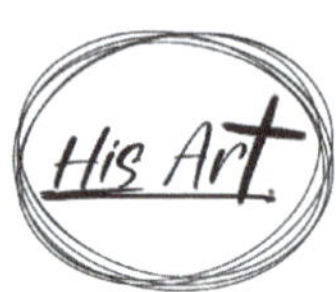

When comparing the language of art design as complete, so are God's elements of design…Complete and nothing to add or subtract. We each have a conscience when something is not quite right in our lives. I am confident you've experienced this! As humans, it is natural to want to control all aspects of our lives. If we are honest with ourselves, we know we possess the ability to search inwardly and identify where the problem is. Seek and ask counsel from the one trustworthy source who can work out solutions in our lives. All answers to life's journey are found in Scripture.

"Search me, O God, and know my heart: try me, and know my thoughts: and see if there be any wicked ways in me, and lead me in the way everlasting" (Psalm 139:23–24).

"And he turned him unto his disciples and said privately, blessed are the eyes which see the things that ye see for I told you that many prophets and kings have desired to see those things which ye see, and have not seen them and to hear those things which ye hear, and have not heard them" (Luke 10:23–24).

Kaleidoscope Click

Take a few moments now to review my His Art Kaleidoscope Guide, located at the beginning of the book. Familiarize yourself with the terms and definitions mentioned. Begin a foundation of learning this language of art and faith. The full guide is provided in the back of the book. Additionally, a free PDF of this resource is available on my website.

The Elements and Principles of Design are complete. Nothing needs to be added and nothing new will ever be required or manufactured by man.

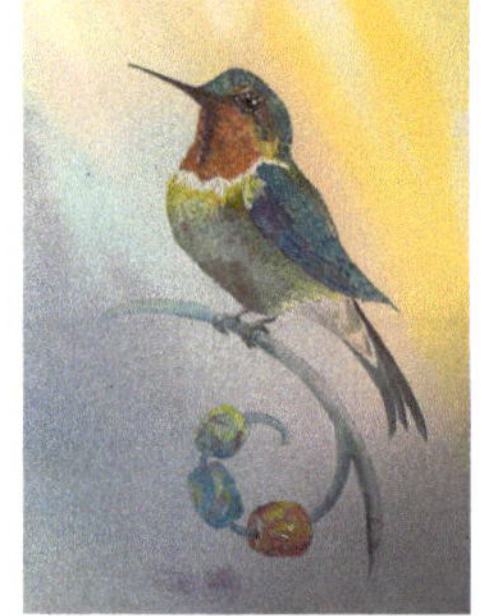

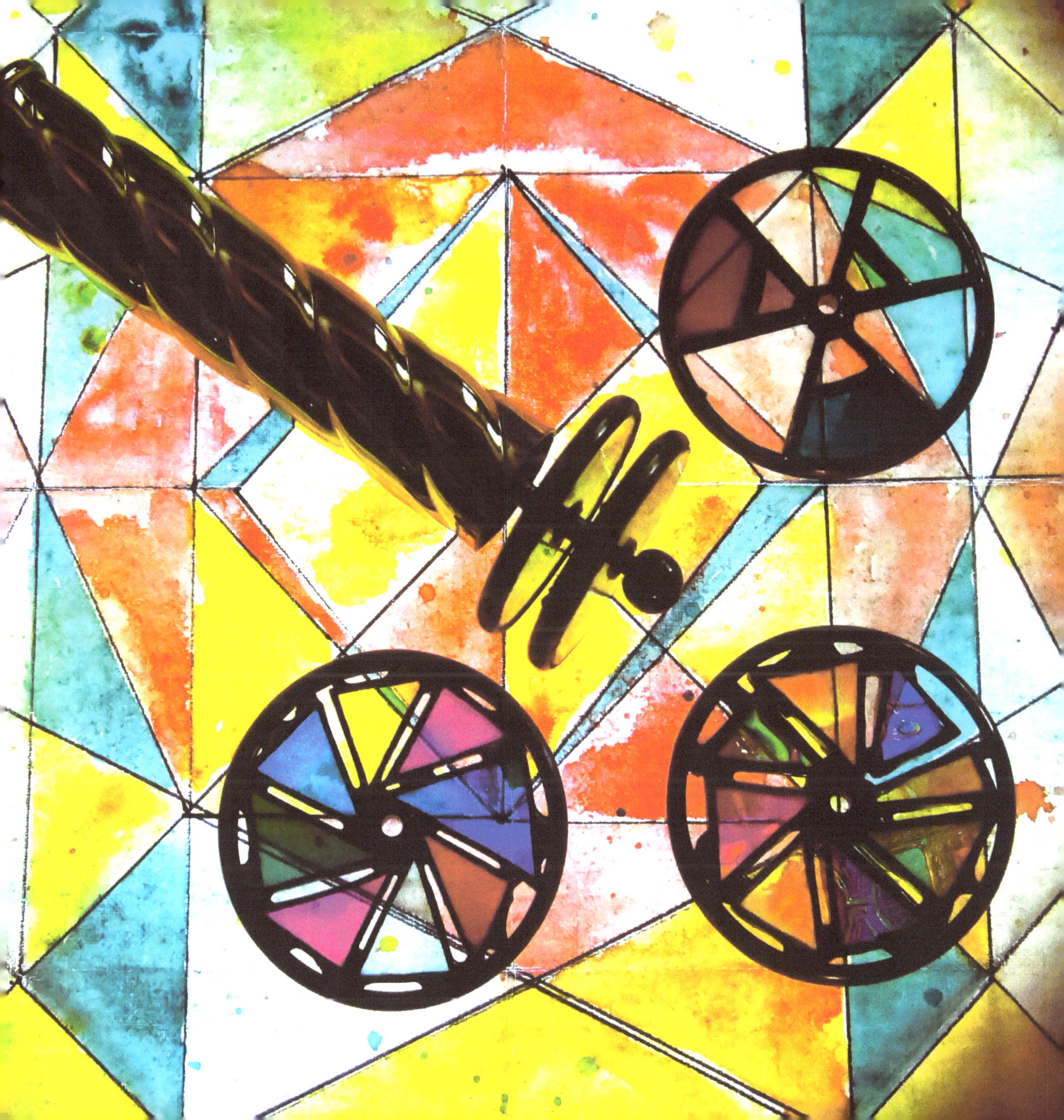

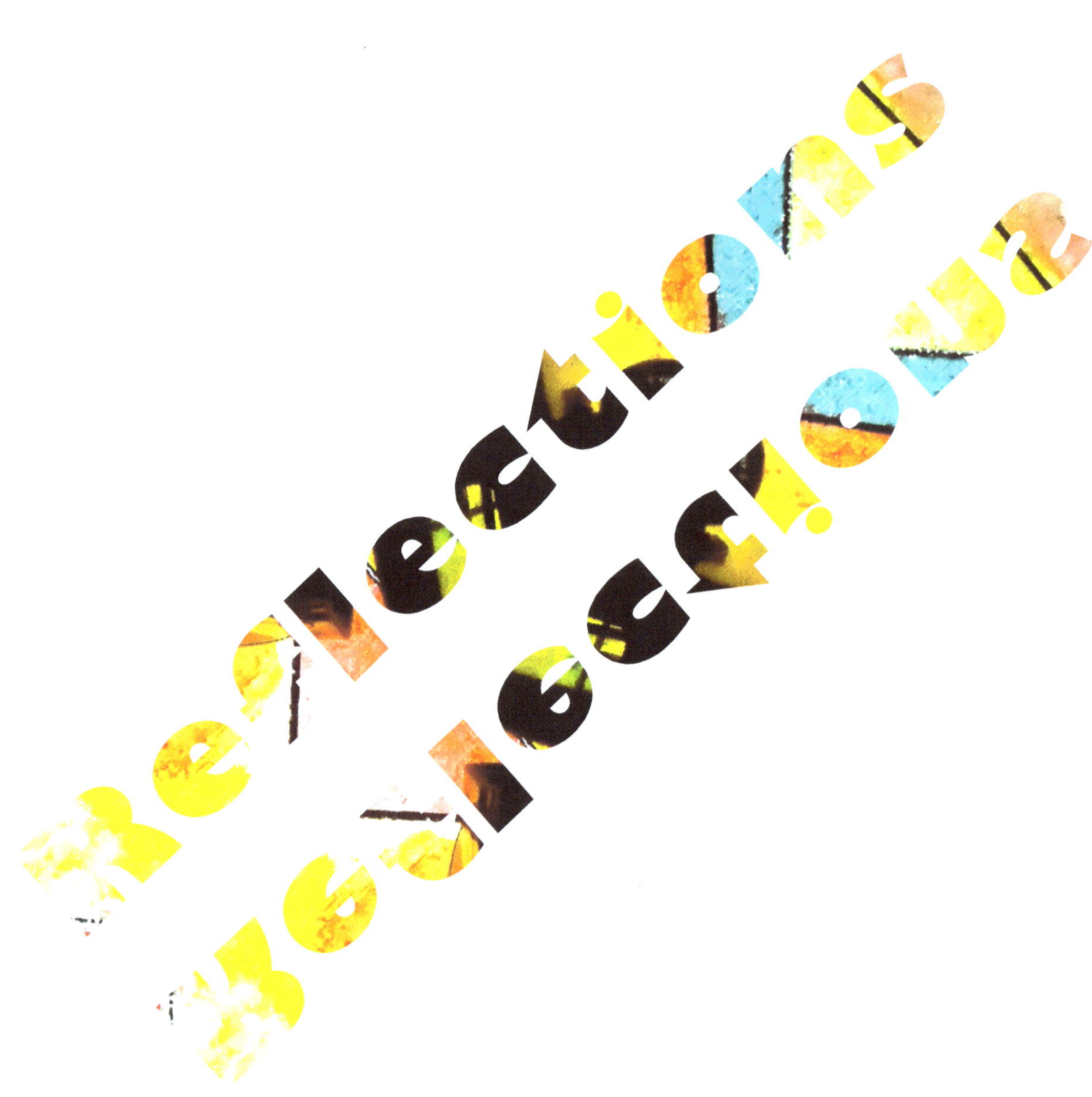
Reflections

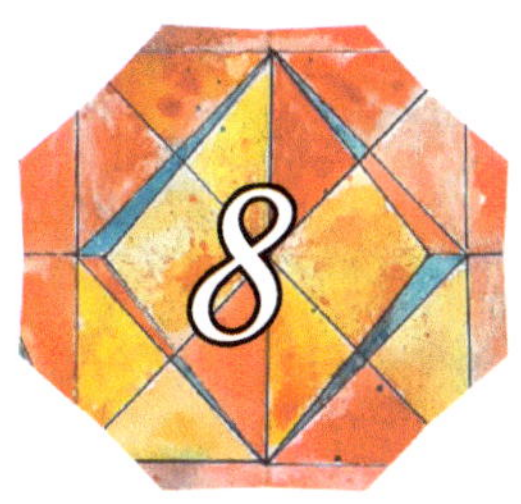

Introduction to The Elements of Design in Comparison to a Kaleidoscope's Glass Crystal Pieces and Mirrored Reflections

The elements of design are key to understanding. It is a standard of comparison. It gives purpose to an orderly, clear, and simple analysis upon which all visual arts are built.

Seven Elements of Design

When I can associate a new idea with something I already have familiarity with, I learn so much easier. Imagine a toolbox containing several different tools – a hammer, screwdriver, tape measure, leveler, nails, screws, and washers. Each one has a particular use; however, you will need all of them to build a project. For example, the hammer is useless if you are missing the nails.

Continuing my vision of the kaleidoscope's inner workings, I see these seven elements, the tools, as fragments of transparent glass crystal chips, pieces of colors, and shapes contained within the enclosed compartment of one end of the cylinder. These minuscule bits may seem to represent nothing as they float randomly within their confines. However, when spinning together, the spectacular bursts of designs are mesmerizing! It is a simple yet complex invention that can be enjoyed by adults and children alike.

So, it is with the seven elements of design. Each has a particular use, but they can achieve a successful painting when these components are working together!

(These first four elements are needed in drawing and sketching.)

1. Line
2. Shape
3. Size
4. Direction

(The remaining three elements are implemented when painting.)

5. Value
6. Color
7. Texture

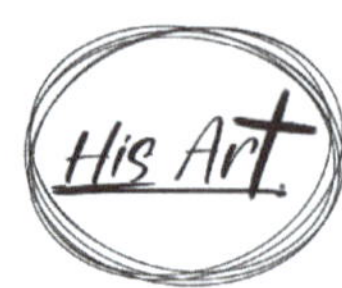

As I studied the comparison of the elements and principles of art design, more biblical truths were revealed. Notice that there are seven recognized elements of design. Furthermore, these elements comprise the vital structure of visual art, sculpture, fiber art, interior design, landscaping, and clothing design. The list goes on and on.

For a painting to be successful, all seven elements must be present. The Principles of Design must also be evident and will be discussed later.

In Scriptures, numbers symbolize several significant meanings. Continuing with my comparison of requiring only seven elements, the number seven represents completion or all.

Kaleidoscope Click

Write out these seven tools on a 3x5 notecard, which I compare to the moving crystal pieces contained within a kaleidoscope. Use this card as a bookmark, and study them in the order given until you know them by heart.

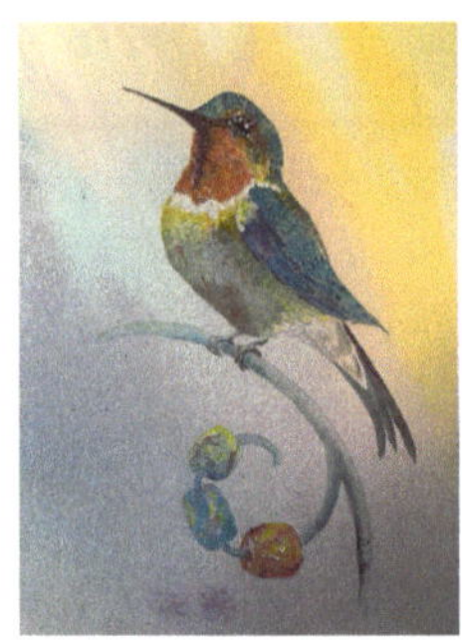

It is not coincidental that the seven elements of design are compared to a scriptural meaning of completion. Consider researching the symbolism of numbers. At the beginning of this journey, this is the first step of searching out the mysteries for yourself. Symbolism is relevant!

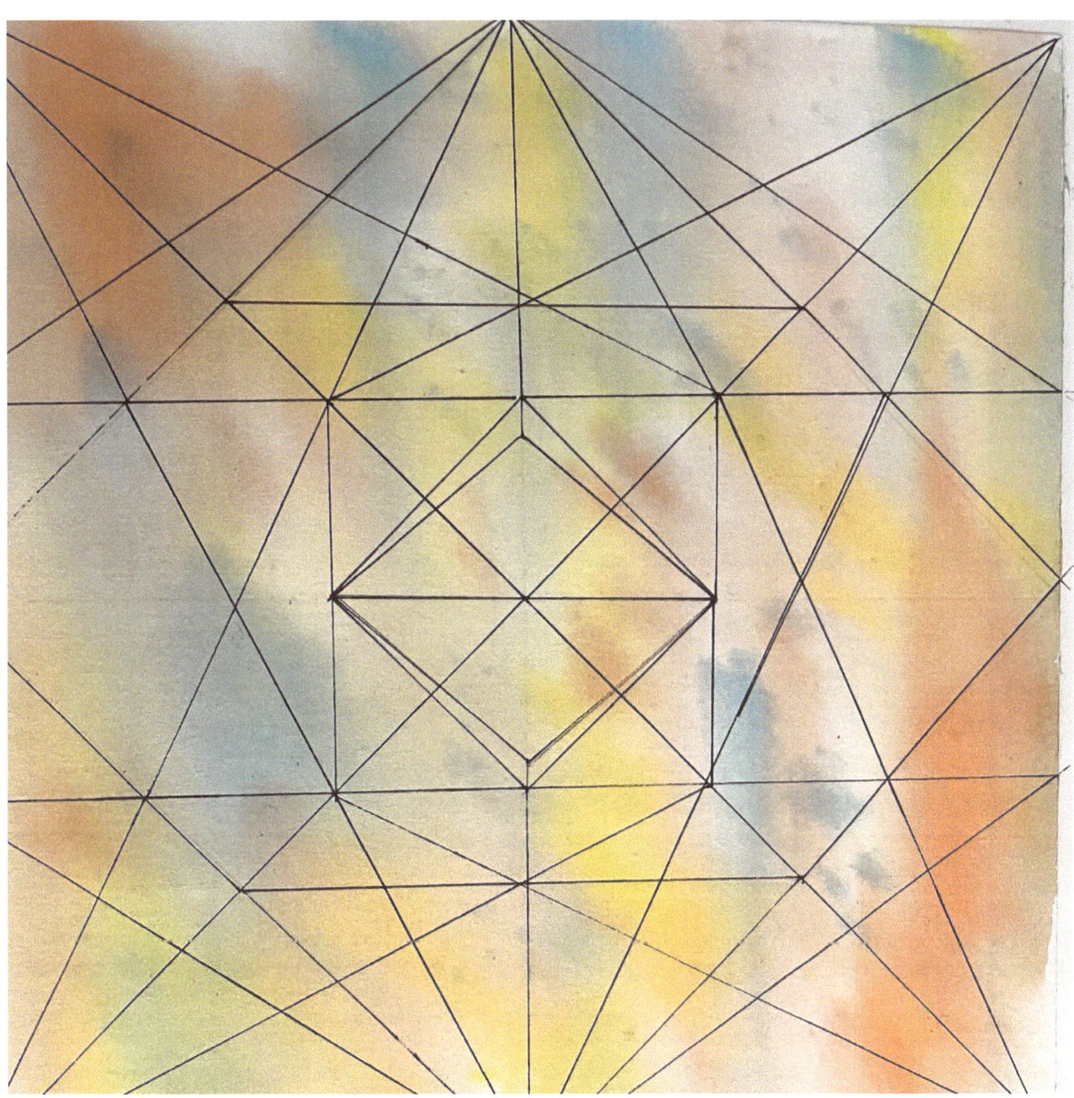

The First Art Element of Seven: LINE

Straight lines, curved lines, or perhaps a combination of both are usually the first marks placed on the paper or canvas. Consider the line as the first crystal bead rolling in the kaleidoscope.

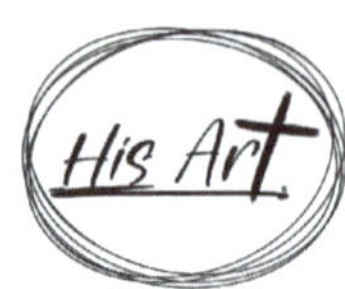

Line in the Scriptures

"Where were you when I laid the foundation of the earth? Tell me, if you have an understanding. Who determines its measurements? Surely you know! Or who stretched the line upon it?" (Job 38:4–5).

There is a line from creation in Genesis to the end of time in Revelation.

Kaleidoscope Click

Find as many LINES as you can. Straight, curved, diagonal, and horizontal. They are everywhere! Trees, branches, railroad tracks, and light poles along the road. Consider eyelashes as curved lines! Can you find more?

The Elements of Design are key to understanding. It is a standard of comparison. They give purpose to an orderly, precise, and simple analysis upon which all visual arts are built

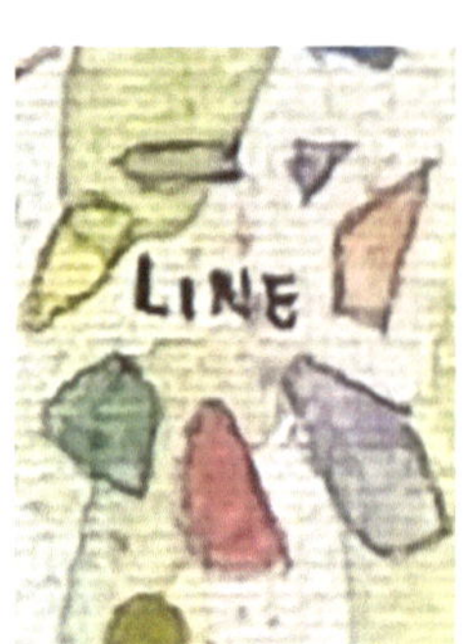

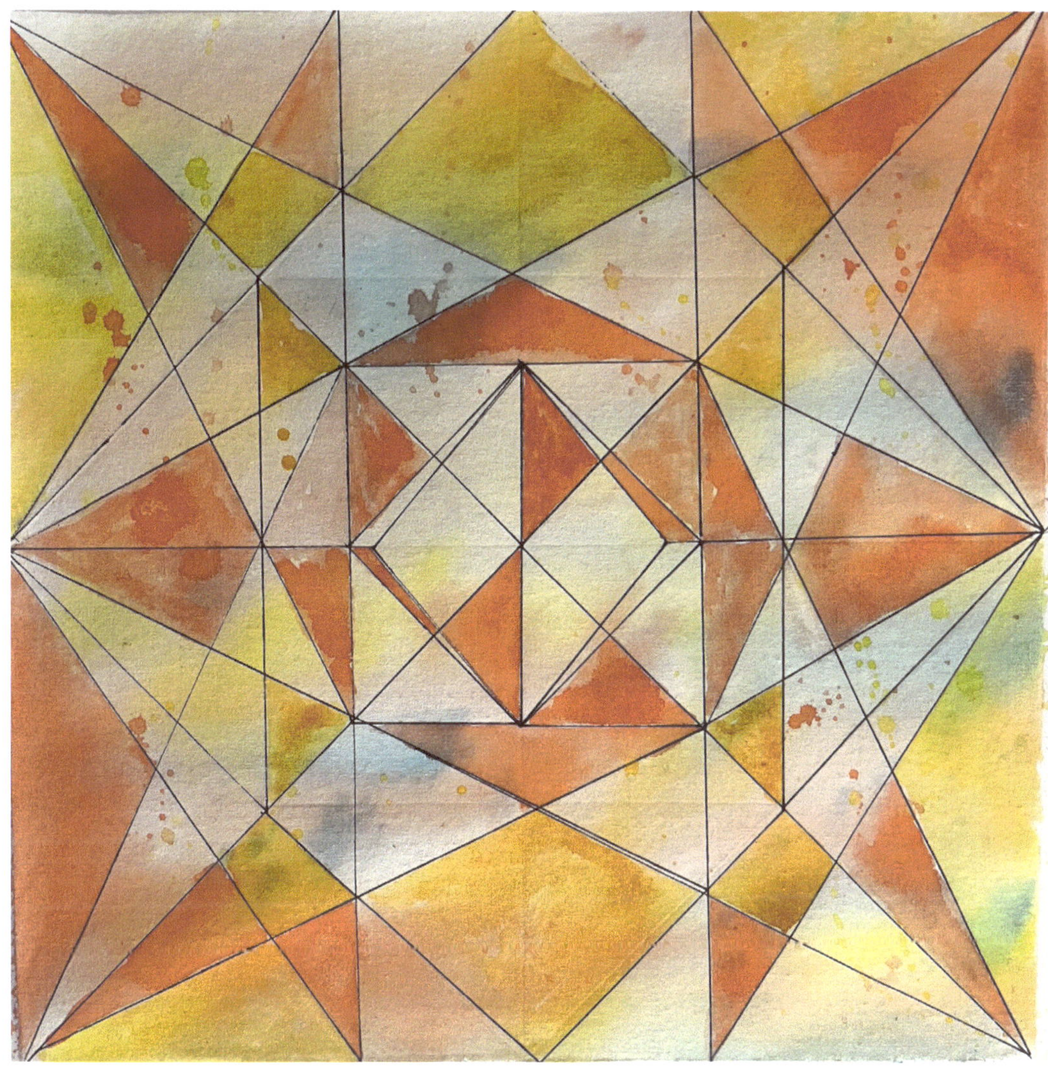

Second Art Element of Seven: SHAPE

With lines, a variety of shapes can be made. There are five primary shapes in nature.

These shapes are square, circle, triangle, a cross or X and spiral. The element of shape is the second crystal piece within the kaleidoscope.

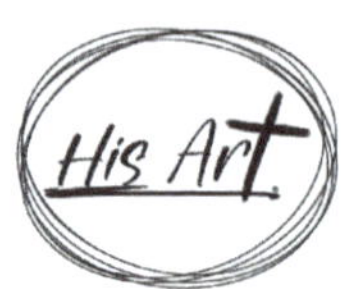

Shapes in the Scripture

"In the beginning God created the heavens and the earth. And earth was without form, and void; and darkness was upon the face of the deep. And the Spirit of God moved upon the face of the waters. And God said Let there be light; and there was light" (Genesis 1:1–3). Shapes in the Bible

Here are just a few examples of shapes mentioned in the Scriptures. There are many more to be discovered!

Rectangles — Noah's Ark Genesis 6:14–16 The First Tabernacle Exodus 25:9—27:9

Circles — Marching around the city of Jericho Joshua 6:3–6 The crown of thorns Matthew 27:29

Triangle — Holy Trinity: Father, Son, Holy Ghost

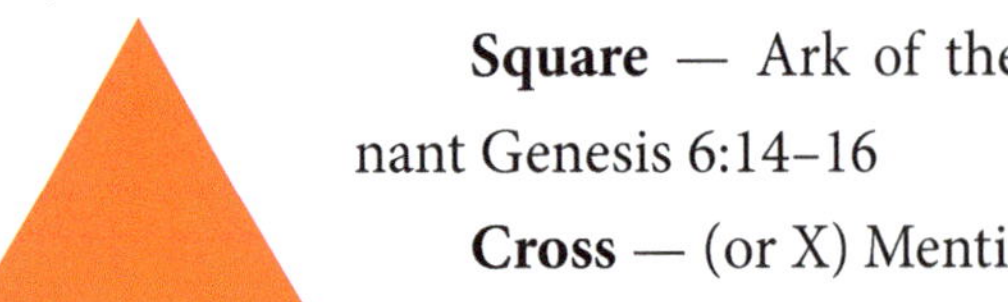

Square — Ark of the Covenant Genesis 6:14–16

Cross — (or X) Mentioned in 28 verses in the New Testament.

As a verb — Unfaithful or disloyal

As a noun — A test of faith, patience, or strength

As an adjective — A cross to bear. As compared to a burden to carry

Kaleidoscope Click

Find as many Shapes as you can. They are everywhere! Cut an apple or orange horizontally for a spiral shape. Your pet's round eyes and cobblestoned pathway are square shapes.

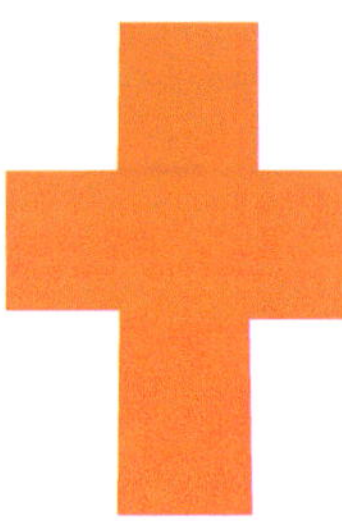

There is a God-shaped hole in the inner man. It can only be fulfilled with the pouring of the Holy Spirit.

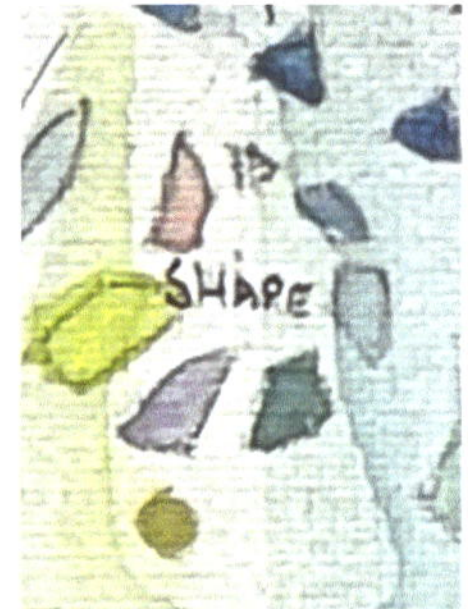

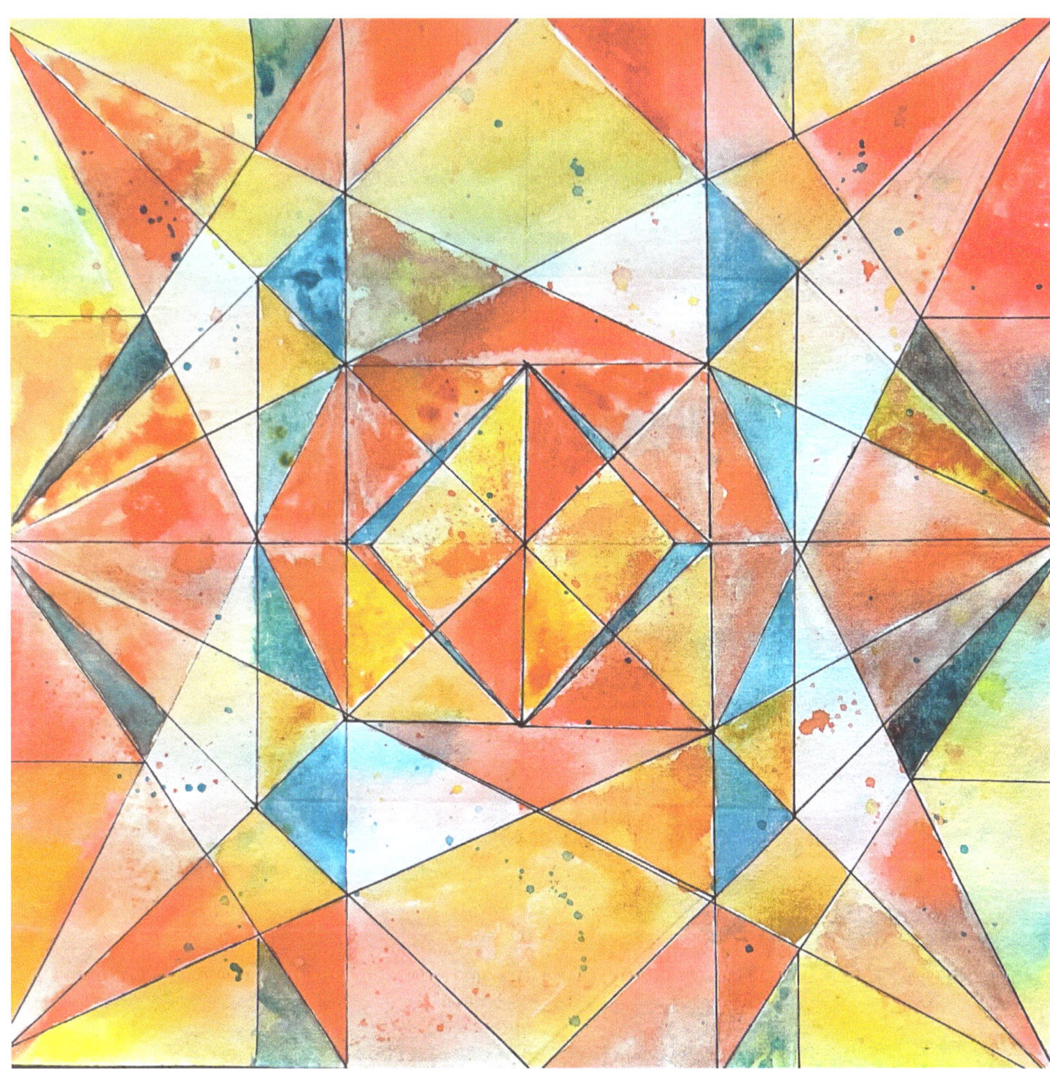

Third Art Element of Seven: SIZE

Different sizes can be created to further organize a work of art from lines and shapes. These sizes can be thick or thin, a large circle versus a medium or small circle.

Size is the third little crystal swirling within the kaleidoscope.

The shape adds dimension to the line.

Form adds depth to shape.

It tells the illusion story on flat paper.

Have you ever wondered, when viewing a painting, "How did the artist create such a realistic work of art?"

You "see" the edges. You "touch" the roundness. You "smell" the flowers. You "hear" the rushing waters.

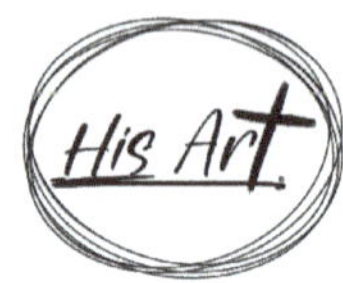

Size in Scripture

"Hast thou not known? Hast thou not heard, that the everlasting God the Lord, the creator of the ends of the earth, fainteth not, neither is weary? There is no searching of his understanding?" (Isaiah 40:28).

Kaleidoscope Click

Look for different sizes: small, medium, and large. Observe adults, children, infants, plants, trees, insects, and horses. Sizes are everywhere!

SIZE tells the ILLUSION StOrY on FLAT PapeR

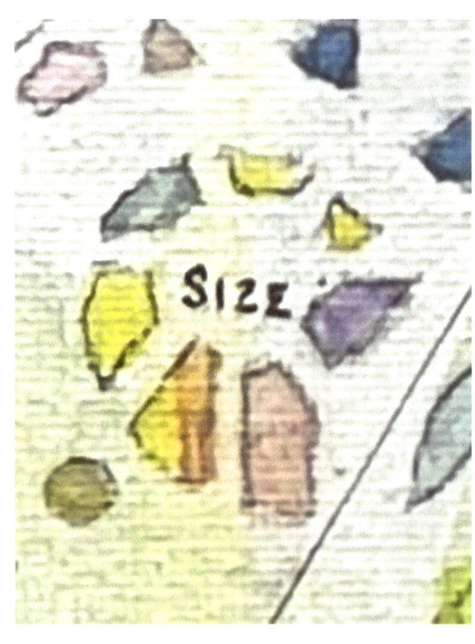

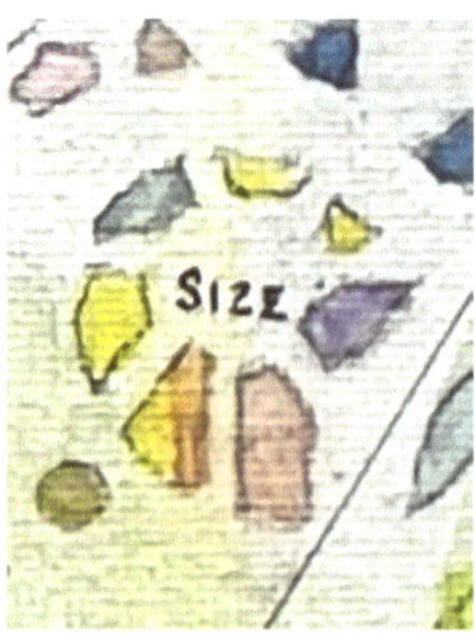

Fourth Art Element of Seven: DIRECTION

Lines, shapes, and sizes can create suggestions of direction. Those directions can be straight across the paper, such as a horizontal line or perhaps a vertical line from top to bottom. A curved line, as in a flower petal, depicts the direction it is leaning. The artist uses the element of direction to guide the viewer through the painting to the main area he wants to share. A well-designed painting will move the viewer around and back again to the focus area to linger there a while longer. The artist begins the story. The viewer continues the story by exploring how the work makes him feel. This element of direction is the fourth piece within the kaleidoscope.

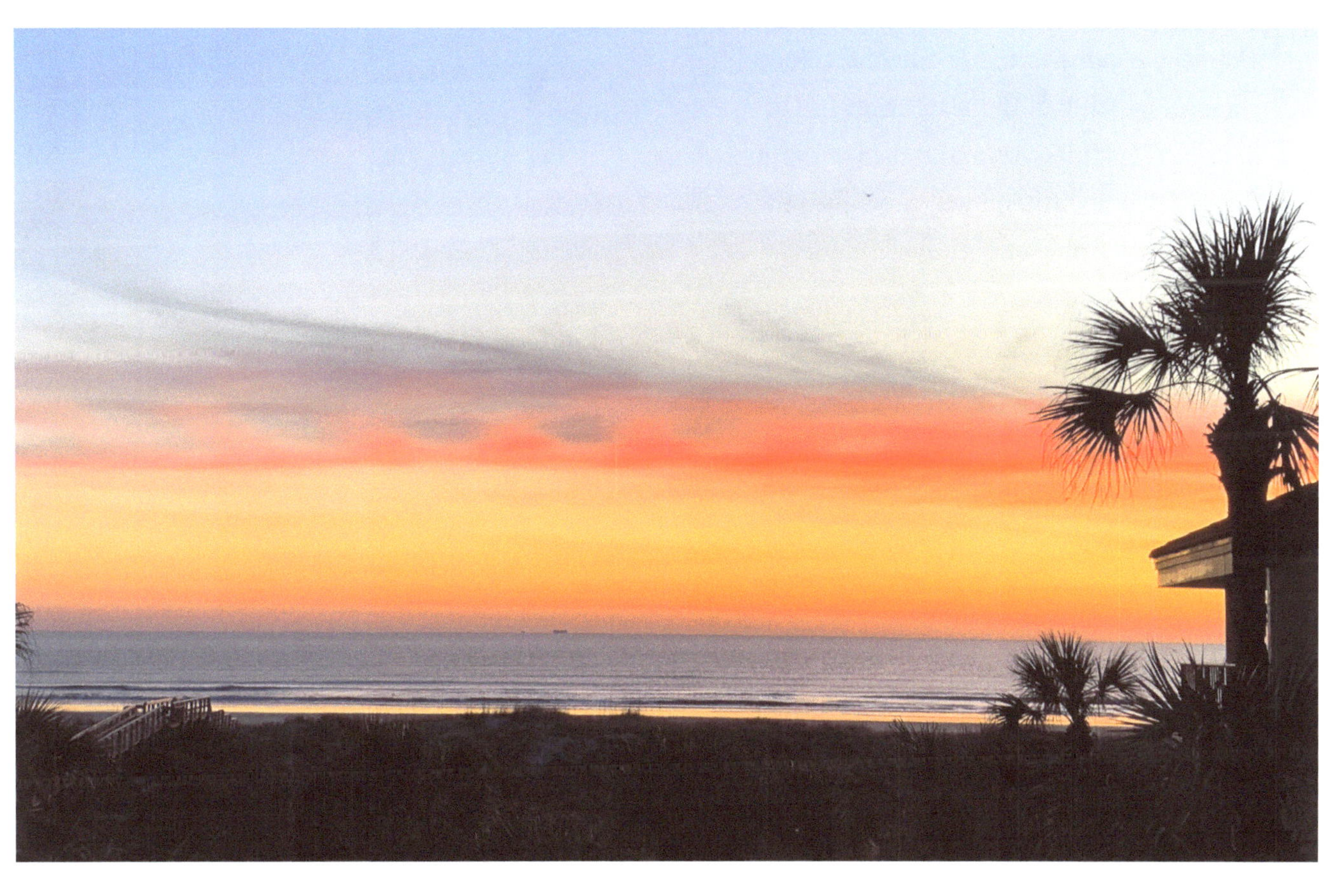

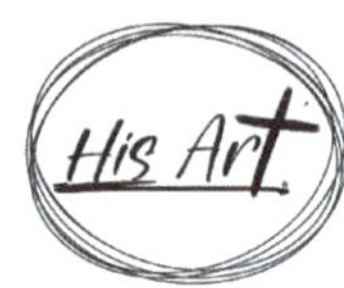

Direction in Scripture

"And they shall come from the east and from the west and from the north and from the south and shall sit down in the kingdom of God" (Luke 13:29).

In the book of Revelation, John paints a picture of a glorious heaven. He shows the bride first (which is us collectively who believe Jesus is the Son of God), but John keeps your focused attention upon Jesus.

"And there came unto me one of the seven angels which had the seven vials full of the seven last plagues, and talked with me, saying, Come hither, I will shew thee the bride, the Lamb's wife" (Revelation 21:9).

Kaleidoscope Click

Look for Directions. They are everywhere! The wind blows the trees, House roof angles, water beads on the windshield, winding roads, and rushing waters. What else can you find?

A well-designed painting will move the viewer's line of vision around and back again to the featured focus area to linger a while longer.

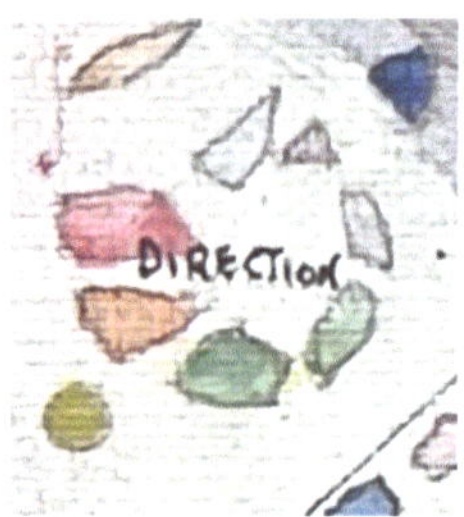

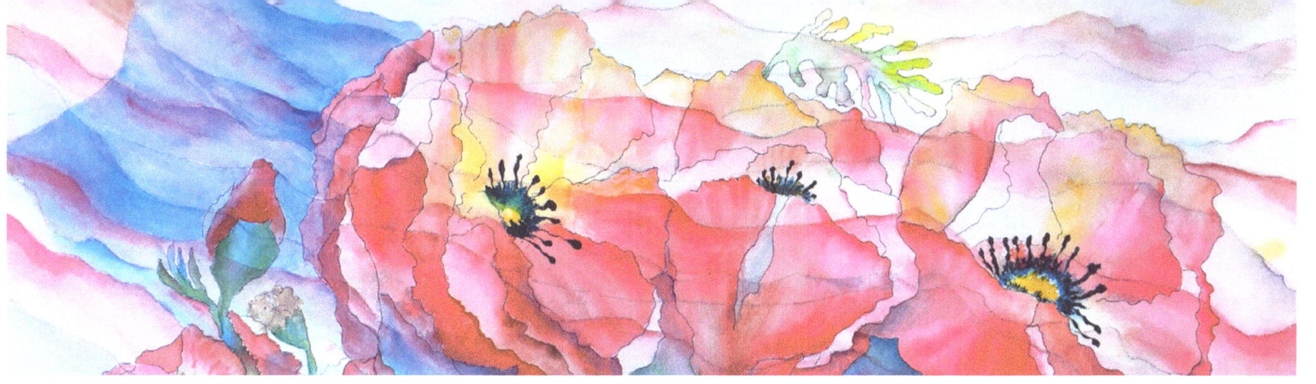

Fifth Art Element of Seven: COLOR

The color concept is a fascinating theory that includes light absorption, interference, reflections, and how our eyes interpret the wide range of natural hues. Warm colors consist of yellow, oranges, reds, and red violets, turning into cool shades of blue violets, blue, blue-green, green, blue, and green, returning to the warmer hue of green-yellow.

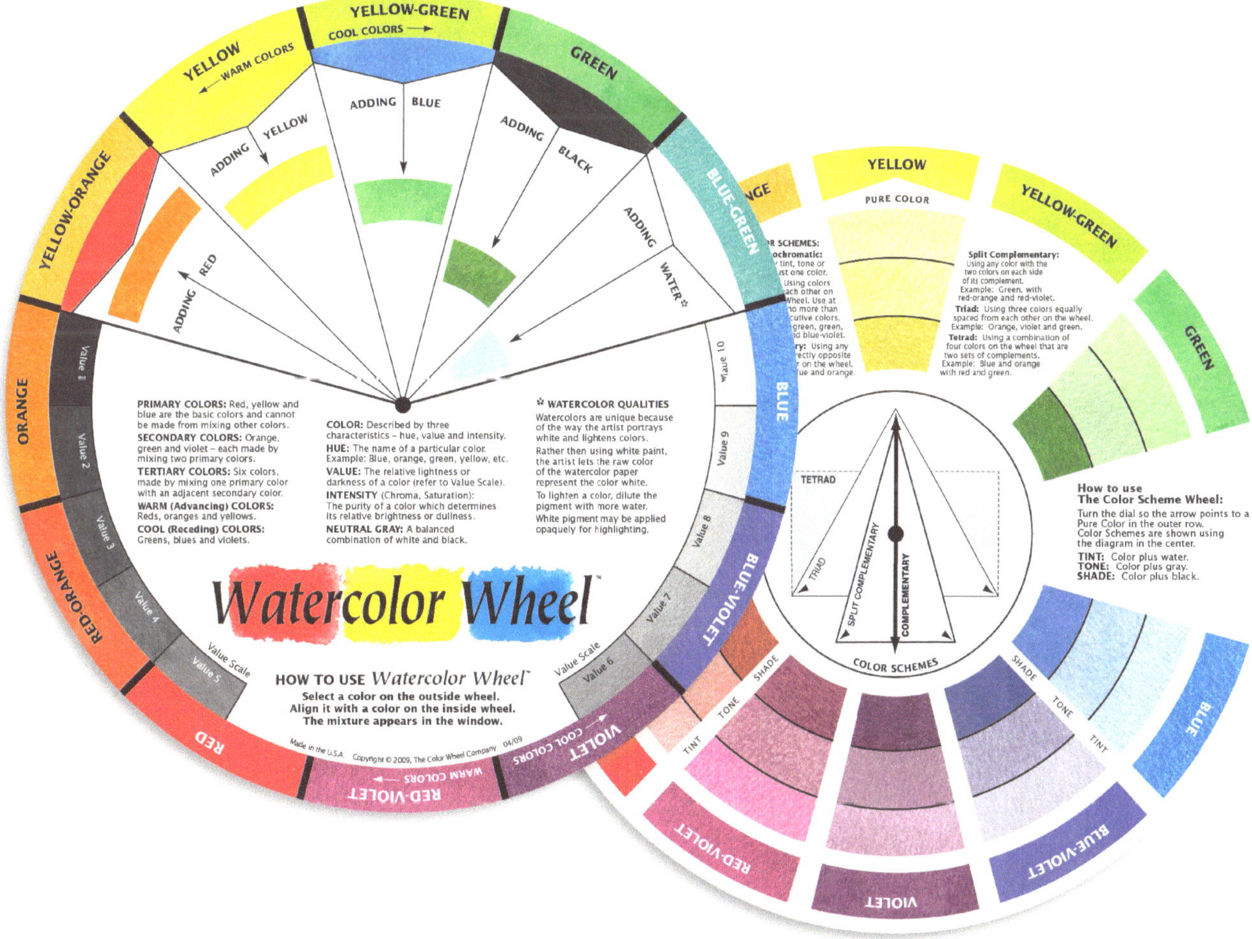

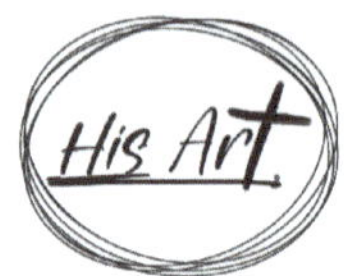

Color in Scripture

"I do set my bow in the clouds and it shall be for a token of a covenant between me and the earth" (Genesis 9:13).

Kaleidoscope Click

Go outside just before sunset and watch how the colors melt into each other. Bring along a color wheel to observe the warm analogous hues of yellows, oranges, and reds blur into their complementary colors of purples and blues, then even deeper tones as the sun drops further out of sight. Experience a glorious morning sunrise. Near the end of a summer's rain, sense the change of the sky's strange brightness and run out to find the rainbow.

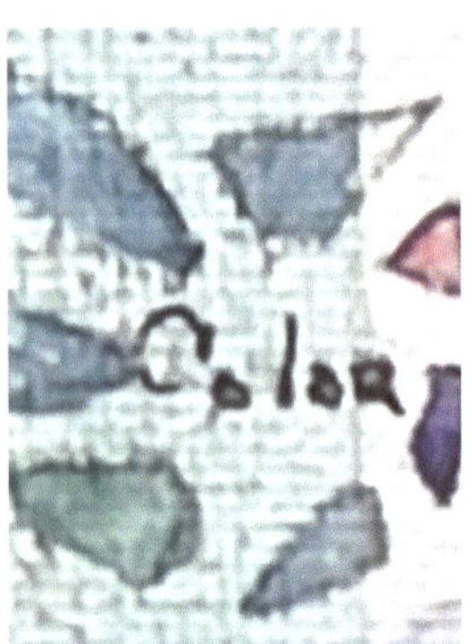

Color receives all the credit. Value does all the work.
~ Author unknown

Sixth Art Element of Seven: VALUE

A line or shape has value— black, white, or various shades of gray.

In art, an artist must have an excellent working knowledge of values and how they strengthen a painting. I remember looking at my painting and not being happy with "something" about it. It was just plain bland, with no exciting, enjoyable area. The technical drawing was good, and the color choices were satisfactory. Then, I learned about values. I was afraid of the dark!

There are light values, medium values, and dark values.

When reflecting off an object, these values reveal gradation, creating the illusion of a highlight on a building or deep, dark shadows under the pine trees.

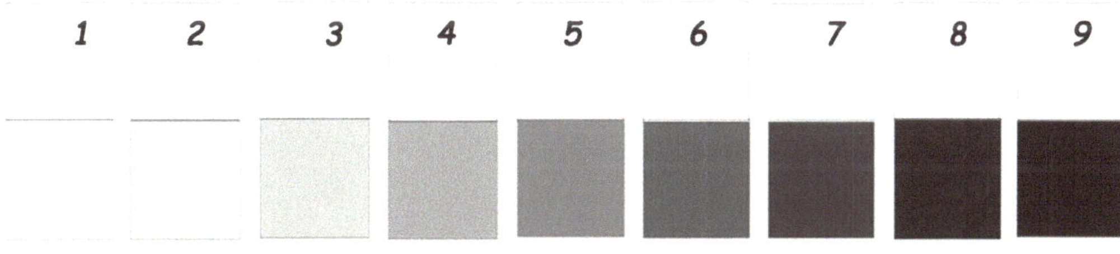

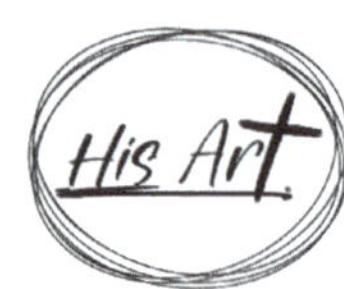

Values in Scripture

If something is not just going quite as planned in my painting, and I will take the time to see what is happening, the problem is usually my choice of values. When reflecting upon my own life, are my life's core values Christ-like?

"Finally, brethren, whatsoever things are true, whatsoever things are honest, whosoever things are just whatsoever, things are pure, whatsoever things are lovely, whatsoever things are of good report; if there by any virtue, and if there be any praise, think on these things" (Philippians 4:8).

"For with thee is the fountain of life; in thy light shall we see light." (Psalms 36:9)

"But if thine eye be evil, thy whole body shall be full of darkness. If therefore the light that is in thee be darkness, how great is that darkness!" (Matthew 6:23).

"Then spake Jesus again unto them, saying, I am the light of the world: he that followeth me shall not walk in darkness, but shall have the light of life" (John 8:12).

Kaleidoscope Click

Look for light, medium, and dark values within the branches of the trees, shadows on the sidewalk, or a flower arrangement. They are everywhere! Where else can you find them?

In my life, are my core values Christ-like?

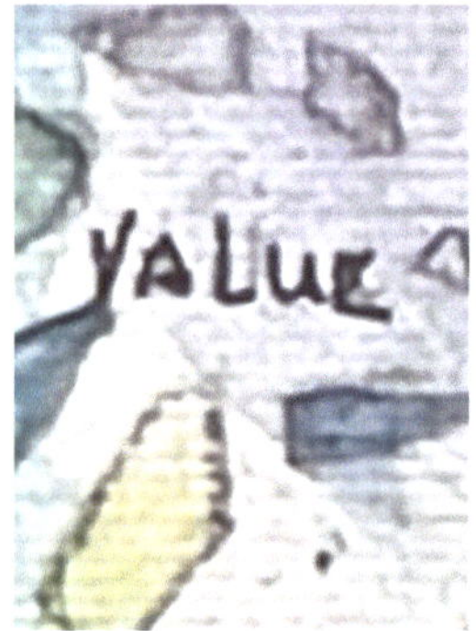

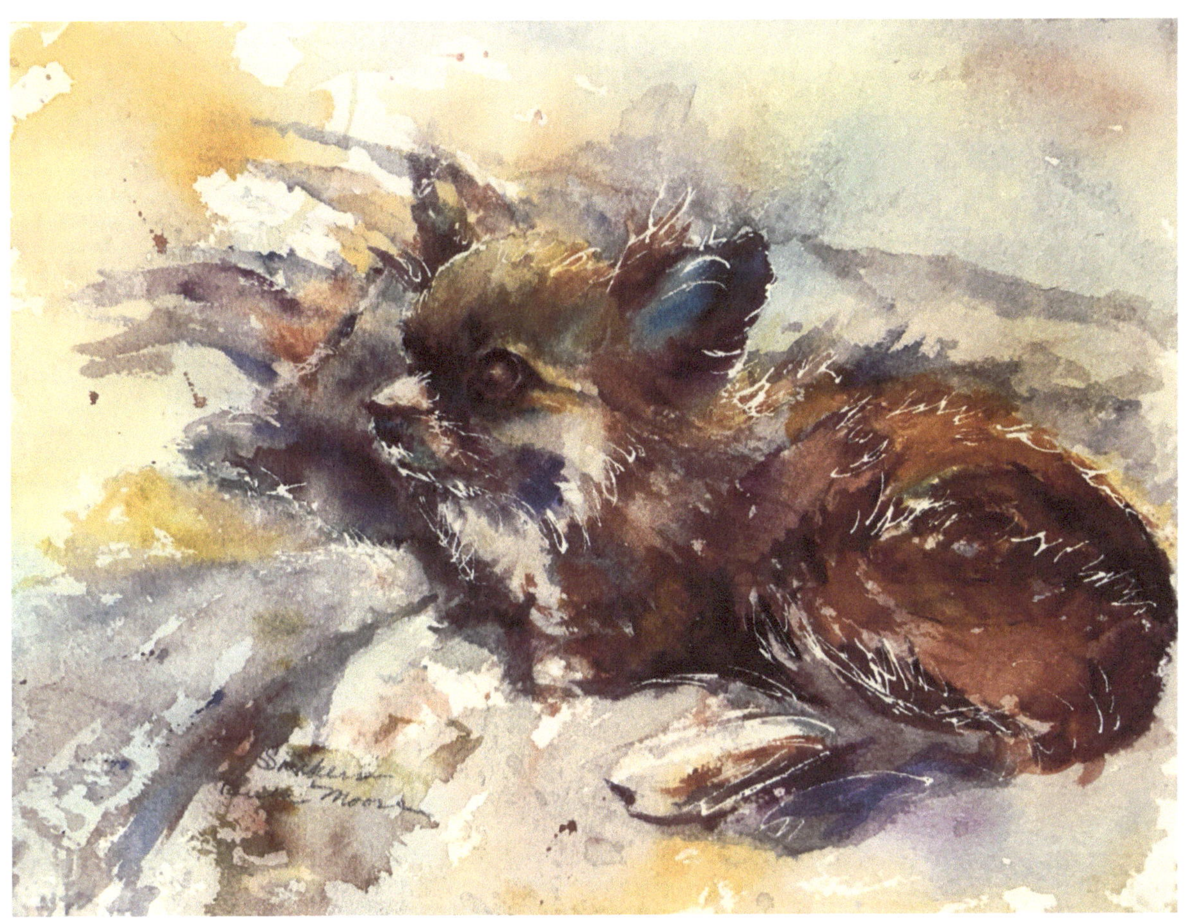

Seventh Art Element of Seven: TEXTURE

Line or shape can be given the illusion of texture, such as the rough tree trunk, soft rabbit fur, or the smooth feel of river round stones.

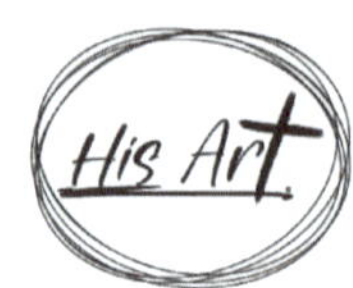

Texture in Scripture

"A soft answer turneth away wrath" (Proverbs 15:1).

"And chose him five smooth stones out of the brook" (1 Samuel 17:40b).

"For God maketh my heart soft and the Almighty troubled me" (Job 23:16).

"Every valley shall be filled and every mountain and hill shall be brought low and the crooked shall be made straight, and the rough ways shall be made smooth; And all flesh shall see the salvation of God" (Luke 3:5–6).

"Again, he limiteth a certain day, saying in David, To day, after so long a time; as it is said, To day if ye will hear his voice, harden not your hearts" (Hebrews 4:7).

"Forasmuch as ye are manifested declared to be the epistle of Christ ministered by us, written not with ink, but with the spirit of God; not in the tables of stone but in fleshy tables of the heart" (2 Corinthians 3:3).

Kaleidoscope Click

Look for texture first by observing, then by touching. It is everywhere! The soft fur of your little dog, the texture on couch cushions, a velvety smooth flower petal. The grassy blade spikes. Practice drawing or painting a textured resemblance of what you see to tell your viewer.

Line provides the illusion of texture.

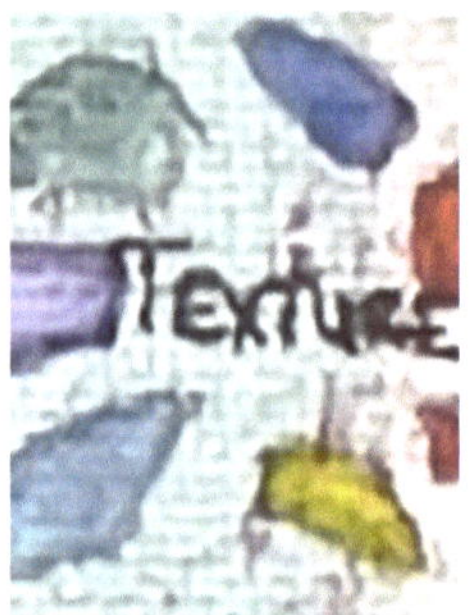

A STUDY OF PERSPECTIVE
per·spec·tive pərˈspektiv

When learning how to draw, perspective must be considered. What methods and techniques are required to produce a lifelike resemblance of your subject matter, whether it be a building, a landscape, or a portrait? The *Merriam-Webster Dictionary* defines perspective as the technique or process of representing on a plane or curved surface the spatial relation of objects as they might appear to the eye. Specifically, representation in a drawing or painting of parallel lines as converging in order to give the illusion of depth and distance.

Thus far in this book, we have reviewed the seven elements in the art design language and how they are each tried and true. Another essential component in the study is your creativity and how you, as an individual, interpret how they work together. Each human being is God's creation and has been given the gift of imagination, a powerful tool that empowers us to create. If I give the same assignment to a room of art students, each will have their own diverse and inspired way to tell the story to the viewer, inspiring us all with their unique perspectives and personal points of view.

I offer my Chickadee painting as a lesson in perspective and my thought process when considering a unique gift for my friend Irene. Irene's homeland is the Bavarian Alps area of Germany, and she showed me faded photos of the years spent there. Once, she also mentioned that her favorite little bird was the chickadee, which also lives in Europe. How could I combine these two special memories into one painting? My imagination dreamed up this small bird resting in the wildflowers and viewing the mountainous landscape in Bavaria. The viewer first sees the bird looking up and is curious to discover what he is viewing, which is the atmospheric perspective through the farmland and villages to the distant mountains. This illusion is accomplished on a flat piece of paper by knowing how to effectively use each element: line, shape, size, direction, value, color, and texture.

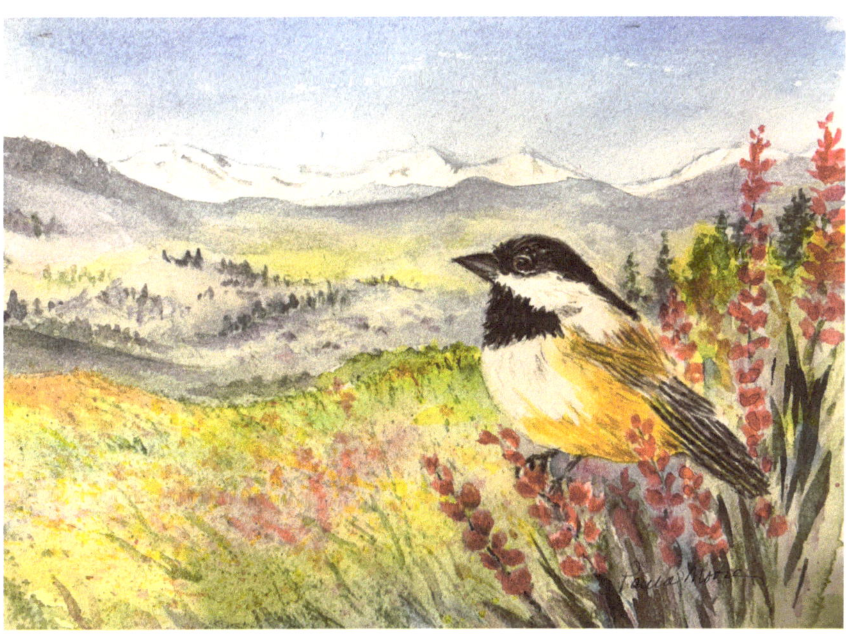

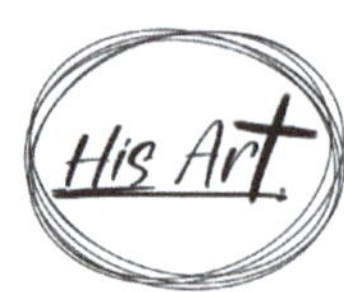

Perspective in Scripture

"For my thoughts are not your thoughts, neither are your ways my ways, saith the LORD. For as the heavens are higher than the earth, so are my ways higher than your ways, and my thoughts than your thoughts" (Isaiah 55: 8–9).

Kaleidoscope Click

Try this: Find perspective in the angles of buildings and observe long roads seemingly getting narrower and smaller in the background. Look from above and look from underneath. Perspective is everywhere. What can you see differently?

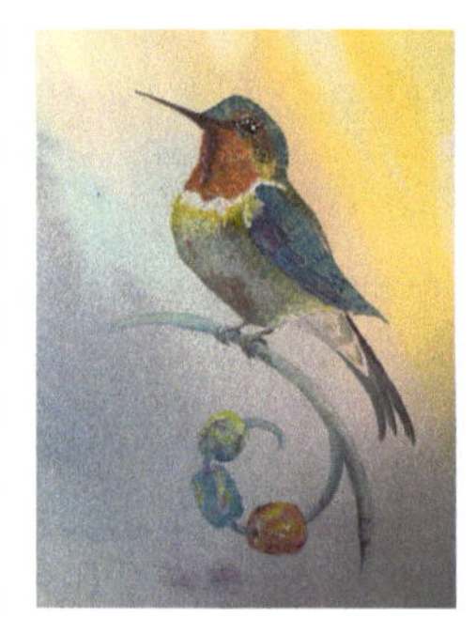

Change your perspective by seeing another angle. Sometimes, just sitting in the chair across the room will help you to consider another solution to an issue. That's why it is phrased: a different point of view.

Part 4

The Eight Principles of Design Comparisons to God's Messages of Truth

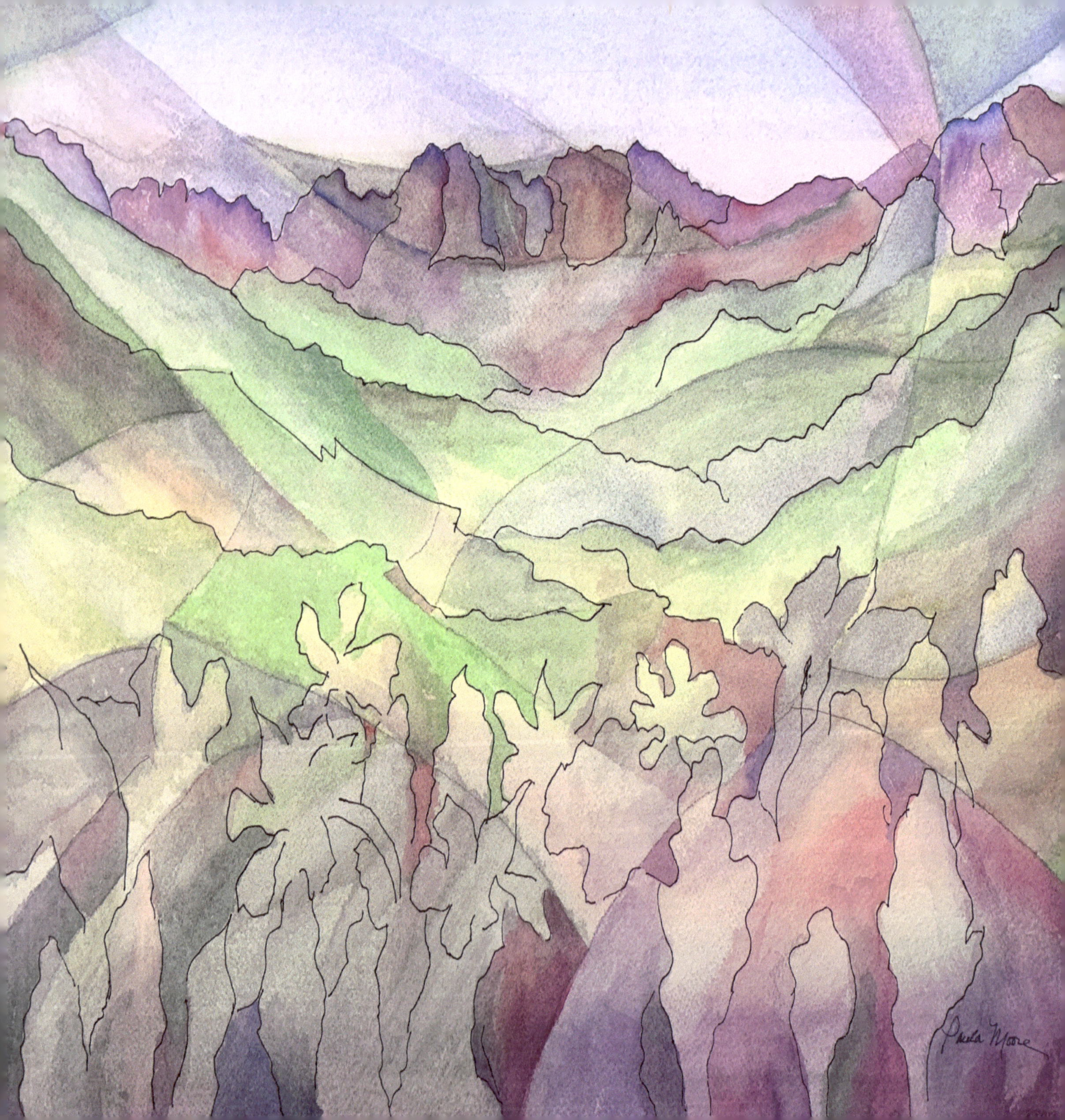
Paula Moore

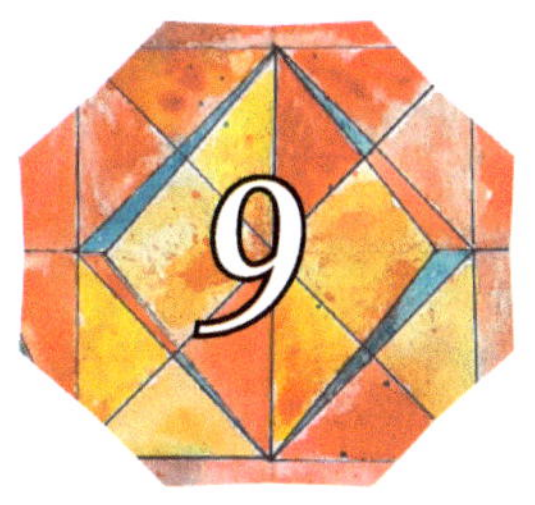

Introduction to the Principles of Design

The structure and boundaries within the kaleidoscope

Design is implementing a plan to organize space, whether that be a living room or a blank canvas

The eight principles of design are:

- Dominance
- Unity
- Repetition
- Harmony
- Balance
- Gradation
- Alternation
- Conflict

When considering the parts of the kaleidoscope, three or more lengths of mirrors, when connected together, create optical illusions of the items held within its borders. These wedged stoic shapes act as the boundaries where the colored chips can bounce at will and create thrilling designs one after another. These wedged mirrored walls are akin to the principles of design.

They remain trustworthy and do not move from their position.

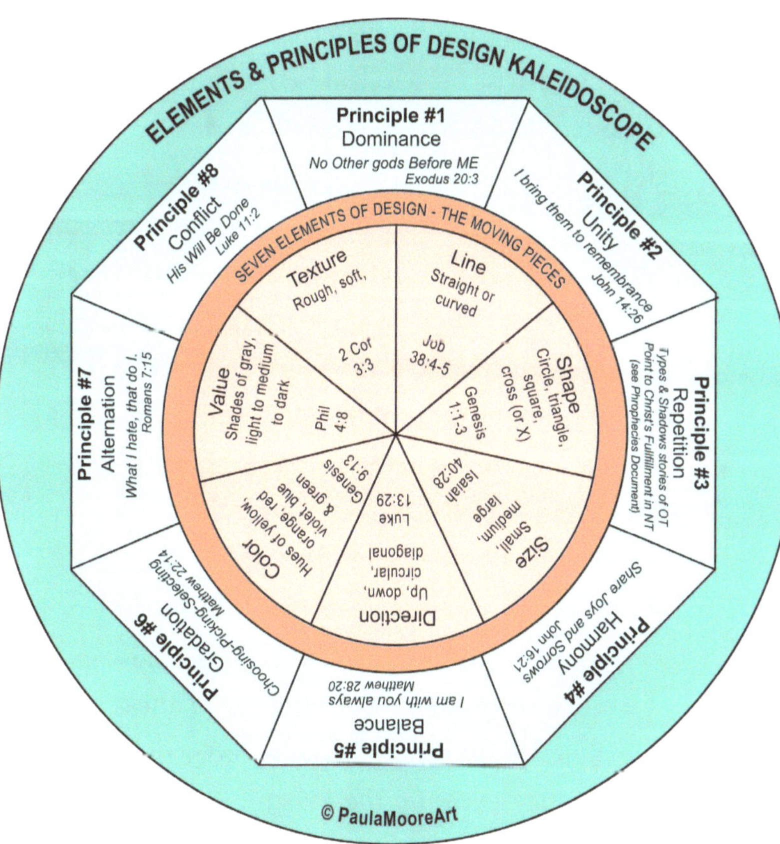

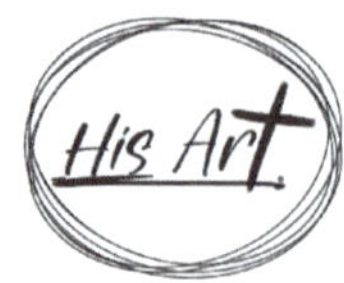

"By faith [that is, with an inherent trust and enduring confidence in the power, wisdom, and goodness of God], we understand that the worlds (universe, ages) were framed and created [formed, put in order, and equipped for their intended purpose] by the word of God so that what is seen was not made out of things which are visible" (Heb 11:3 AMP).

Kaleidoscope Click

Return to the Elements and Principles of Design Comparison to a Kaleidoscope Guide. You have reviewed the inner circle and the seven elements of design. Can you recall all of them in order?

Now for this exercise. Review the outer ring holding the eight structure principles that contain the elements. The principles are the outside walls where all our elements can move and play. Pretend that the outer rim is spinning. The inner crystal elements are moving in this contained space. Are you beginning to realize the concept?

Remember the 3x5 index card I asked you to jot down the seven elements (the tools or the small crystal pieces contained within a kaleidoscope)? Take that same card and write down these eight principles of design in the same order mentioned above. They make up the structure that holds the movable bits, providing the boundaries and structures where they can freely move together. As you review the kaleidoscope guide, Picture this framework in your mind's eye, holding the elements. Sketch out a diagram to train your artistic eye to see.

Is the concept beginning to click?

These wedged mirrored walls are akin to the principles of design. They remain trustworthy and do not move from their position.

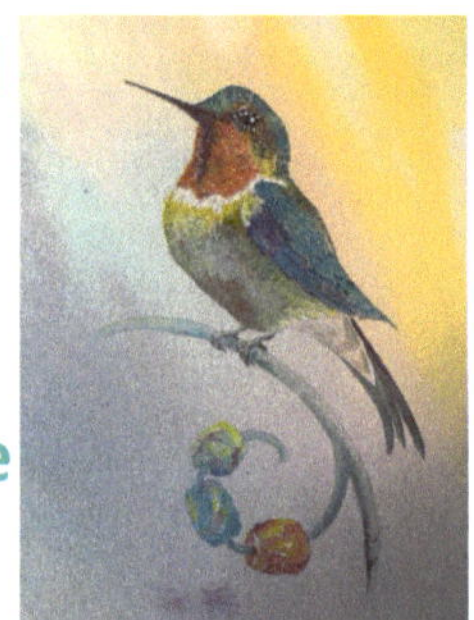

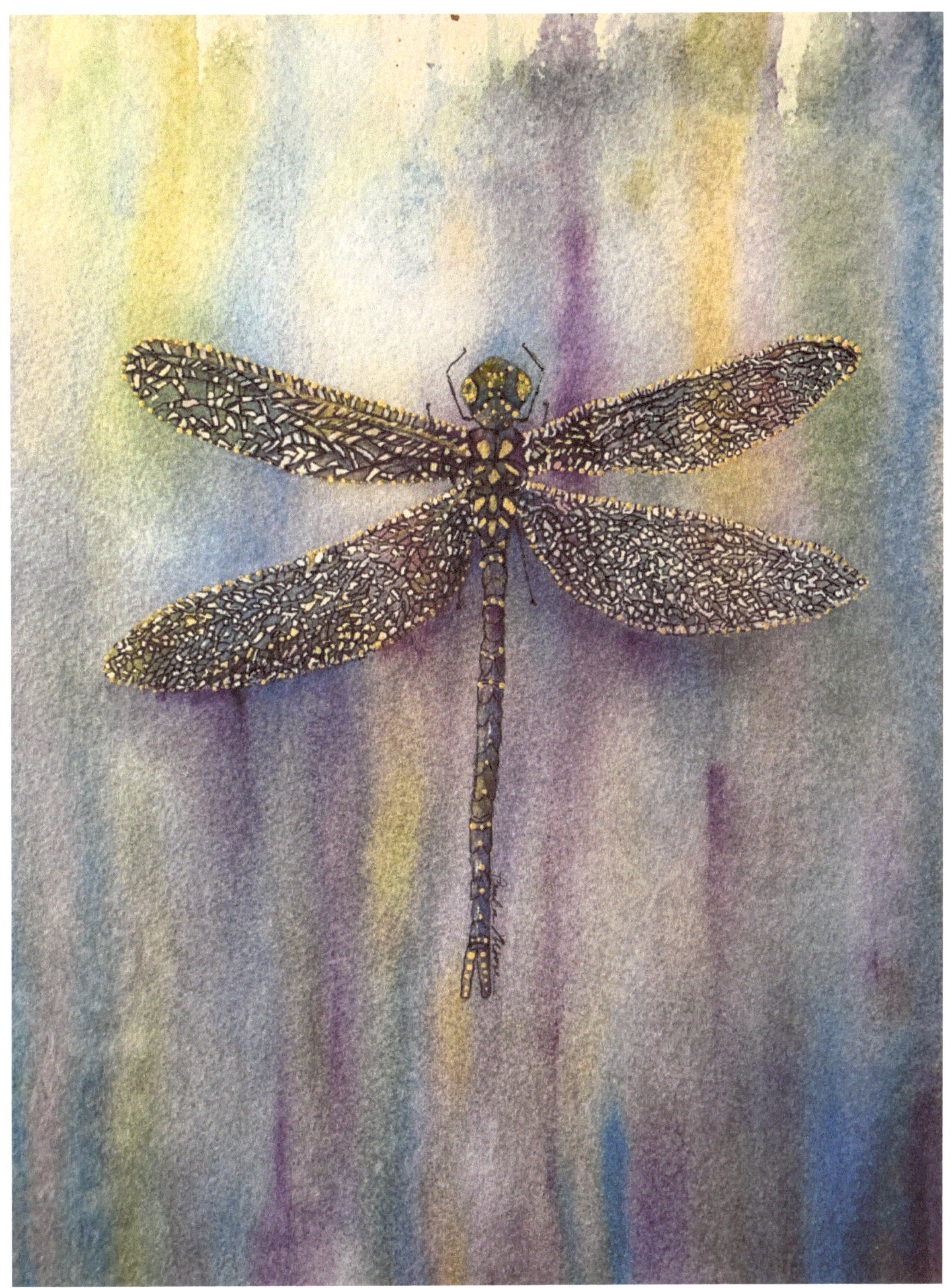

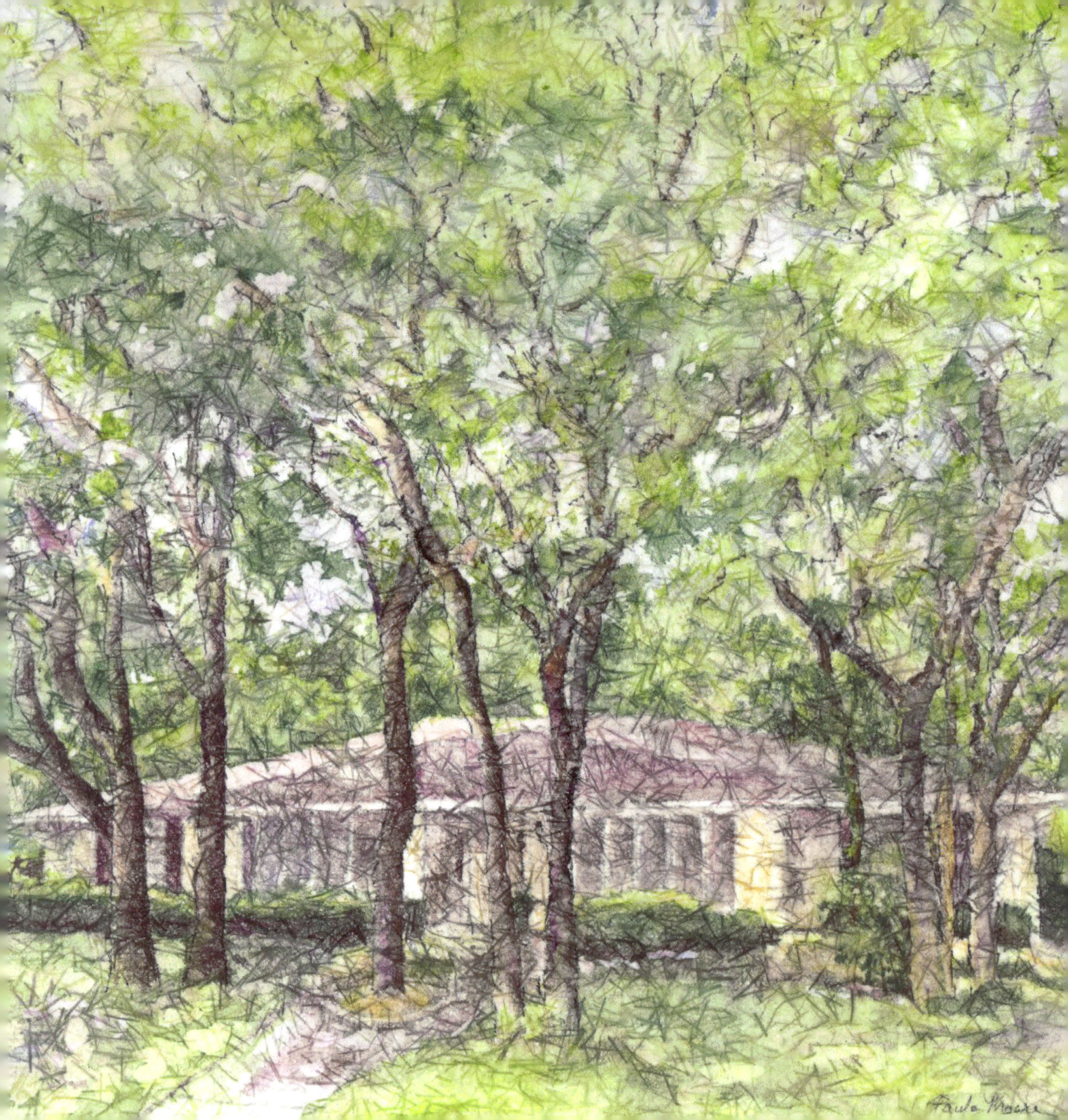

First of Eight Principles: Dominance

For a successful work of art, there must be a dominance, which is to say, the evidence of each element's important role. Just as a house being built begins with the structure of a strong foundation and framing room layouts to guarantee that your home will flow as you hope for many years to come. With no foundational planning, the structure will be weak and fall apart. Consider the following synonyms, "more" or "larger," instead of the word dominance when thinking about the design elements. In your painting, there must be more of, or larger, of a type of line, more of one kind of shape used, and more of a particular size, such as five large, three middle sizes, and two small. The painting should have a clear direction where it leads the viewer's eye. Is it angular or curved? There should be more than one color in your color scheme, and more than one value should be presented. For example, is it a painting capturing a sunny day or a night scene? For a sunlit day, your color scheme choice might be bright blues and yellow sun rays. For an evening painting, the deep purple sky holds a silvery blue moon and stars while suggesting the long shadows playing between dark green pine trees. Lastly, there should be evidence of more texture. Do you have very soft flower petals or rough tree bark as the most important role in the painting?

If you understand only one of the eight principles, to me, dominance is the most important. Everything else will find its place when you have a strong dominance in each of the elements. Otherwise, the painting will be disorganized and not hold together successfully. You will be disappointed with your efforts.

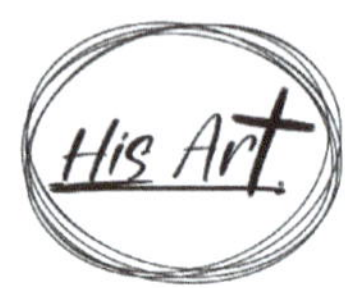

Dominance in Scripture

Such as in life, we must have a central theme. The individual has a lord to worship: Either the ways of this sinful world or Christ.

"Thou shalt have no other gods before me" (Exodus 20:3).

Kaleidoscope Click

Look for the dominant color in a room, which usually means, what do you see more of? Do you see what value is dominant in your kitchen? More white cabinets or medium-valued floors. There is dominance everywhere! What else can you discover in your home or in nature?

Everything else will find its place when you have a strong dominance in each of the elements.

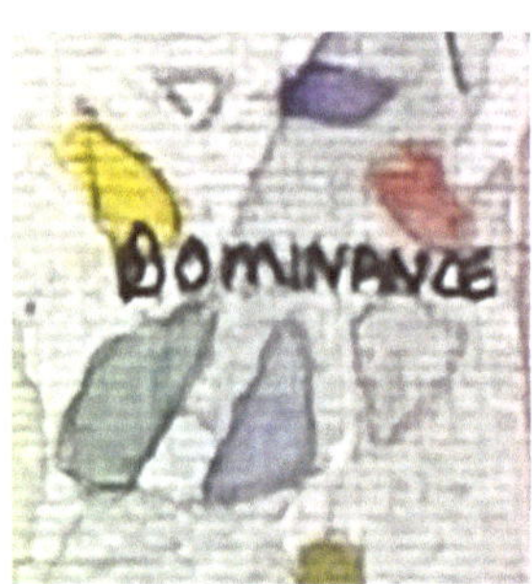

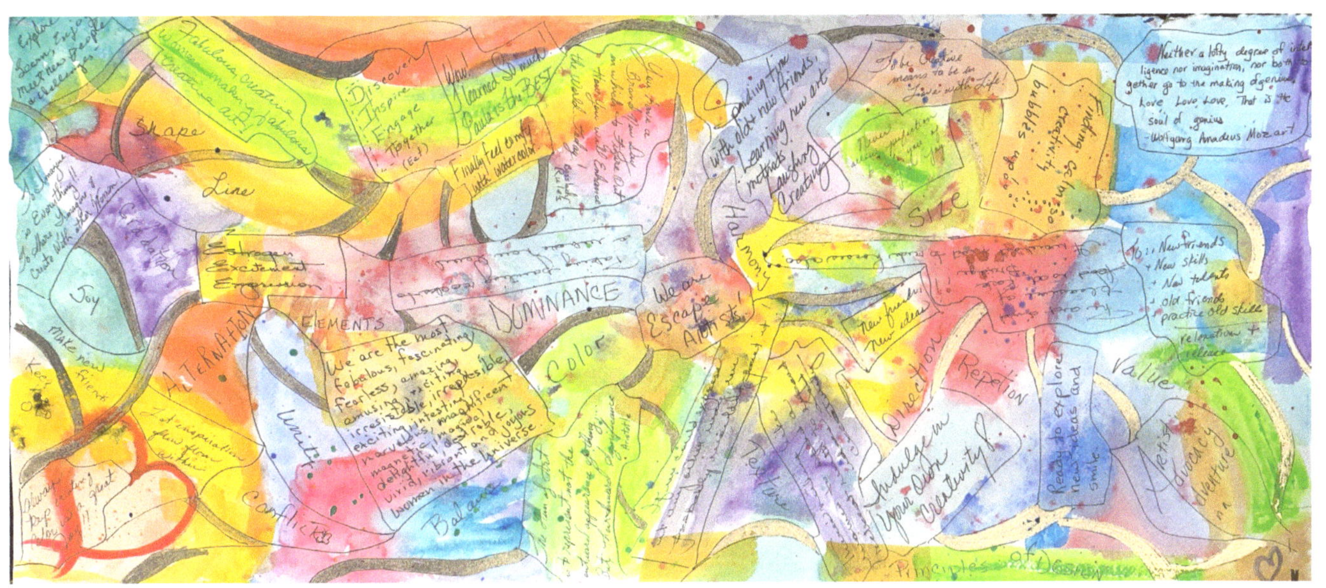

Second of Eight Principles: Unity

Think of a time when you were in a situation where many people participated in the same activity. For example, a music concert, where everyone is watching the band and singing every word of the lyrics by memory. Or perhaps a basketball game where each member has a role to play. Hours of practicing unify these confident players as they race down the court, passing the ball back and forth, giving us yet another thrilling three-pointer basket.

In a painting, each element must be united, confidently playing together to achieve a common goal. As in the basketball team, honing the fundamentals of design language skills will determine whether the artist makes the A team or sits on the bench.

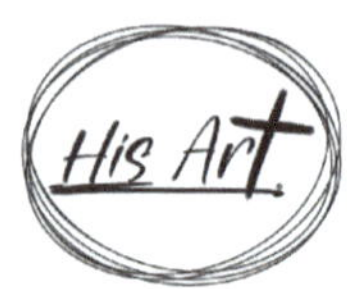

Unity in Scripture

"There is one body, and one Spirit, even as ye are called in one hope of your calling; One Lord, one faith, one baptism, One God and Father of all, who is above all, and through all, and in you all" (Ephesians 4:4).

When several activities are happening simultaneously, such as the music concert or sports game I described, we also witness every detail of it. It's the same as with a painting at first observance. You see the cohesive, whole picture, and then your eyes simultaneously explore and see different areas of the same scene.

I wrote of this study of the book of Revelation earlier in the book. Note: it is only One

Revelation and not multiple! Since you are reading my book about a kaleidoscope comparison of the design language and Biblical truths, I invite you to find a quiet place and mindfully read the passages of Revelation. Particularly, turn your focus to Chapters 11, 13, and 19:11.

I hope you start to see the magnificent scenes unfolding!

Kaleidoscope Click

The next time you visit a produce department, look for unity. Glance overall, then zoom into each area of fruits and vegetables. Even the signage is in unity. What else can you find?

In a painting, each element must be united confidently, playing together to achieve a common goal: to create a successful painting.

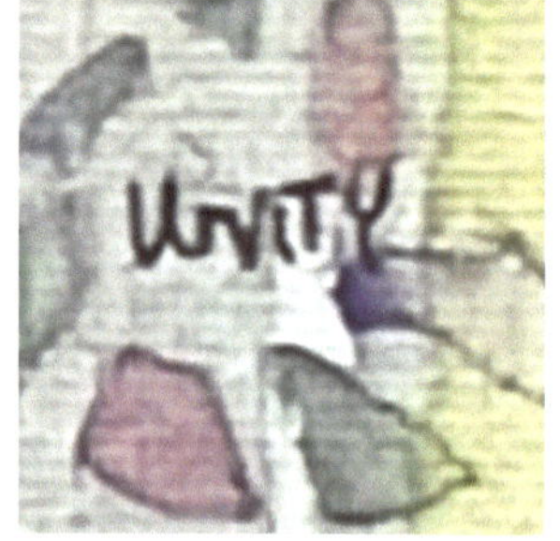

Third of Eight Principles: Repetition

Do you have a woven basket close by? Please pick it up and observe the design created by simply weaving a strand over and under, over and under. Notice the shaping and the variety of designs it has taken to complete the basket. (Do you also see evidence of the other principles of dominance and unity?) A work of art must have repetition and rhythm to give it variety and interest. I have painted a refrain of musical notes as flowers, secretly singing a favorite song lyric. Other associations are footprints on the sandy beach and cloud shapes repeating across the sky.

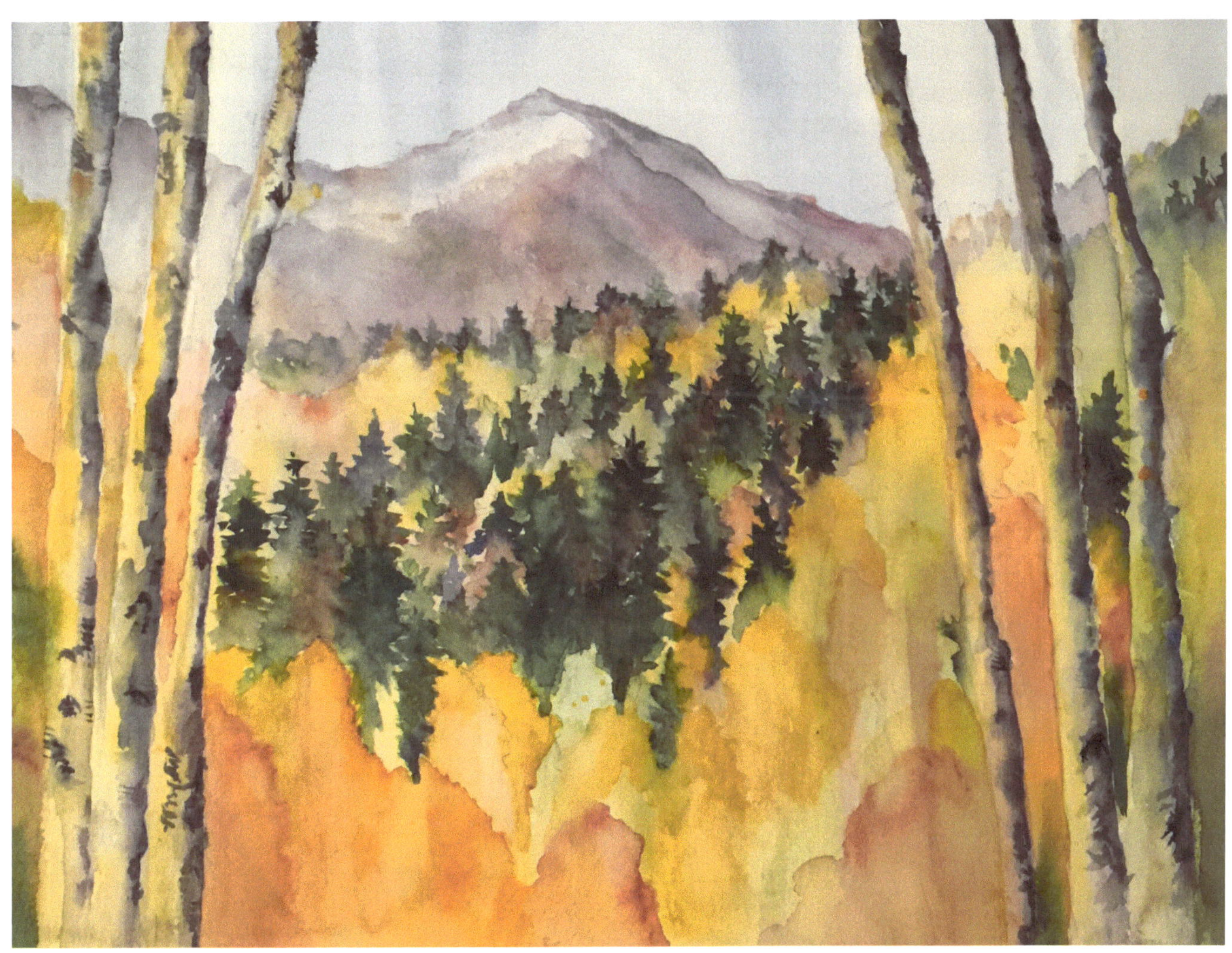

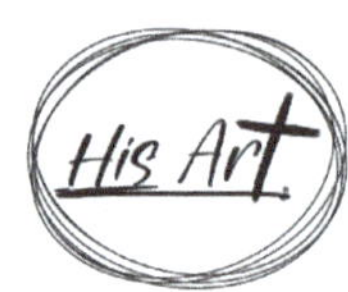

Repetition in Scripture

"Of whom we have many things to say, and hard to be uttered, seeing ye are dull of hearing. For when for the time ye ought to be teachers, ye have need that one teach you again which be the first principles of the oracles of God; and are become such as have need of milk, and not of strong meat. For every one that useth milk is skillful in the word of righteousness: for he is a babe. But strong meat belongeth to them that are of full age, even those who by reason of use have their senses exercised to discern both good and evil" (Hebrews 5:11-14).

"In all things shewing thyself a pattern of good works: in doctrine shewing uncorruptness, gravity and sincerity" (Titus 2:7).

Kaleidoscope Click

REPETITION is everywhere! The wallpaper pattern, the black and white piano keys, or a large cluster of maple leaves—what else can you find?

A work of art must have repetition and rhythm to give it variety and interest.

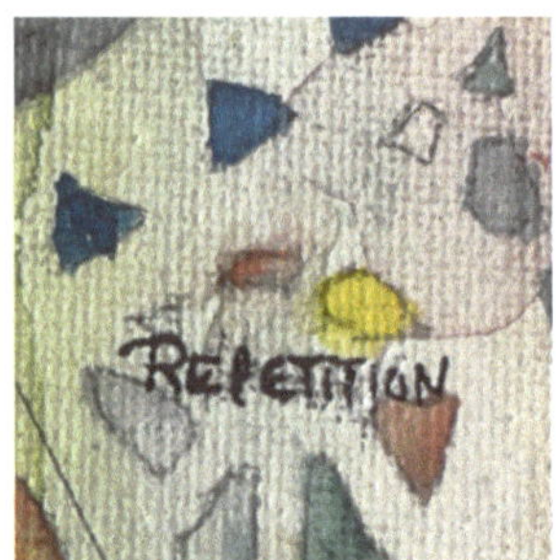

Fourth of Eight Principles: Harmony

This could be defined as a pleasing melody made up of a medley of musical notes in repetition and rhythm. Consider a group of small children playing together in a sandbox. Everyone gets along, sharing their imagination, oblivious to what time it is and of the supervising adults sitting close by. Everyone is in harmony.

The party ends when someone gets mad, takes their dump truck, and leaves. Similarly, all the elements in a piece of art should play well together, recognizing all of the elements with nothing symbolically yelling at the viewer, such as a messy paint blob or a strange angle that needs adjustment.

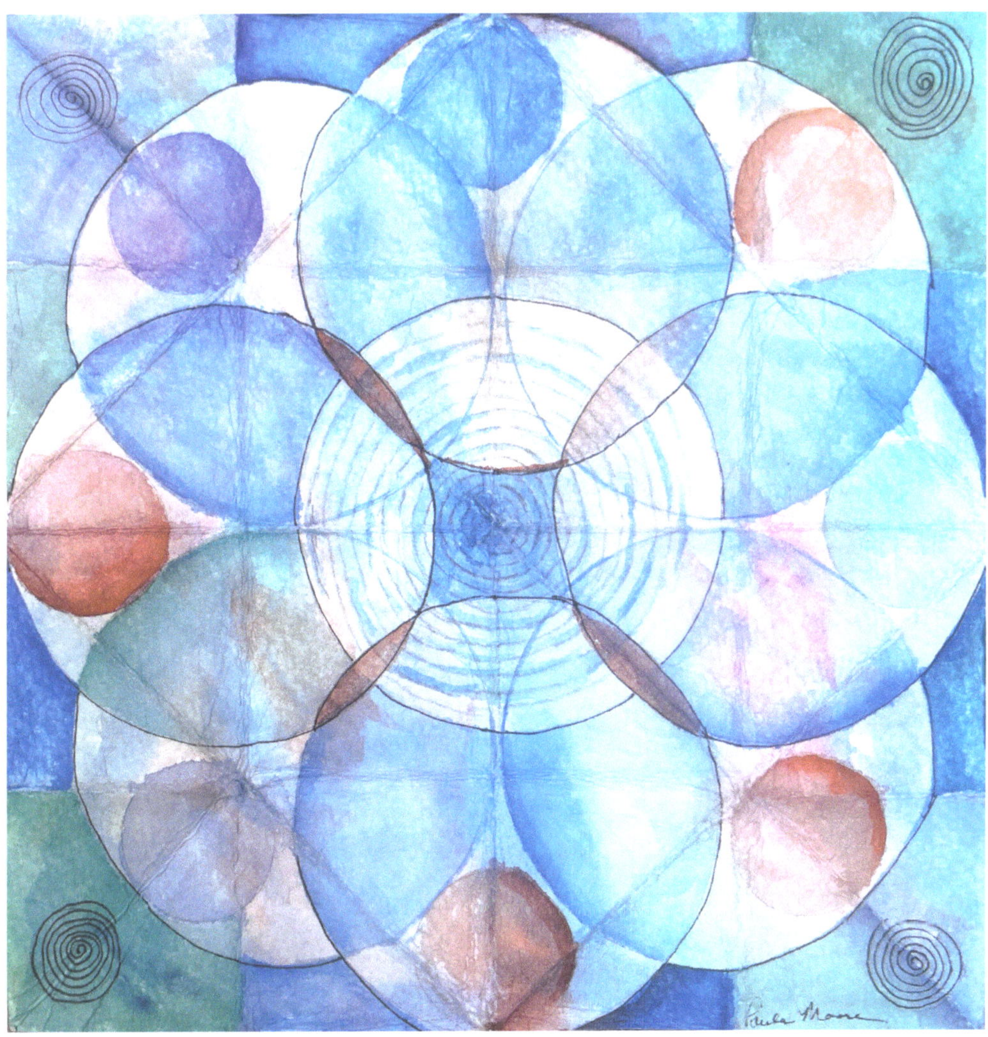

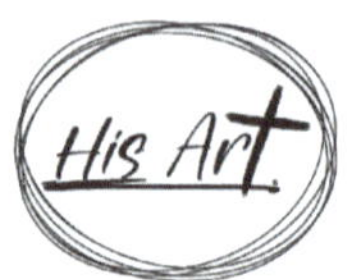

Harmony in the Scriptures

There is harmony in the Scriptures. The same story told in the Old Testament are the types and shadows of what is to come to pass in the New Testament and beyond. Everything points to Christ. All Scriptures fit together perfectly, presenting the beautiful, intricate details of the Creator's masterful yet straightforward plan. Christ is the perfect one and the only sacrifice required to restore the relationship between God and us individually. It is not a concept that can be reasoned with our intellectual thoughts. Only by faith believing will the painting of Christ be revealed. God is not a God of confusion, and his principles are true. On the contrary, the enemy, Satan, is the father of lies and deception, roaming around to find who they can devour. Please do not doubt that he and his demons are alive and well on planet Earth. One of his favorite weapons is to whisper just a suggestion of doubt. Be sure you are listening to the voice of truth!

"Be of the same mind one toward another. Mind not high things, but condescend to men of low estate. Be not wise in your own conceits. Recompense to no man evil for evil. Provide things honest in the sight of all men. If it be possible, as much as lieth in you, live peaceably with all men. Dearly beloved, avenge not yourselves, but rather give place unto wrath: for it is written, Vengeance is mine; I will repay, saith the Lord. Therefore, if thine enemy hunger, feed him; if he thirst, give him drink: for in so doing thou shalt heap coals of fire on his head. Be not overcome of evil, but overcome evil with good. Be kindly affectioned one to another with brotherly love; in honour preferring one another" (Romans 12:16–21) .

Kaleidoscope Click

The principle of HARMONY is everywhere! Look for analogous colors of yellow, orange, and red that play well together. Observe red roses surrounded by their dark green leaves complement. What else can you discover?

All the elements in a piece of art should play well together. When they do, you will recognize all the elements with nothing symbolically yelling at the viewer. This is akin to when a musician stops to tune his guitar. He can discern there is a string out of tune.

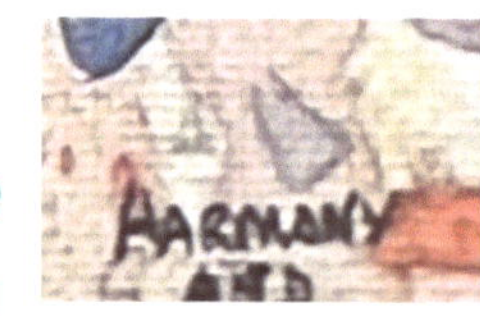

Fifth of Eight Principles: Balance

Balance can be asymmetrical or symmetrical. It can be rigid and formal or take a more casual, informal appearance. There is also another type of balance that automatically happens. An example is the flamingo bird's instinct to balance perfectly on one foot.

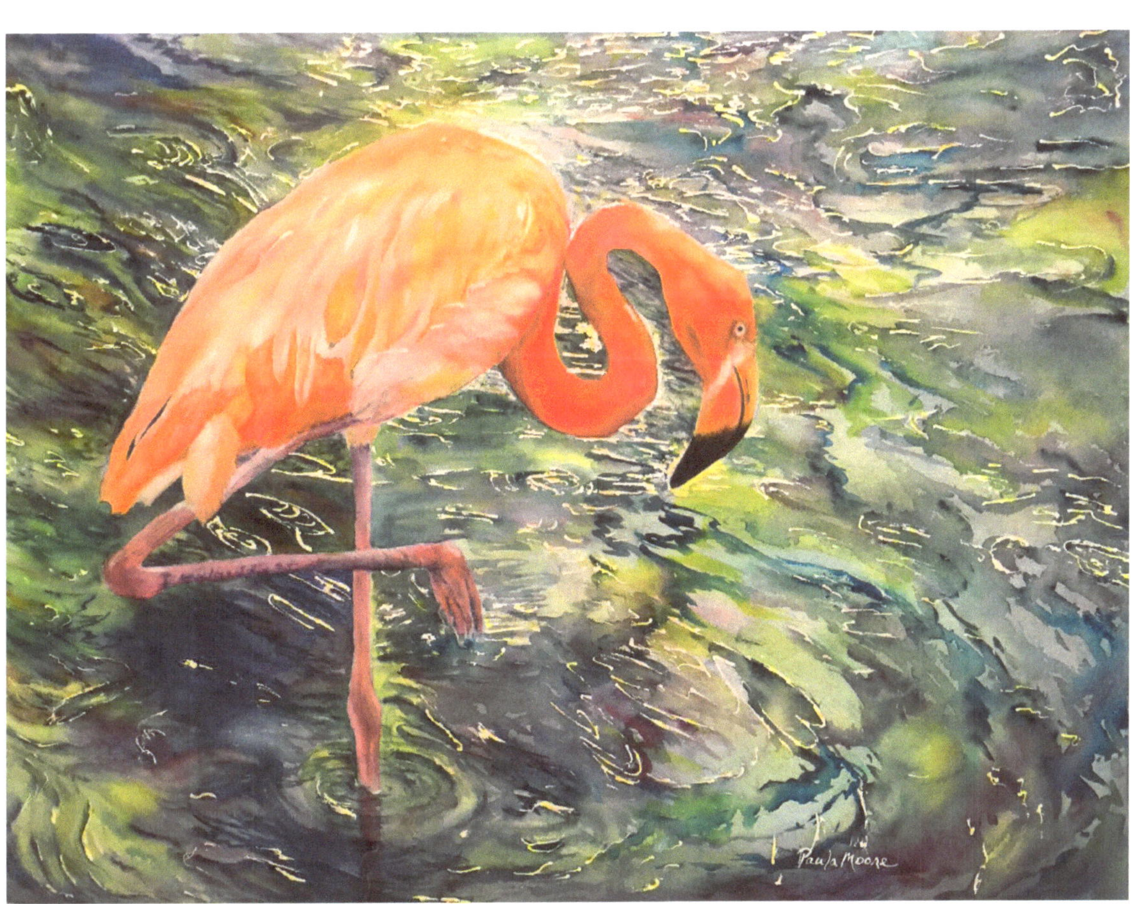

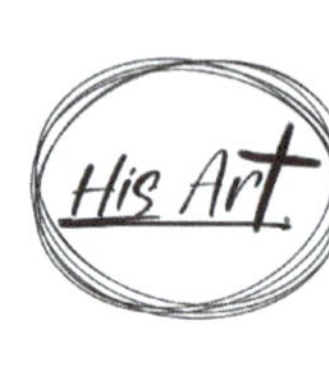

Balance in Scripture

"Carry each other's burdens, and in this way, you will fulfill the law of Christ" (Galatians 6:2 NIV).

Kaleidoscope Click

The balance principle is everywhere. Teeter totters. The interior design tip is having an odd number of items. Three, five, or seven make an interesting arrangement. A formal table setting for eight. What else can you find?

The flamingo bird's instinctive nature is to balance on one foot.

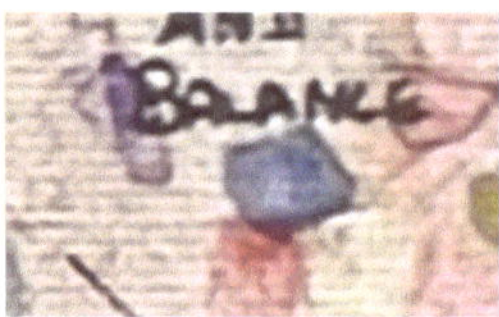

Sixth of Eight Principles: Gradation

Recall a gradual transition of a beautiful sunset moving seamlessly from one color to the next.

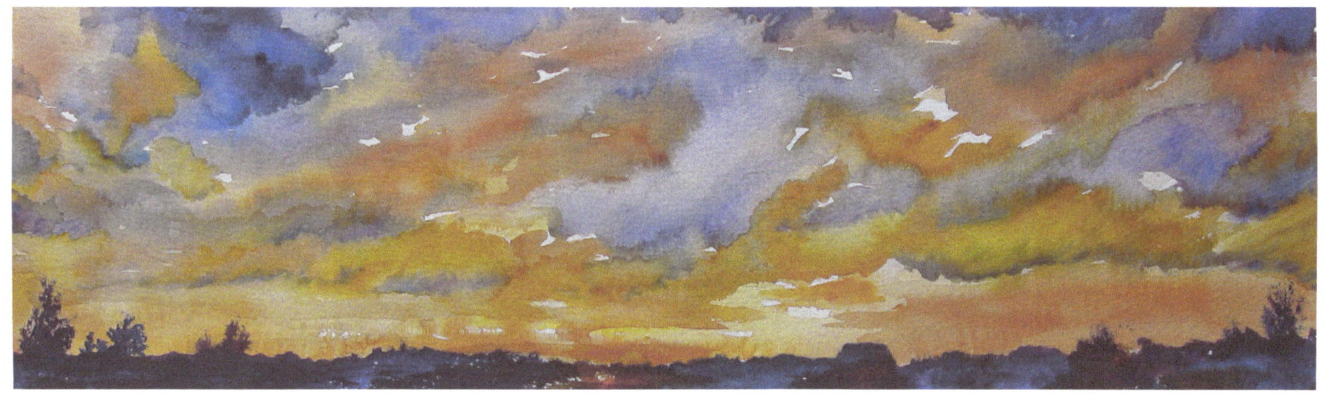

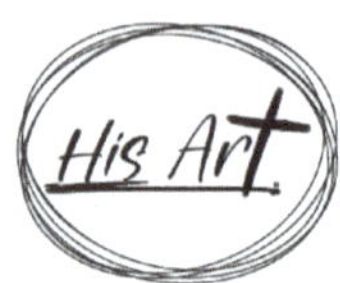

Gradation in Scripture

He is with us through dark times of life, from grays of doubt to bright sunshine days. Through sorrow and joy!

"Teaching them to observe all things whatsoever I have commanded you: and, lo, I am with you alway, even unto the end of the world. Amen" (Matthew 28:20).

"Nevertheless I tell you the truth; It is expedient for you that I go away: for if I go not away, the Comforter will not come unto you; but if I depart, I will send him unto you" (John 16:7).

Kaleidoscope Click

I love to watch the sunrise come up each morning from the eastern sky and then experience a glorious sunset in the west, watching colors melt into each other. I recall an inspiring exercise in one of the beginning watercolor painting courses where I participated. We would take a break at sunset to watch the Master Painter splash his natural color wheel across the sky. This is your assignment today, friend. With a color wheel in hand to critique his painting, watch the colors change. Find analogous color schemes which are colors side by side on the color wheels: yellows, oranges, and reds. Then anticipate just for a few moments and watch the colors change gradually to their complements. (Test it against the color wheel and find the colors directly across from each other on the color wheel,) into blues hues to deep purples. Be sure to consider the sunset against the deep green colors of a tree-lined avenue. Of course, sunrises and sunsets are routine daily. If you are like me that summer evening, today's sunset will be different in that it will take your breath away. I hope you realize that these daily sky paintings are anything but ordinary! You are witnessing God's messages of truth through the principles and elements of design.

Watch a sunset melt into the evening. Watch a sunrise bloom into the day.

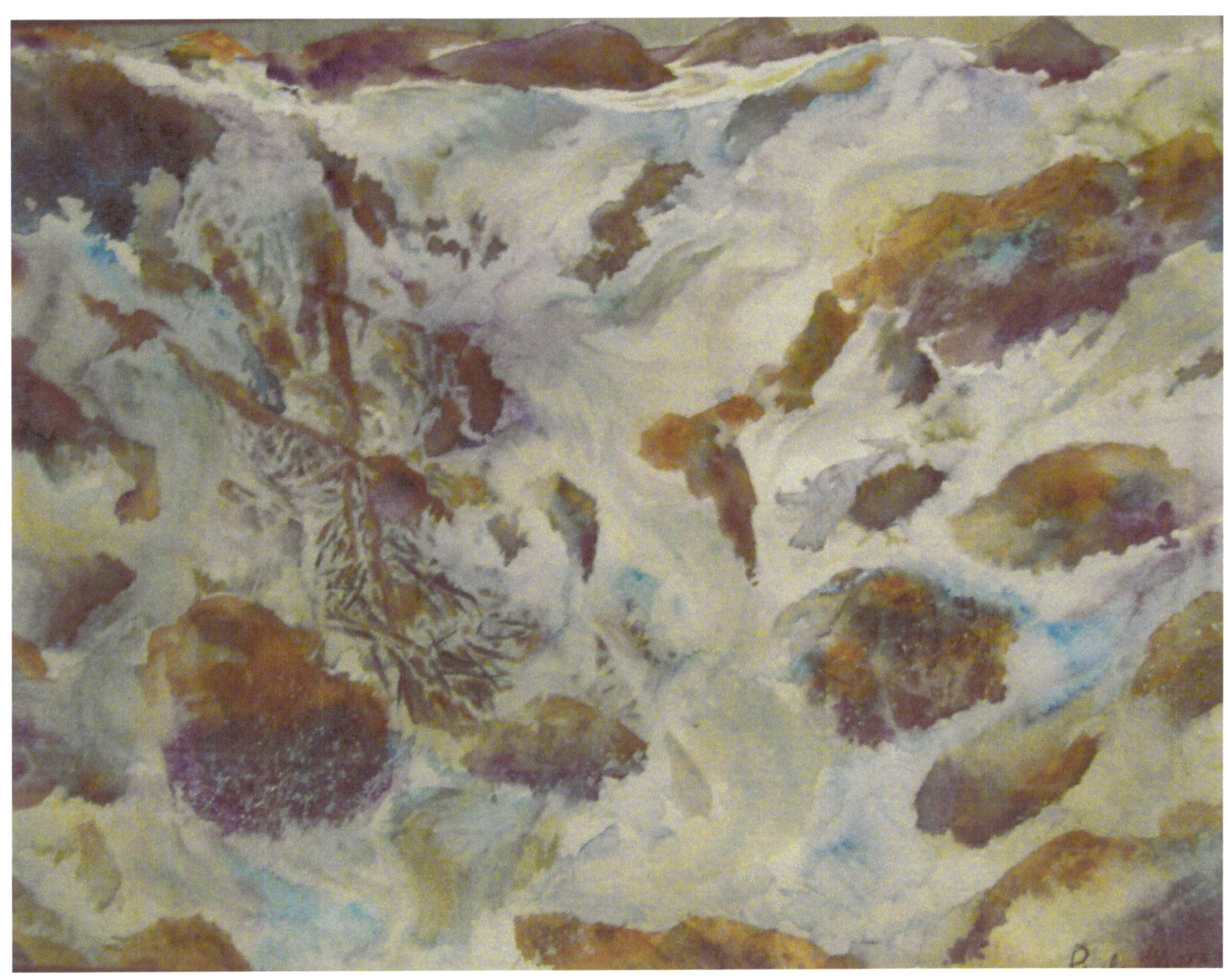

Seventh of Eight Principles: Alternation

Successive change from one thing or state to another and back again. A trill is a rapid alternation between two notes. It is choosing-picking-selecting.

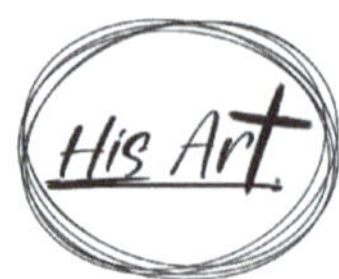

Alternation in Scripture

"To everything there is a season, and a time to every purpose under the heaven: A time to be born, and a time to die; a time to plant, and a time to pluck up that which is planted; A time to kill, and a time to heal; a time to break down, and a time to build up; A time to weep, and a time to laugh; a time to mourn, and a time to dance; A time to cast away stones, and a time to gather stones together; a time to embrace, and a time to refrain from embracing; A time to get, and a time to lose; a time to keep, and a time to cast away; A time to rend, and a time to sew; a time to keep silence, and a time to speak; A time to love, and a time to hate; a time of war, and a time of peace" (Ecclesiastics 3:1–8).

Kaleidoscope Click

For me, I consider this principle of alternation as braiding or weaving two or more elements together. Find alternation on a tiled pattern. Can you find more?

When considering these principles, it is helpful to visualize a descriptive picture in your mind. I jot down these Art Words in my notes, such as lacy leaves, rough tree trunks, and spiky grasses. These art words help train your artist's mind to mimic the word as you paint.

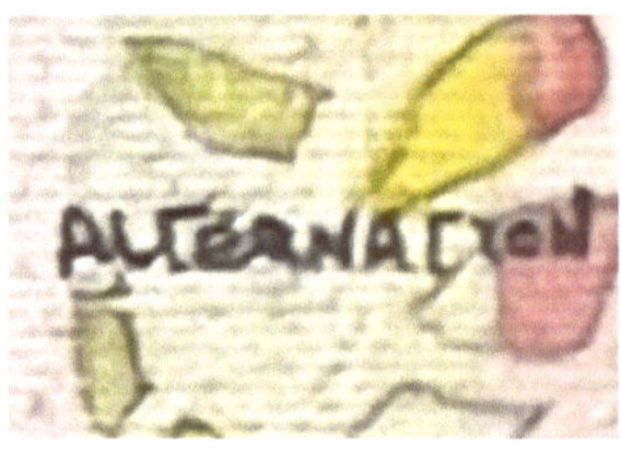

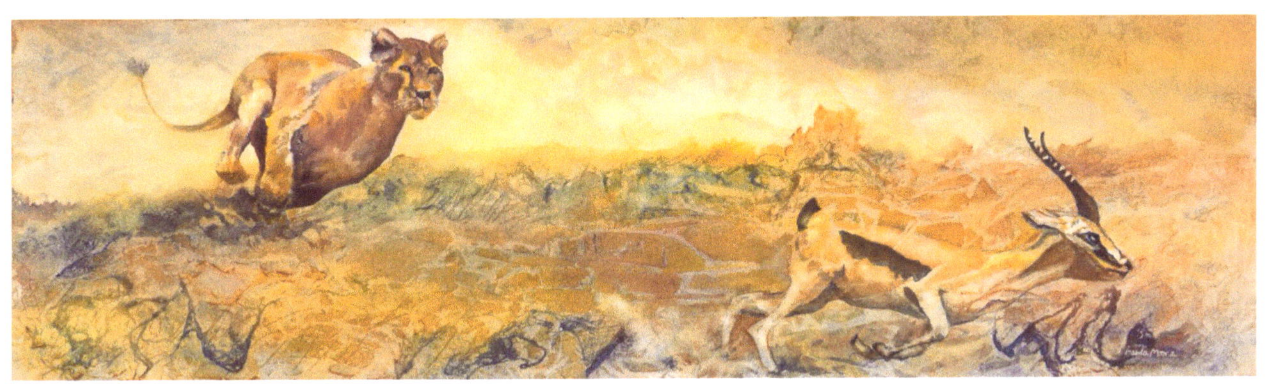

Eighth of Eight Principles: Conflict

Examples of these conflicts could be:

In Line: straight versus curved,

In Shape: round versus angular,

In Size: large versus small,

In Color: a discord of hues

In Value: light versus Dark,

In Direction: diagonal and vertical

In Texture: rough versus smooth

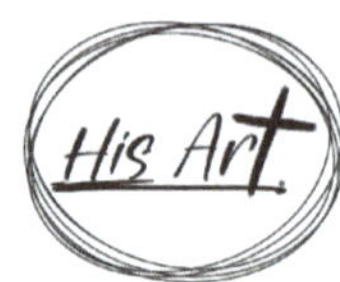

Conflict in Scripture

"We know that the law is spiritual; but I am unspiritual, sold as a slave to sin. I do not understand what I do. For what I want to do I do not do, but what I hate I do. And if I do what I do not want to do, I agree that the law is good. As it is, it is no longer I myself who do it, but it is sin living in me. For I know that good itself does not dwell in me, that is, in my sinful nature. For I have the desire to do what is good, but I cannot carry it out. For I do not do the good I want to do, but the evil I do not want to do—this I keep on doing. Now if I do what I do not want to do, it is no longer I who do it, but it is sin living in me that does it. So I find this law at work: Although I want to do good, evil is right there with me. For in my inner being I delight in God's law; but I see another law at work in me, waging war against the law of my mind and making me a prisoner of the law of sin at work within me. What a wretched man I am! Who will rescue me from this body that is subject to death? Thanks be to God, who delivers me through Jesus Christ our Lord! So then, I myself in my mind am a slave to God's law, but in my sinful nature a slave to the law of sin" (Romans 7:14–25 NIV).

Kaleidoscope Click

The principle of CONFLICT is everywhere.

A square-shaped pillow on the couch, among several other round cushions.

One dead brown bush is in a row of several lush green bushes.

What else can you discover?

**"Peace is not the absence of conflict. It is the ability to handle conflict by peaceful means."
~ Ronald Reagan**

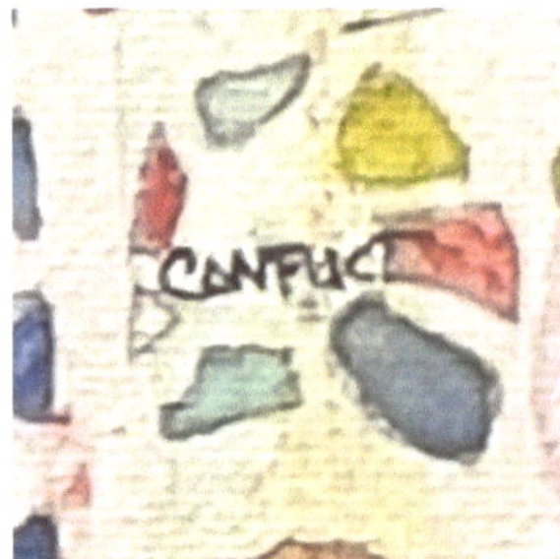

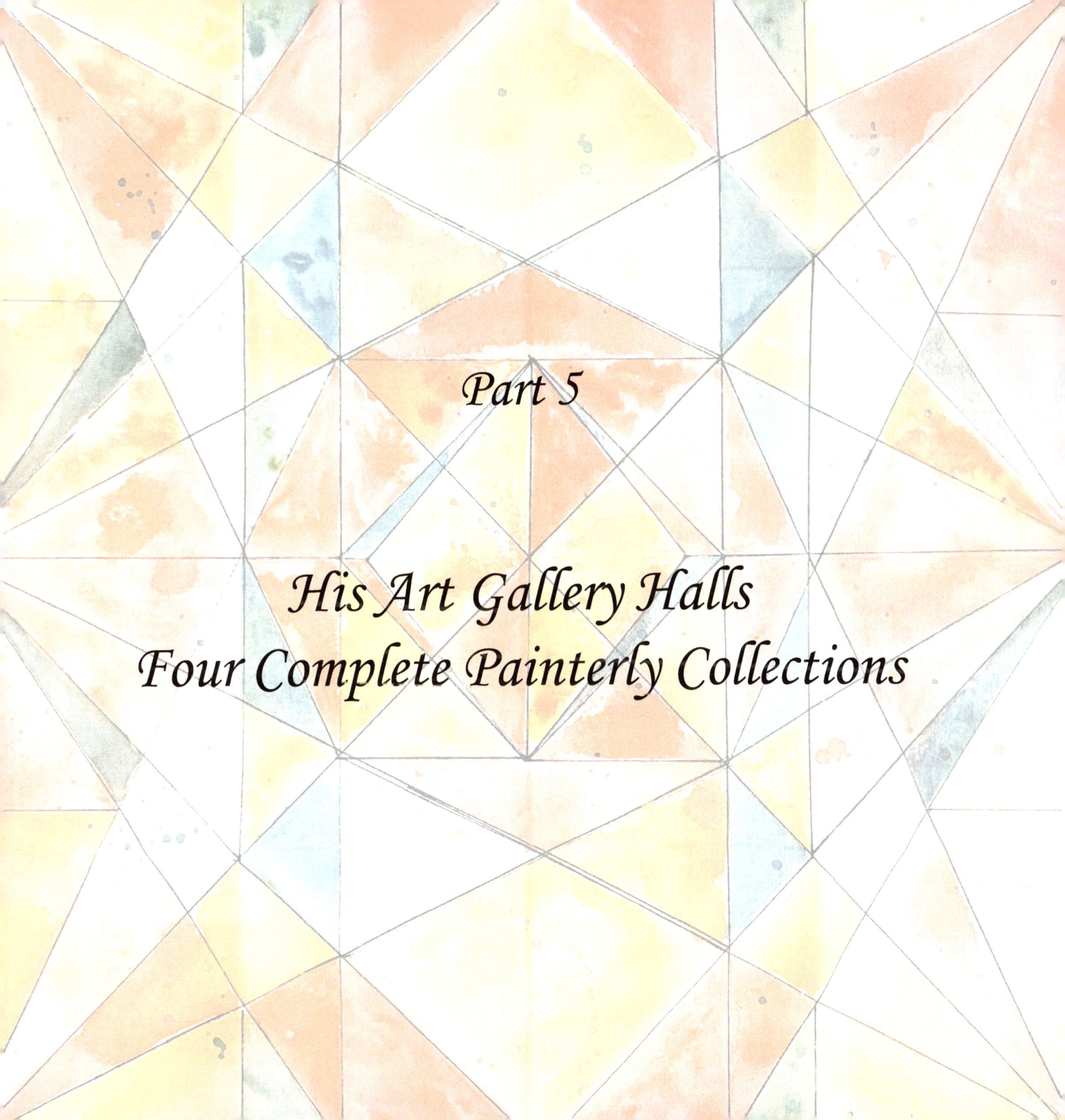

Part 5

His Art Gallery Halls
Four Complete Painterly Collections

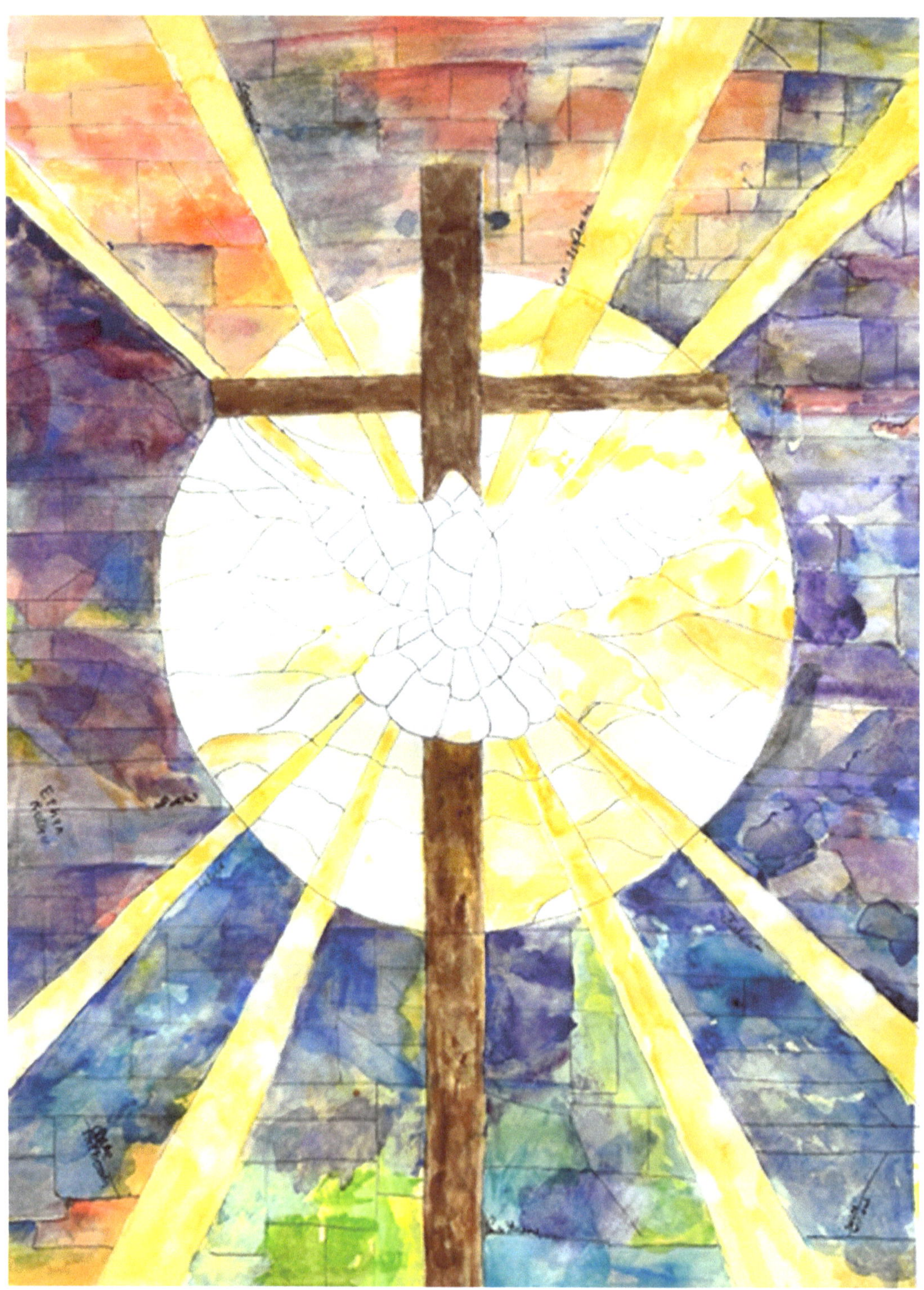

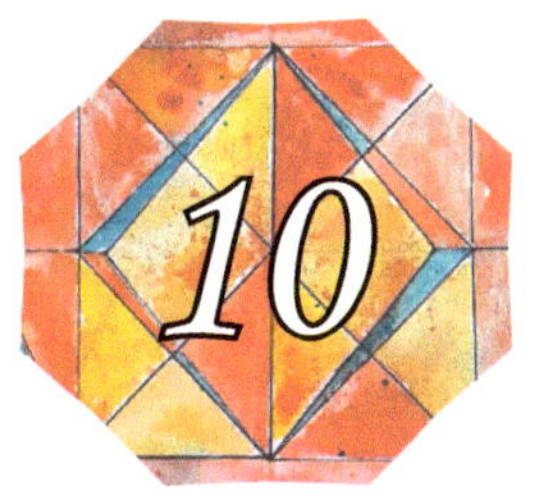

His Art Gallery: A Field Trip for Artists

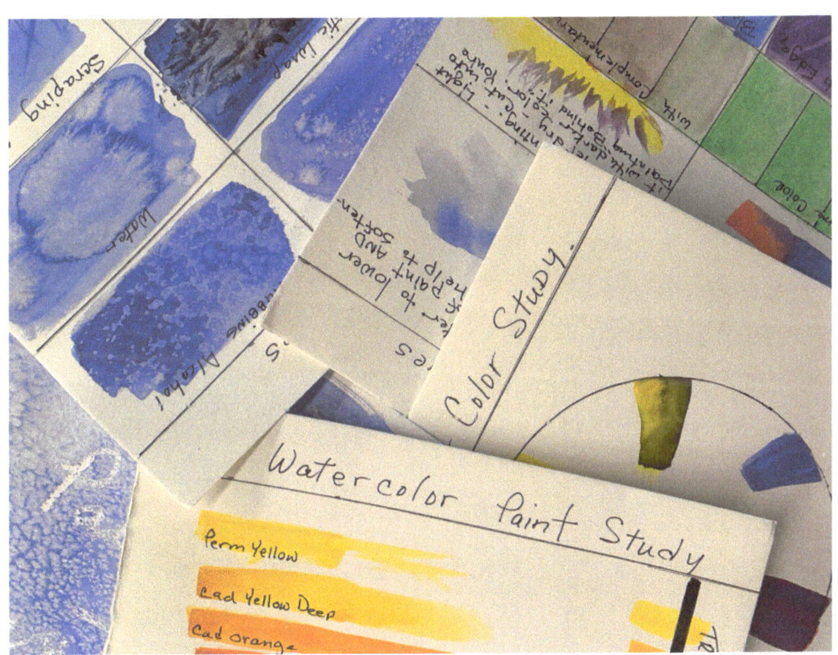

Southwest Missouri Springfield Art Museum features the Watercolor USA Competition each summer. Only the best watercolor paintings from several hundred entries have been selected for display. It is a free exhibit, and everyone is invited to see the works of art. Different styles are represented, including Abstract, Realism, and Impressionism. Many subjects, from landscapes and florals to portraits, are excellent examples of the artist's imagination and creativity.

Each Spring, I teach an Introduction to Watercolor for Beginners series of classes. My students listen, watch my demonstrations, and practice as they become familiar with their new brushes, paints, techniques, and tips. Each week's lesson builds confidence in painting distant mountains' atmospheric perspective in the backgrounds and organizing the middle-ground and textured details in the foregrounds. The design language is gradually introduced, explaining the essential concepts such as light, middle, and dark values and color theory. I enjoy watching the new artists' faces light up as they discover the knack of painting with watercolors. Last year, I wondered, however, if these enthusiastic students truly comprehended the design language, so I suggested a field trip to the Watercolor USA Exhibit to study the entries together. When we met at the museum a few days later, I presented each eager student with a scavenger hunt list of all the techniques they had been learning. They were to seek and find evidence of the elements and principles they had been pursuing in my classes. I was delighted to watch them pause with each painting, looking for clues of the story the artist wanted to tell. That message is carried away with the viewer so that they can consider the meaning. My students intently observed, discussed, and leaned in close as they considered each masterpiece on its merit before stepping to the next framed painting, waiting patiently for their undivided attention. The practiced projects we had completed as a class suddenly came into focus as the students recognized familiar brush strokes, color schemes, and techniques in these fine art pieces. My students were excited to realize these beautiful, award-winning paintings were created with the very same basic techniques they were mastering. I was thrilled my scavenger hunt had served its purpose. My new watercolorists were seeing the mysteries of art on their own.

Elements of Design (the tools)

Line	Color
Shape	Value
Size	Texture
Direction	

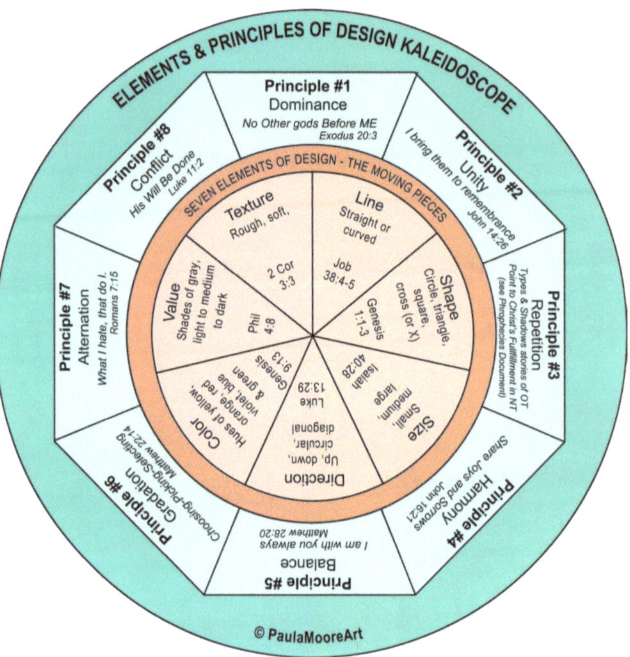

The Principles of Design
(What we can do with the tools)

Dominance	Balance
Unity	Gradation
Repetition	Alternation
Harmony	Conflict

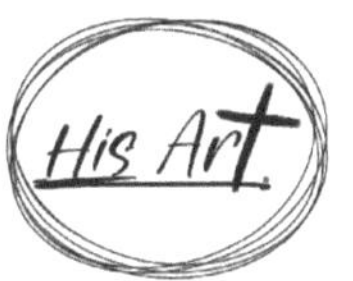

There will be a moment in each person's life—I'm not able to give you an exact time—when you will have a longing well up in your soul, a need to understand more about the mysteries of God, Jesus, and the Holy Spirit, not just from hearsay from others around you, but rather a deeper dive to grasp the meanings for yourself. There will be a need to personally comprehend about how these mysteries spin and work together, unlike the kaleidoscope image, throughout this writing. There will be a calling from God himself inviting you to seek and find him. He will be there drawing you, leading you, showing you the way. "What things do I need to do?" you will ask. My friend, there is nothing in your power you can do! Only follow in obedience what he asks of you and believe in all that he is.

When I was a child, I asked my mother, "When will I know that I am lost? Separated from God?"

She always answered back, "You'll know."

"Well then, Mother…when will I know when I'm saved? Adopted into God's family?"

The answer was always, "You'll know that too."

There are four passages an individual goes through in their search to know God personally.

<u>The first is Self-Reliance</u>—believing they can be good enough on their own merit that God will call him his own. Or self-reliant that they have no use of God.

<u>The second is Conviction</u>—An inward knowing you are separated from God. This is him drawing you closer, asking you to follow. Although this is uncomfortable, it is wonderfully exciting! That pull from the deepest part of your soul is God inviting you to trust in him fully. I encourage you to not run from this calling, instead run towards him willingly.

<u>The third is Repentance</u>—Confessing that you are a sinner and realizing within your spirit that you can do nothing without God in your life. This is the only offering that he does not despise.

<u>The fourth is Sweet Surrender</u>—Salvation. The "know-so" faith that you are his and he is yours forever. Take pause here. You do not have to keep it or be concerned that you can lose it. He writes your name in his Book of Life and keeps the reconciliation safe within his arms. I will share a precious memory of little Aiden, listening intently in a primary class I taught several years ago. His little arm shot up in the air and excitedly exclaimed the profound truth he had come up with on his own, "AND he writes it in permanent ink!"

> "Draw nigh to God, and he will draw nigh to you. Cleanse your hands, ye sinner and purify your hearts, ye double minded" (James 4:8).

Kaleidoscope Click

This quest is two-fold. For the artist, visit your local art museum. There will be many examples of beautiful paintings, sculptures, and drawings. I suggest bringing a small notebook to take notes regarding what art medium intrigues you most. Is it the watercolors or oils? Do you like abstract paintings expressing emotions, realism, or impressionism? Your notes give clues on what to consider next in your artistic endeavors. Inspiration is everywhere!

For the His Art seeker, I invite you to read the following passage. A friend once suggested that I read scripture as a letter to myself…because it is just that! I particularly like to read this passage because the words jump off the page. It takes my breath away to realize these were the words of Jesus, written down as a letter to me and to you. Your assignment, then, is to read your own name where appropriate. I challenge you to try this with other Scriptures as well!

Dearest ______________

Do not let your heart be troubled: ye believe in God, believe also in me.

In my Father's house are many mansions: if it were not so, I would have told you, _________.

I go to prepare a place for you.

And if I go and prepare a place for you, I will come again, and receive you, ____________

Unto myself: that where I am, there ye, __________ may be also. And whither I go ye know and the way ye know, _________.

Love Always – Jesus

John 14:1–4 (variation added by me)

You'll Know.

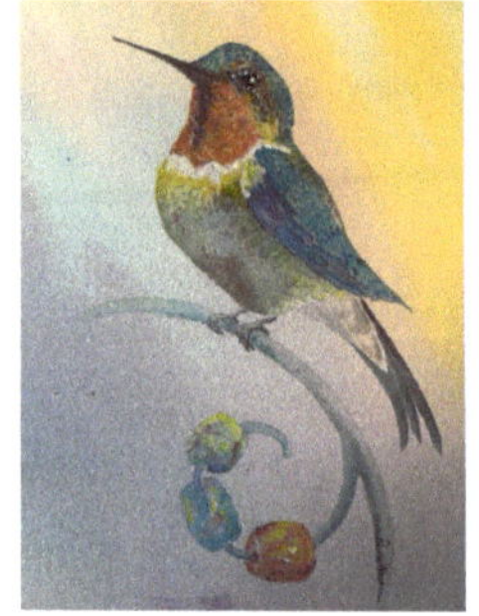

BUILD ON YOUR STRENGTHS
NOT ON YOUR WEAKNESSES

PUSH BACK!
Wow Wow Wow!

ELEMENTS

"Even I Make
Mistakes"

You mean
WHAT ARE YOU SAYING?

PRINCIPLES

Unity

Cool-
WARM
Cool-Warm

DOMINANCE

Sign it!

details only in the value change

Hokey Pokey?

I'm afraid
to start!

But I like lollypops and potatoes!!!

LINE

Repetition

Shape

60% - 20% - 32%
= 100
WHAT!!?!!

-Warm-Dark
You can
fix
everything

(unless you can't.
then collage it)

Jane Jones
Plain Air Workshop Lake City Co
September 20th 24th 2021

HARMONY

Dark-Warm-Lite-Warm-Cool

Soooo Much Detail!
Why did you make those grasses??

No
diddly
watts!!
(except sometimes)

SIZE

WHEN YOU CAN COUNT
SOMETHING... CONNECT IT!

Keep
Different
Widths

Balance

Gradation

Jane's Way

Whats up here

Cool-Warm-Cool-Warm-Cool-Warm

Put down
there

DIRECTION

Simplify

Interlocking shapes

YOU are the impressionist
YOU are the symbol maker!

Alternation

COLOR

Keep going

cool- warm

VALUE

Broken Light. Broken Color

CONFLICT

Just keep working

TEXTURE

Lights 1-2-3
MID 4-5-6
Darks 7-8-9-10

Looose
An
Edge

You have
to have

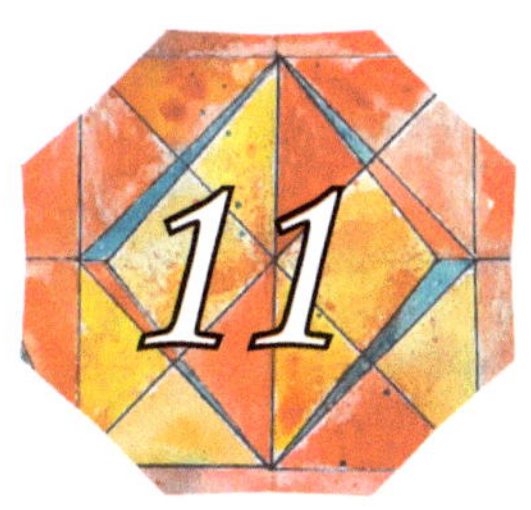

Your Personal Invitation to the Gallery Hall of His Art

You, the reader, have invested several hours in my writing. You are well acquainted with the Elements and Principles of Design, both in art theory and in evidence in scriptures.

This next section is your special invitation to the His Art Gallery, a collection of sixteen painterly essays written over several years. Please note that just as the paintings previously mentioned in the art exhibit were each a stand-alone painting, each essay is quite different from the next. Each has a particular style and message offered to you. I suggest refraining from rushing through these stories because you could be confused about jumping from one topic to another. Instead, enter this gallery as you would any other, with anticipation and mindfulness within a teachable spirit. Seek out what you like, perhaps aspects you question, and parts you might want to emulate in your own life's story. In other words, have a quiet heart-to-heart conversation with each of His Art gallery painted essays before engaging with the following story awaiting you on the next page.

The entrance to this exquisite hall is free to all, and the entrance fee has been fully paid for all who will come. There will be many others who will claim they will take you through or they know a shortcut. Be warned and wait. The Master Creator of the Universe will be available to guide you through when you are ready. The hall is a long, narrow room, enough for all to pass through. There is only one entrance in and one entrance out. Once you enter, you cannot turn back. Do not be discouraged or fearful. Many others throughout history have made this walk before you. The Holy Spirit wants none to perish. Instead, there is the everlasting prize for everyone. There is the promise of hope just beyond the last door. It was prepared from the beginning of time and waits for you on a table holding God-shaped pure crystals engraved with Christ's blood. You will receive one personalized with your name written permanently upon it.

You'll undoubtedly witness other seekers headed for the door. You do not have to wait for them; continue to seek out the Holy One who will lead you through. You'll observe many others hesitant to take that first step inside. Stay focused on why you are there which is to experience his grace and mercy for yourself. When you cross the entryway, realize you enter as an individual, on your own, lost and undone. Others will encourage you and point the way; however, you must follow his lead to the other side. There will be darkness of uncertainty, but continue to follow his Light throughout to the end.

The grand hall is divided into four separate exhibits. You cannot jump ahead; however, you are not limited in how long you must stay. I strongly recommend not wasting time. Some make this passage in an instant. Others linger for months and years. It depends on following his lead or trying to make your own way out. You'll see others searching for evidence, lingering, and procrastinating at each painterly exhibit. You'll see others attempting to move through the Grand Hall convinced they can succeed on their own wits and understanding. Be aware they may entice you to join them on their fruitless attempt to make their way out on their own. This is impossible to do! So be assured you've been called by the Master of the Universe to be here. Trust his way through.

As children, we are introduced to scriptures gently with little songs about sunbeams and hearing that Jesus loves us. They listen to fantastic stories of Noah's floating zoo, rainbows, baby Jesus, and a little boy who shared his lunch at a big picnic. Like my new watercolorists, the head knowledge turns into spiritual understandings that still ring true centuries later.

Here is a little scene of my then four-year old daughter as she attempted to tie her shoes. The impatient mama, me, wanted to hurry her along so I started to do it for her. I backed off when this determined little girl reacted to my involvement. "Mamma, let me help me!"

Isn't that what we usually do to ourself or to others? Do we tend to rush the process? Try to manage our life our way. One little fellow said, "You're not the boss, I'M the boss!" You can witness this phenomenon even in an innocent smiling toddler disobeying while their little eyes are locked on their parent. The child daring the parent just how far he or she can push the envelope of disobedience. How does that little one know in an instant how to come up with a fib? We do not have to teach them to lie; they know innately since mankind inherited disobedient traits from our ancestors, Adam and Eve when they doubted God. The God-sized hole can only be filled with our true faith in Jesus Christ being the ultimate sacrifice for our sins.

At the beginning of this book, I shared my Dream Purpose of the necessity to write the messages of God's truth to you through the Elements and Principles of Design. I was inspired to pen my Dream Purpose because it is my why. I cannot comprehend that these written thoughts will ripple out past my lifetime to further God's Kingdom. I desire to lead you to this book's messages of truth so that you might want to find, recognize, experience it, and claim God's messages as they speak to you personally as your own.

Each of us, God's masterpiece created in his image, is born with a God-size hole in our spiritual hearts. Mankind vainly attempts to search to find lasting happiness remedies on their own. Only turning to God can provide the lasting peace that passes all understanding. Approximately 1,000 years before Christ died as the ultimate sacrifice for us, David, in Psalm 51:17, with eyes of faith saw beyond the required blood sacrifices of innocent lambs and bulls. He understood they were only a symbol of a redeemer who would be the ultimate, last sacrifice to fulfill God's requirement.

He so elegantly wrote what the acceptable sacrifice is and summed up what is required:

David wrote to us: "My [only] sacrifice [acceptable] to God is a broken spirit; a broken and contrite heart [broken with sorrow for sin, thoroughly penitent], such, O God, You will not despise" (Psalm 51:17AMP).

This restored relationship has nothing to do with our ancestral heritage, our importance, or our accomplishments; it is what Christ willingly did for us, becoming the perfect sacrifice foretold in the Old Testament writings. This is the perfect healing love poured into our souls when we fully trust our mind, body, and spirit that he is who he says he is. We are eternally adopted into the kingdom.

Are you ready to walk through the His Art Gallery Hall? You are expectant of its glorious mysteries, and you have studied how to enter. All those pages of singing hymns, bible stories, Christmas pageants, Easter mornings, sermons, prayers, even perhaps something read in this book. Something in your soul will click and you'll see the plan all fitting together perfectly.

As I wrote this section for you, much thought went into how to organize the essays. I sat them out as I do when preparing a gallery wall in my home, searching for all those principles of design you've learned. I go about organizing these paintings in a cohesive plan, pondering how best to present them for you to see this kaleidoscope comparison of art and God. For each painterly essay, is there a featured dominance? Are all the principles, unity, repetition, harmony, balance, alternation, and conflict evident? How do I do this best, Lord? Then the answer, his answer, came to me. Build the essay paintings around Psalm 51:17 writing to us.

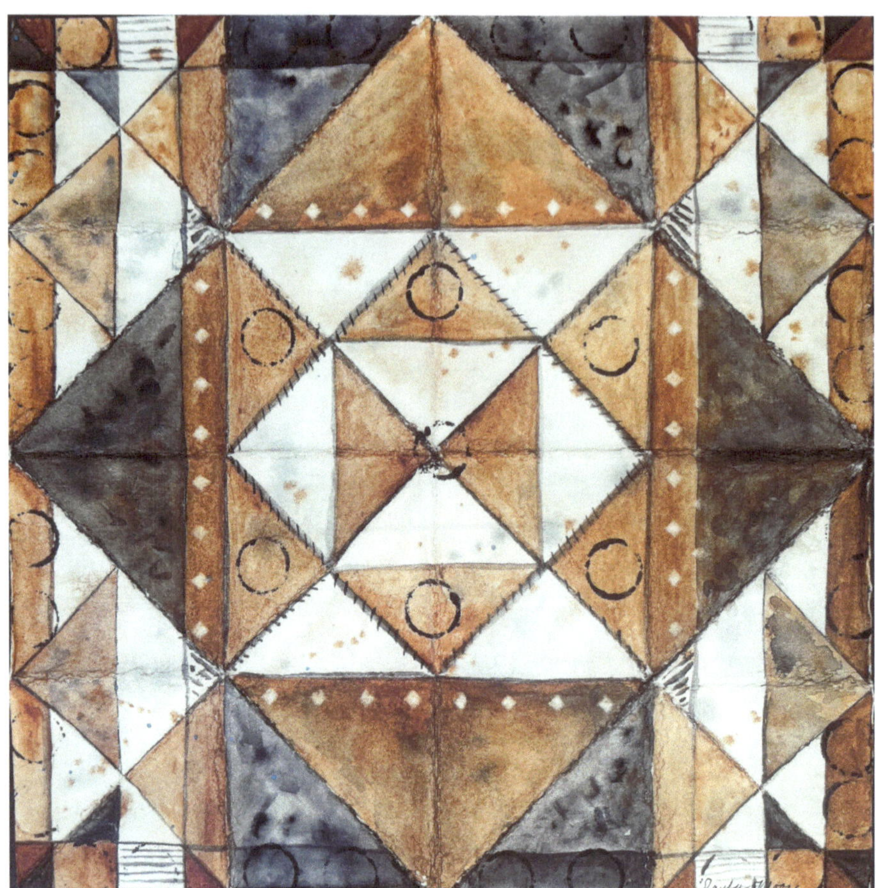

The painting essays are structured around four significant themes. It is an allegory describing the passage we must individually navigate to find peace with God.

Self-Reliance - Let Me Help Me

Leaky Elbows

Stay on Task, Mamma

Looks Like a Chicken

Conviction – I Do Need You to Help Me

Second Glance, Second Chance

Winding Curves Ahead

Then Why Take the Workshop

Repentance – Let Me Depend upon You

Portrait of a Gracious Woman

Gift of the Giver

New Winkle in Owl B'Wayn

Like Riding a Bike

Having a Conversation—Talking and Listening

Sweet Surrender- I Trust You to Help Me

Losing an Edge

Types and Shadows Versus Reality

Reflections of His Love

The Last Finishing Touch

The Final Critique —Is it WOW Worthy?

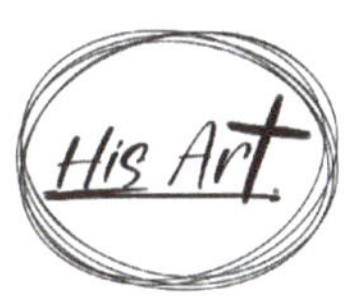

"But seek ye first the kingdom of God, and his righteousness and all these things shall be added unto you" (Matthew 6:33).
"At the same time came the disciples unto Jesus, saying, Who is the greatest in the kingdom of heaven? And Jesus called a little child unto him, and set him in the midst of them, And said, Verily I say unto you, Except ye be converted, and become as little children, ye shall not enter into the kingdom of heaven. Whosoever therefore shall humble himself as this little child, the same is greatest in the kingdom of heaven. And whoso shall receive one such little child in my name receiveth me" (Matthew 18:1–5).

Kaleidoscope Click

It may have been a while, or perhaps never, since you have read a Children's Bible storybook or a Children's Bible written in simple story form. Approaching God's Word in this manner is a perfect way to begin when you want a refresher to fall in love with the stories again. Check with your local libraries and bookstores. Searching for children's bible stories and videos online is another way to start. Volunteer on Sunday mornings during the little one's Sunday school session. Participate by listening to the stories, learning the songs, and engaging in the activities. Then, take yourself and perhaps a trusted friend on a maturity growth scripture scavenger hunt for the deeper meanings. Join a Bible Study or attend a service. Just as my novice artists, you will quickly begin seeing with new eyes of faith how scriptures all work together to paint pictures of Christ. As the Holy Spirit draws you, you will yearn to learn more.

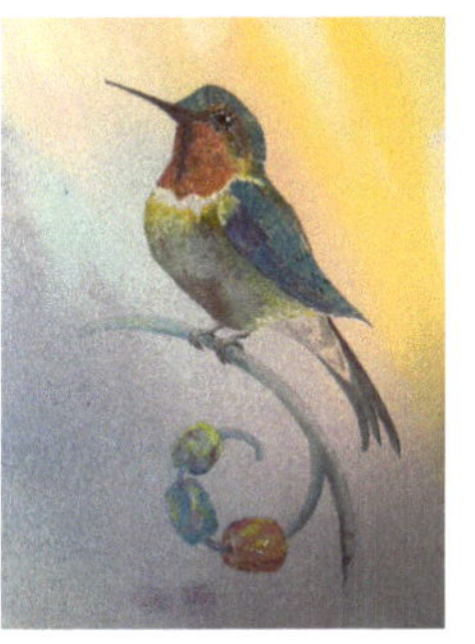

Self-Reliance—Let Me Help Me
Conviction— I Do Need You to Help Me
Repentance—Let Me Depend upon You
Sweet Surrender—I Trust You to Help Me

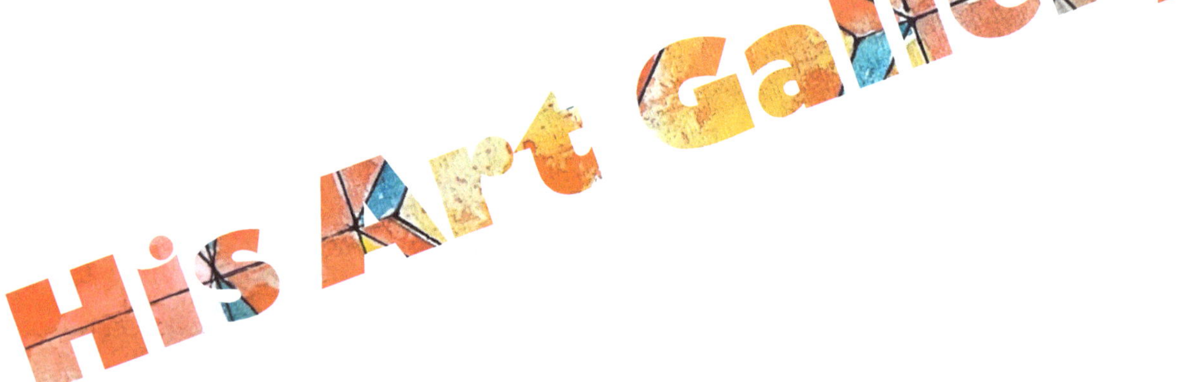
His Art Gallery

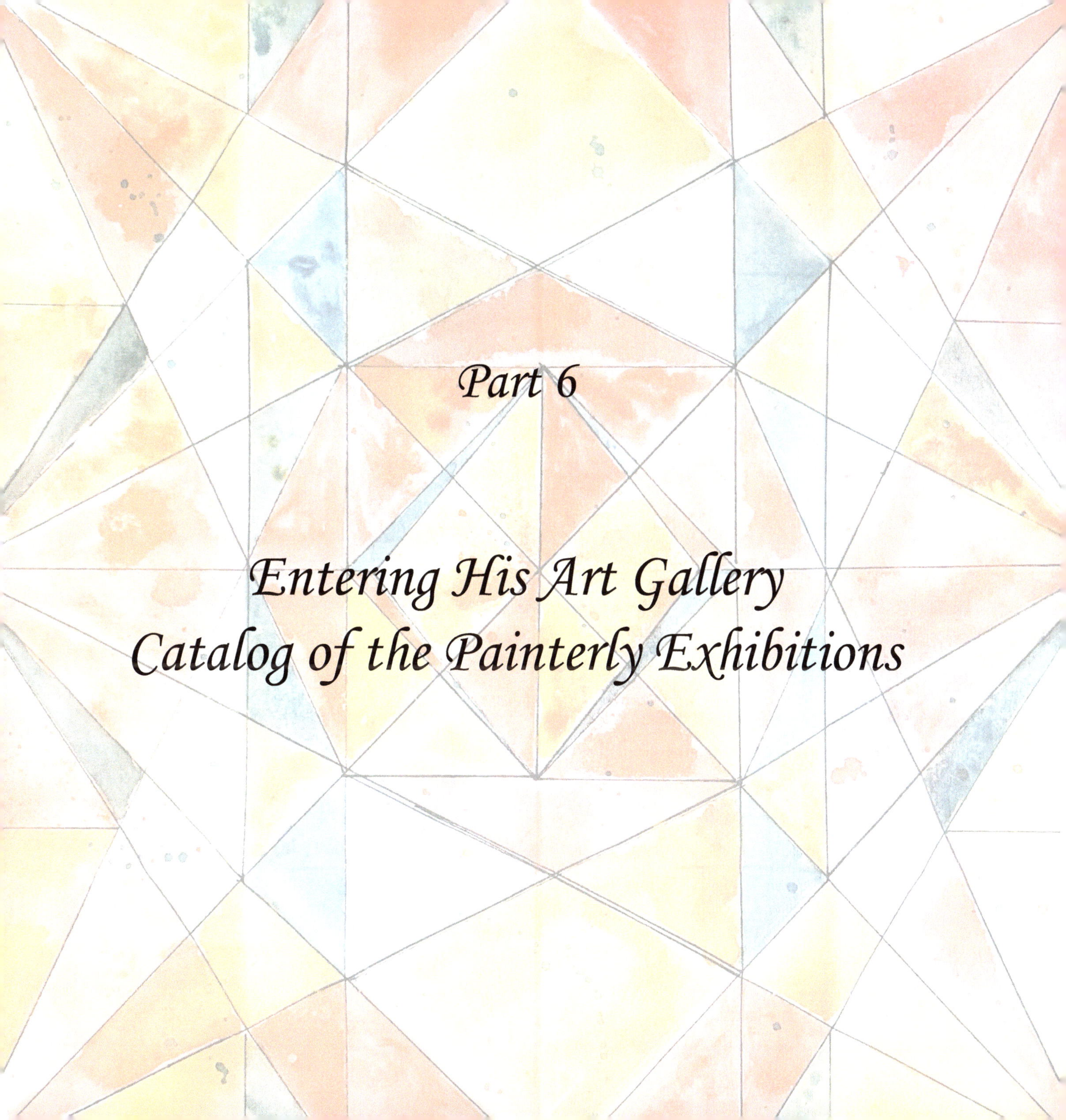

Part 6

Entering His Art Gallery
Catalog of the Painterly Exhibitions

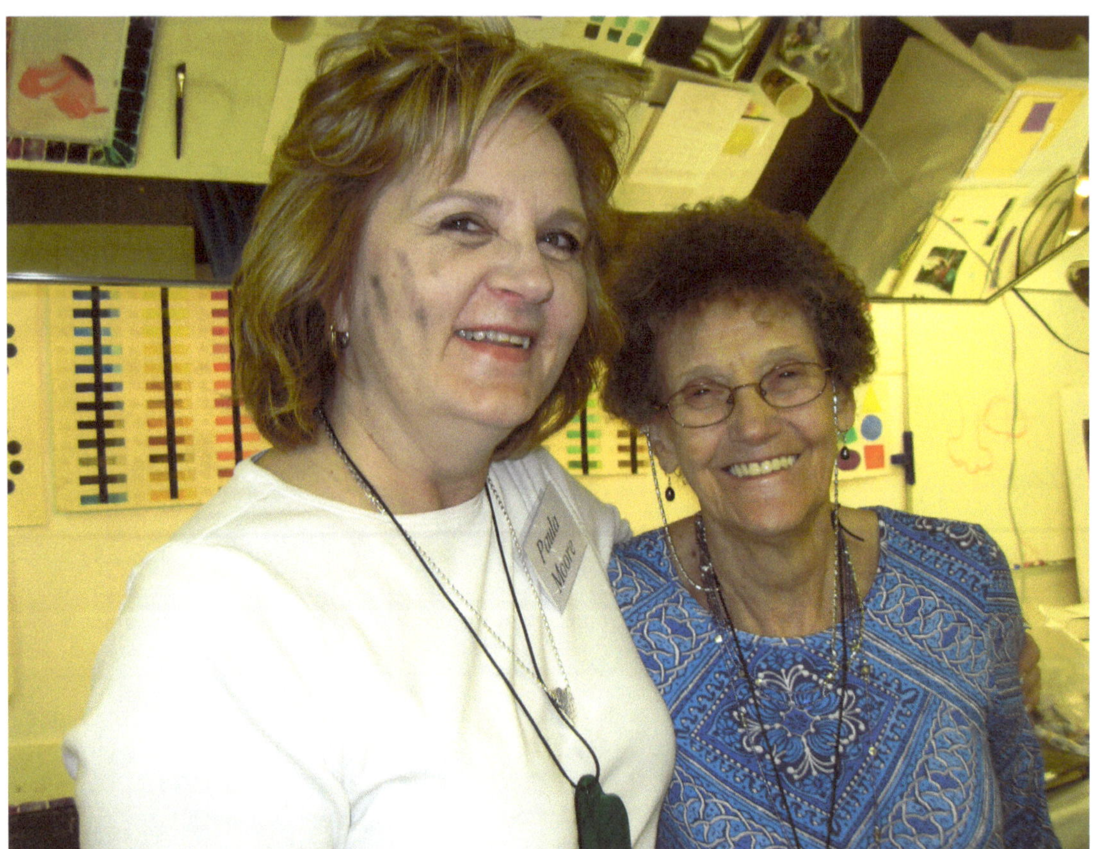

Self-Reliance — Let Me Help Me

Leaky Elbow Syndrome

There is an actual, contagious, chronic condition that I personally and many of us live undiagnosed. I can lapse easily into this mindset if I'm not careful. Both in art and in life! I first heard of this limitation during a painting workshop with Jane. As we gathered around her demonstration table, she carefully explained and fully demonstrated the painting skill she wanted us to master. Confident we had the head knowledge of what she had just shared, we made our way to our easels to try the technique. We all failed miserably! Jane walked around to view our messes, sighed, stomped her little foot, and exclaimed, "You all have Leaky Elbows!!" What?? "I gave you all the information on how to paint, and before it can travel through your brain, through your hand to your paintbrush, it leaks out through your elbows!" We all had a good laugh, and Jane asked us to come on back for another lesson. We practiced, asked questions, and listened intently until we finally understood the technique by heart.

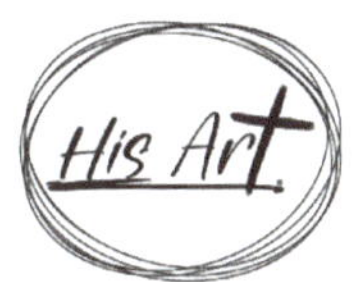

We can go to Sunday School, sit under thousands of sermons, and sing every word of the hymns. The old stories are in our heads; however, the message leaks out before it reaches our soul's heart. Distractions, wrought readings, insincere prayers that bounce off the church's high ceilings and go no further.

There is a distinct difference between knowing about Jesus and knowing Jesus spiritually.

Scriptures warn us, and I fear many good people will miss Heaven as their eternal home by only an eighteen-inch span between the mind and one's heart. How sad to miss Heaven by this small measurement: the distance between the Head Knowledge of Jesus and Knowing him in your soul of your Heart.

"My son [and daughter], if you receive my words and treasure up my commandments with you, making your ear attentive to wisdom and inclining your heart to understanding; yes, if you call out for insight and raise your voice for understanding, if you seek it like silver and search for it as for hidden treasures, then you will understand the fear of the Lord and find the knowledge of God. For the Lord gives wisdom; from his mouth come knowledge and understanding; he stores up sound wisdom for the upright; he is a shield to those who walk in integrity, guarding the paths of justice and watching over the way of his saints. Then you will understand righteousness and justice and equity, every good path; for wisdom will come into your heart, and knowledge will be pleasant to your soul; discretion will watch over you, understanding will guard you" (Proverbs 2:1–11).

Kaleidoscope Click

Turn down the noise in your mind. Then, you'll be able to tune into the small voice of the Holy Spirit. Choose a brand-new journal and write your prayers as you seek his counsel.

When you are willing to listen, I am confident unique ideas will bubble up like a fountain. I suggest you quickly write or sketch them down as they are presented. For me, often, those ideas come in the quiet early hours of the morning. My friends ask, where do you come up with all your innovative ideas for classes and studies? Now you know my technique. I merely keep tuned into the Holy Spirit leading and guiding.

Information before it can travel through your brain, through your hand to your paintbrush, it leaks out through your elbow!

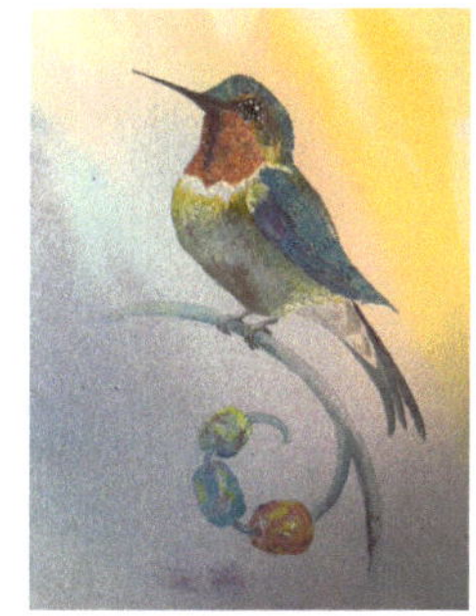

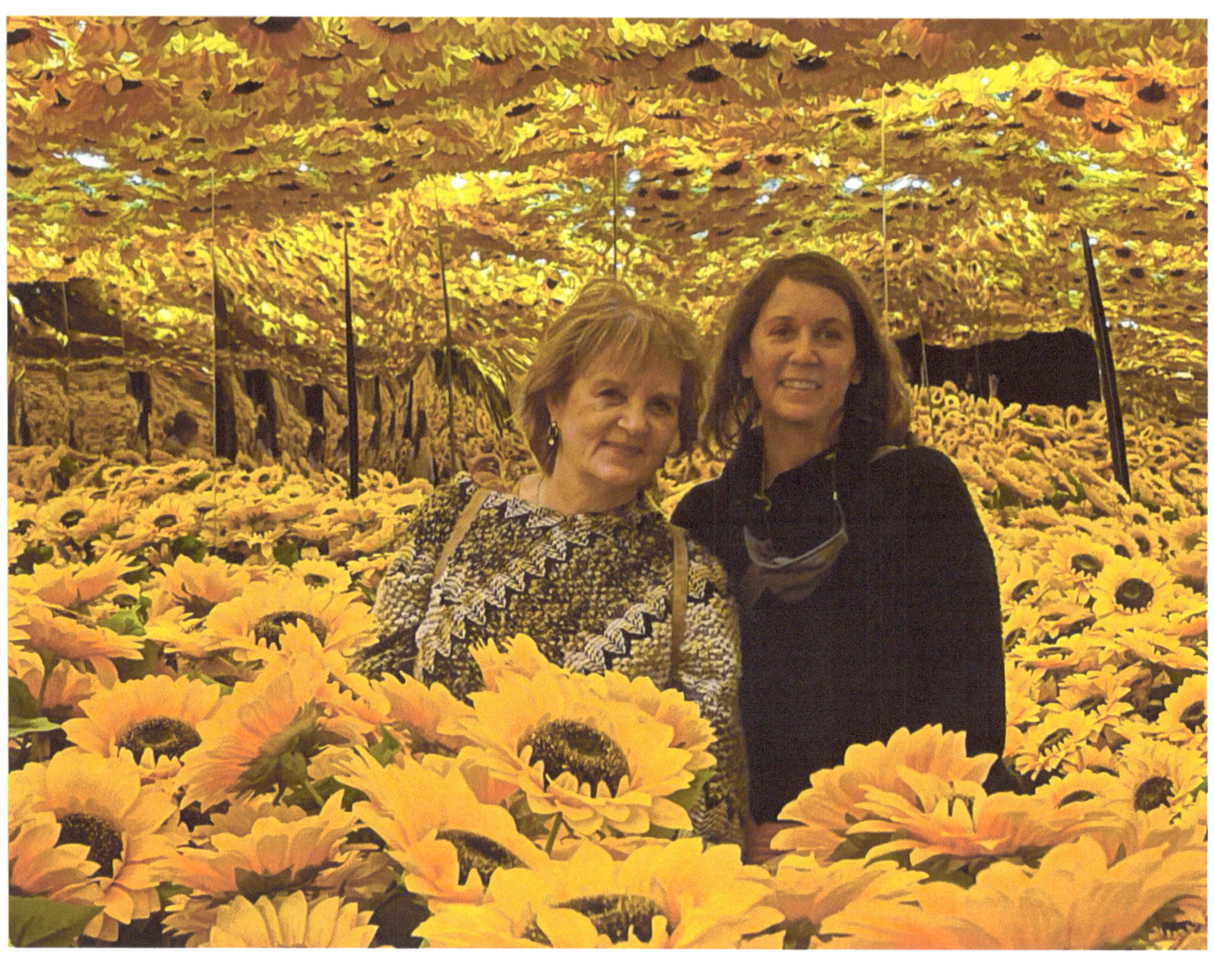

Self-Reliance — Let Me Help Me

Stay on Task, Mama, Stay on Task
(What's most important)

Medical scientists continue to analyze how the extraordinary human brain organizes thoughts and ideas. In the most basic brain studies, there are two lobes. I comprehend that the left lobe is for analytical thoughts, and the right is for creative abstract thinking. Usually, one area is stronger than the other; however, we certainly use both sides of the brain. Therapy for stroke victims often includes exercises to strengthen the brain, encouraging stimulation of connections.

As you may have surmised, I tend to have several projects going on at the same time. Several years ago, my then-teenage daughter observed me multitasking several activities hurriedly, all at the same time. She calmly and quietly said to me, "Stay on task, Mamma. Stay on task." We had a good chuckle together; however, she had a point! We all simultaneously juggle family activities, work, church, and hobbies. Some are better at it than others, and yes, I drop the ball sometimes. As a little girl, I remember being mesmerized watching a black and white television as a man tried his best to keep all the porcelain plates spinning on rotating wobbly, thin dowel rods. He would half run one way and then the other in his fitful attempt to keep everything balanced. We could all see a plate that wouldn't make it, shouting a warning to him as if he could hear us through the screen! Undoubtedly, a plate would crash to the floor in scattering bits. We'd laugh as he picked up another new plate and started it again.

Many of my coworkers, and perhaps you as well, will make a linear list of things to do. Unless it's a grocery list laid out in categories, that system frankly did not ring true to me. I wanted to "see" the full project in its entirety and understand how each component aided the next. In my banking career, during a management training seminar, I was introduced to an organizing method called "mind-mapping." It was so much like my kaleidoscope theory; it was uncanny! Whether organizing my art studio, ideas for this book, or packing for a trip, the mind-mapping method works for this creative soul. I can see what activities will move me closer to my goals of serving my art students, my family, and my church. I see the big picture simultaneously and keep the activities spinning…most of the time. If not, I pencil it back in and keep the kaleidoscope spinning.

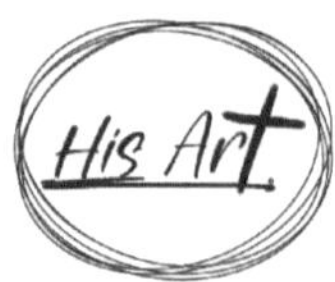

At this writing, my heart's dream progresses slowly as the kaleidoscope of my life continues to reveal yet another direction presented to me. I sense a change moving inside my soul, like a breeze blowing slightly stronger and from a different direction. I ponder how this will fit into what I'm doing now with the heartfelt prayer, "Lord, where do I go from here? You gave me this dream, and I need to hear from you that I'm on the right track. I want to hurry this dream along! A little help here, please?" You can talk to God like this, you realize. He already knows what you're thinking. However, he desires you to consult him so you both know you're partnering in agreement for the next phase.

From the beginning, the Creator yearned for a deep relationship with mankind. I recommend reading the book of Psalms, a collection of conversational prayers, poems, and songs, many written by David, a man of war, an adulterer, and a murderer. Yet he was also a man after God's own heart. Story after story tells us about David returning to God for relationship restoration. In my opinion, I would offer that effort in developing close relationships is the very center of life. When there is a close relationship, it just feels right. The other side of that feeling is unsettling, knowing there's an underlying current of trouble. This truth rings true in your close relationships with God, your spouse, family, friends, church, community, and worldwide. When Jesus ascended back to Heaven, he sent the Comforter to the entire world. The Holy Spirit who lives among us actually dwells within the believer's soul. This close friendship with the Holy Spirit is a precious gift God has offered since the beginning. It is then where we can quiet our spirit and filter out the noise in our heads. In my mind's eye, I imagine myself curled up close to him on the couch, or the essence of leisurely walking hand-in-hand on a quiet beach at sunset, relishing an easy conversation. Actually, it is a continual conversation throughout the entire day if we make ourselves available. He is always there. This is a two-way discussion that requires listening and talking. I'm good at talking and giving him my never-ending list of demands. The listening, waiting and doing, I'm still working on. Perhaps this is the reason for our human experience: the continual pursuit of staying in the middle of his will. I do better when I take a moment to quiet myself, thank him for his mercies, and then present my needs to him. Like turning that kaleidoscope cylinder, I'll continue fine-tuning the wheel to stay focused, knowing he is working his plan through me.

I received the whispered answer to my "a little help here, please!" prayer in the wee hours of the morning between sleep and waking.

Stay on Task, Daughter, Stay on Task.

"I press toward the mark for the prize of the high calling of God in Christ Jesus" (Philippians 3:14).

Kaleidoscope Click

While writing this book, I found myself distracted by too many other activities, which pulled me away from finishing the manuscript. I was rushing it to publication. I continued to discern, knowing that it wasn't quite ready yet.

These activities were all beautiful parts of my life; however, I needed to step back and find areas where I could revise my daily schedule to find the time to write. So, I had a business meeting with the Holy Spirit and explored the "What Ifs?"

It was a bit scary to think about giving something up, even though I knew it needed to be done. To take the sting out of the process, I wrote in pencil on an ordinary piece of lined paper to jot down different scenarios. I used an eraser frequently and ran the income figures. Since none of these ideas were written in permanent ink, I could freely keep an open mind and heart. I poured out my thoughts and considered the worst that could happen if I laid down my busy teaching schedule for a while, which would give me several hours a week to write.

By rushing, it would have been my way to publication. By trusting, it is his.

God does not want us to be overwhelmed with activities. I am just learning that even though I may be working for God, there may be areas where the current project should be set aside for a while when it's not in alignment with his dream purpose. The final result? Well, my friend, you are holding the book in your hands.

Are you feeling stressed instead of blessed? Each season of life brings with it new happy times and struggles. We all deal with daily challenges and decisions, the "what ifs." Even the word *life* cannot be written without the *if* in the middle!

Your kaleidoscope click is to find a pencil with a good eraser and a lined notebook. Then, schedule a regular business meeting with the Holy Spirit to review all your what-ifs.

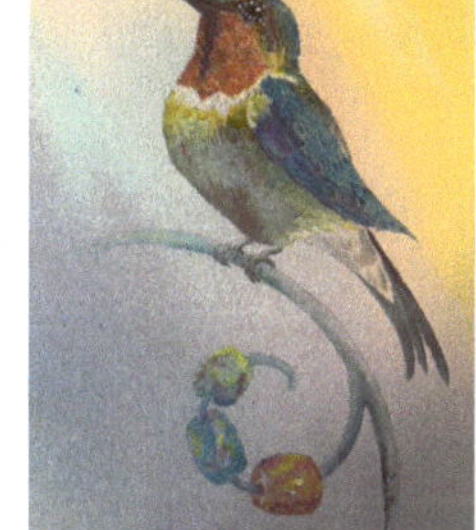

Stay on Task, Daughter, Stay on Task

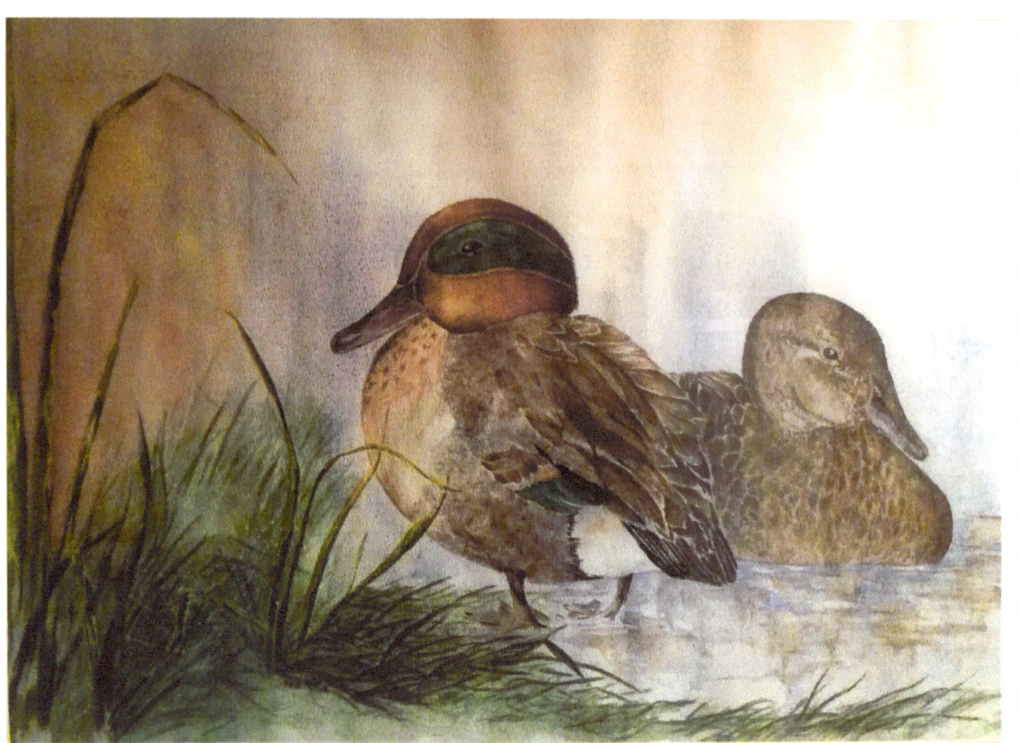

room, observing me hunched over, focused on yet another way to paint feathers. He said, "Don't you think you're ready to start painting?" He was right. I was stalling, rethinking, second-guessing, and questioning whether I could really do this. Who did I think I was? An Artist?

So, I took a deep breath and finalized my ambitious design of a green teal couple contemplating a delicious spider breakfast perched on her woven web glistening in the cattails. I recall the moment I used my fingerprint lines pressed in the paper for the delicate neck feathers. I had poured myself into those watercolor ducks that now were before me. Terry walked through just as I finished, and I asked him, "What do you think?" imploring him for his valued opinion……

"Yep…. Looks like a chicken!"

His comic one-liner broke all semblance of my serious effort to create those perfect feathered ducks. I was laughing so hard, I was crying. The painting was framed and submitted for the juried show. I didn't win; however, my entry wasn't the

Self-Reliance—Let Me Help Me

Looks Like a Chicken!

Several years ago, I threw my painting skills in the Missouri Conservation Duck Stamp Contest. The winning painting would be chosen for the prestigious award of having the image for that year's duck hunting stamp and fundraiser. The subject was the green-winged teal duck. I researched, sketched, and observed actual pairs of the feather fowls. I focused on all this in preparation before actually beginning the painting. The piles of paper drawings of beaks to feathers mounded over the dining table turned art studio. The entry deadline was fast approaching. My Sweet Terry strolled through the worst either. My valuable prize was learning the process of pondering what I wanted my painting to be, yet not stepping over to the point of confusion and doubt. I gained experience making decisions, discerning the next step, committing to splashing paint to paper, and not taking myself too seriously during the process. One workshop instructor called it the economy of brush strokes, mindfully considering how and where to paint next. Decades later, when I show Terry my latest masterpiece, whether it be a mountain scene or a pet portrait, I'll give you one guess of his cheeky comment. "Yep, Looks like a chicken!"

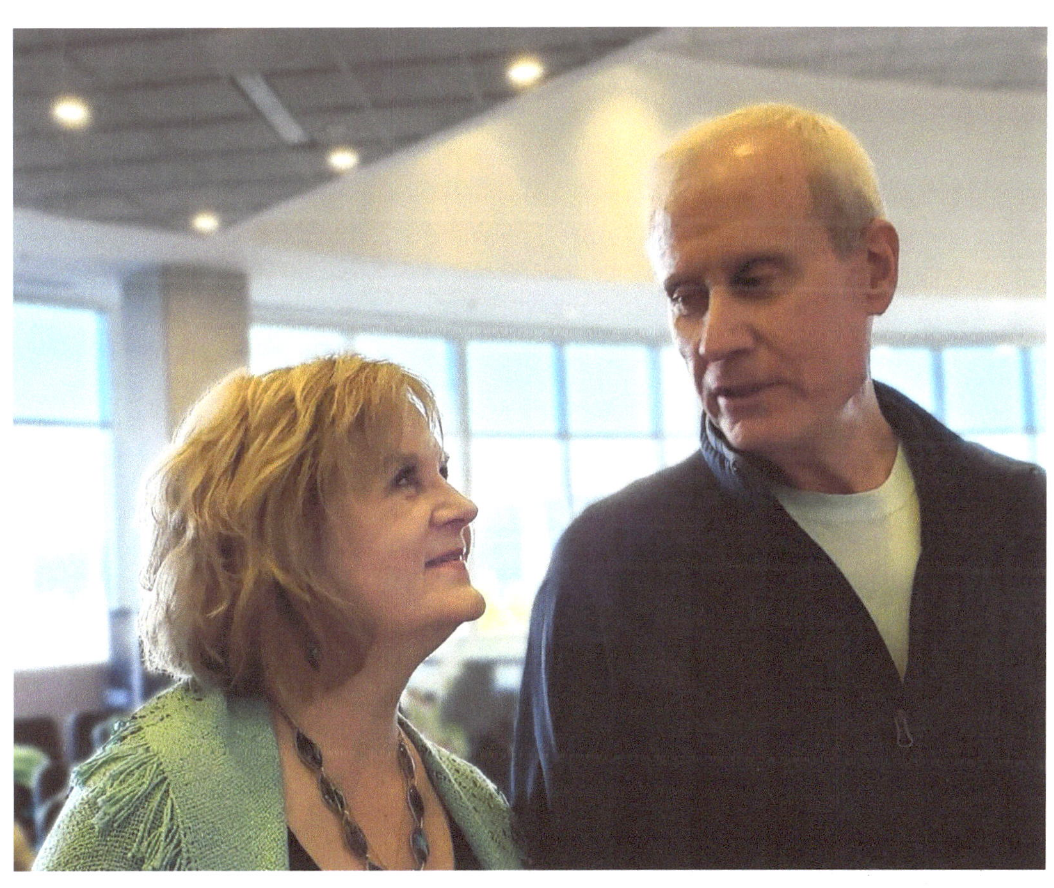

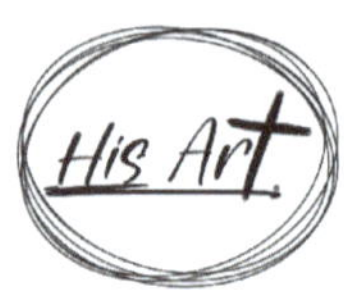

Ponder (Verb) 1.) to weigh in the mind. 2.) to think about: reflect on

"But while he thought on these things, behold, the angel of the Lord appeared unto him in a dream, saying, Joseph, thou son of David, fear not to take unto thee Mary thy wife: for that which is conceived in her is of the Holy Ghost" (Matthew 1:20).

Like in my painting story, Joseph had a dilemma and needed answers quickly. He was anxious about how his life and Mary's were seemingly being torn to bits. With an open heart and mind, he took heed of the advice of the angel of the Lord and took confident action.

Kaleidoscope Click

Yes, we certainly need to consider different scenarios, options, and consequences. Seek opinions from trusted friends and reliable sources. Most importantly, consult God himself until there is a holy nudge on where and when to take the next step. Then, with quiet assurance, take that step! Commit to it! So often, we ponder to the point of confusion and discouragement. (Remember my pile of rejected drawing ideas?) Settle your thoughts, take a breath, discern the next step, move forward with it, and then wait for the next.

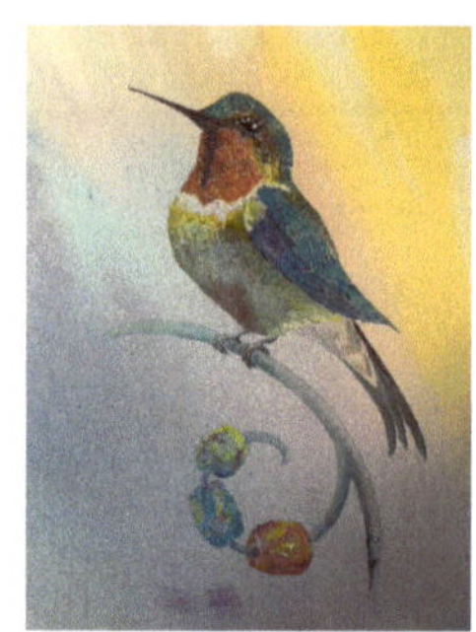

Learn the process of pondering to the point of recognizing the next step yet not stepping over to a point of confusion and doubt.

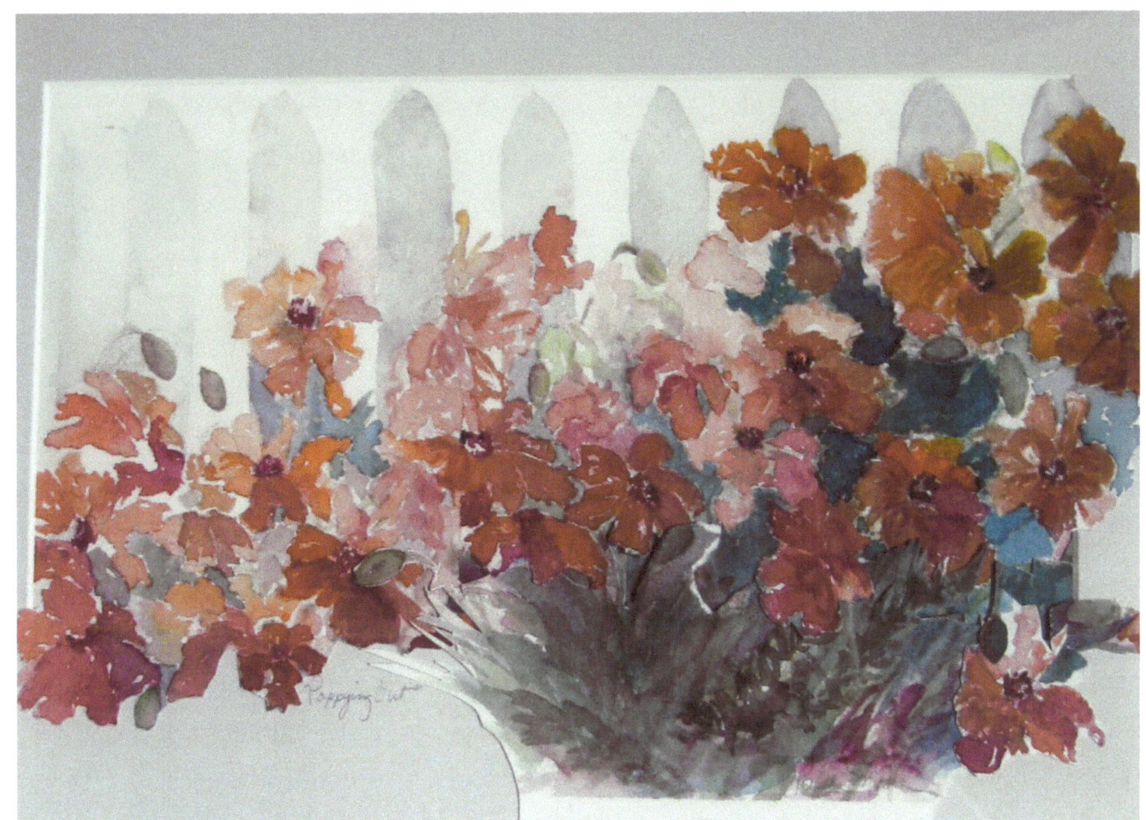

Conviction — I Do Need You to Help Me

Second Glance, Second Chance
What if I coulda woulda shoulda

I very much liked parts of my poppy painting. They were inspired by the red poppies playing a wild game of peekaboo in and around the white picket fence. If I had been paying closer attention, I would have had a better composition design. As it was, it was lopsided—too much green here and not enough poppies on the other side. I wasn't sure it was worth saving, so it set in my drawer of rejections, waiting for another chance to become something worthwhile.

Years later, I was learning some collage techniques and remembered the poppy painting. Since it was my painting, I was the only one who could take ownership to make the drastic change I was considering. My choices were to try an idea to morph it into something new and unique, keep it stuck in the drawer, or throw it away. Watercolor paper is expensive, and I am reluctant to trash it.

I glanced at the paper again, still thinking: I really liked parts of this poppy painting. Could I try a new thing? I placed my hand over the offending section, just like I remembered how Jane would temporarily do when assessing her painting. "Better," she would mutter under her breath. What if I moved this dark green foliage over here?

WhatifIcouldawouldashoulda.

Years ago, our teenage son could always entertain us with his funny adlib one-liners and antics. Upon our impromptu request, I can still picture his lanky, uncoordinated frame breaking into a command performance of his hilarious River Dance rendition. His focused eyes were straight ahead, not matching his solemn jawline, quivering on the verge of breaking into a silly grin. His fancy footwork, twirls, and high steps were never quite the same routine. One afternoon after football practice, making his way to the refrigerator, he announced he had made up a new phrase:

"Yagottaknowyawannacan." He said it so fast I didn't catch it, and I asked him to break it down for me: Ya Gotta Know Ya Wanna Can. This hopeful saying is still a favorite in our household.

Glancing at my poppy painting again, I had an idea; however, I wasn't sure if it would work, but I least wanted to try. Drastic paintings take drastic measures sometimes. I sketched out my change on a separate paper and loved it! With careful precision, I snipped out the section that needed to be moved into a new place. There was hope, but I needed assistance to finish my vision. I was confident it would work; however, I needed help holding and weaving it into place. I knew just the kind man who would help me unconditionally.

At the time, I taught classes at a local craft shop and had good friends who I relied on in the framing department. I called my friend Roger, telling him I would like to schedule surgery for my poppy painting project. "Sure!" he said. I knew he would be interested in seeing my crazy scheme. I arrived at the appointed time and shared my unorthodox plan and vision for this second-chance painting. He listened without judgment, took measurements, headed to his mat-cutting machine, and returned with a perfect but oddly shaped mat. I had brought my surgical scalpel scissors from home, and together, Roger and I huddled over our paper patient, who willingly lay quietly on the operating table. A clip here, a scoot there, we pushed the promising painting up and through to its new position. One last bit of glue was placed for stability. Then, suddenly, the work was done. The surgery was a success. The patient had a new life to live. I even gave it a new name!

"Poppying Out"! The title was a play on words describing the happy red poppies weaving in and out of the white fencing and finally popping out over the mat, attempting to move on to new adventures. They could not be contained. They were singing me a familiar song of gratitude— "YaGotta-KnowYaWannaCan!" I have had offers from clients to purchase this unusual painting with its odd title. I keep it in my private collection to remind me to try something new and not give up.

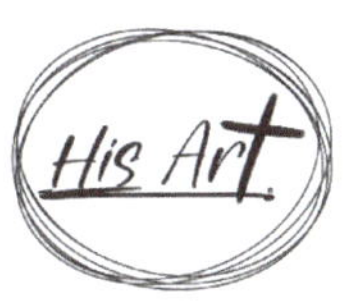

"I can do all things through Christ which strengtheneth me" (Philippians 4:13).
"Delight thyself also in the Lord: and he shall give thee the desires of thine heart" (Psalm 37:4).
"Trust in the Lord with all thine heart; and lean not unto thine own understanding" (Proverbs 3:5).

Kaleidoscope Click

Have you found yourself here? You're going along, painting a pretty little scene of your life. You stand back to take it all in and realize you've got yourself into one hot mess. The moral lines have gradually become a muddied blur. The faded dreams are not taking shape fast enough. Principles and defined values are now shades of gray. That little white lie has steadily slipped into center stage as the focal point. No amount of scrubbing it out will remedy the issue – it only threatens to tear a larger hole in your very fiber. They are the noisy critical voices in your head confirming the fact of failure; it's no use. Who do you think you are? Why waste the time? We toss our purpose in shame's dark drawer where it is abandoned. Sure, you have the option to stay there forever tucked away in the Regrets and Rejections File……or maybe, just maybe, consider a second glance at possibilities.

No one is perfect, and we all make mistakes. Thank God for his gifts of long-suffering and forgiveness! Otherwise, we all would be thrown on the trash heap. Be willing to take your sorry life's painting and present it to the God of Second Chances. (I will add that there are infinite chances throughout your lifespan!) There is one time an individual comes to God for salvation. However, from that moment in time, the line of communication has always been open no matter how far away you are from him. All you have to do is cry out for help, and he will be there. Trust as you sense his plan to do the work. Don't be surprised when he hands the paintbrush right back to you! He will guide you through the revisions when you stay close—not dropping behind or racing in front. Just one brushstroke of the process at a time. This awareness is not only in the big troubles you face. It is in the everyday little details that the Holy Spirit desires to be a counselor in your life. What is beautiful about this relationship is that there is no force or requisition forms to complete. Earnestly seek and ask because there is absolute hope. Imagine yourself as the original hopeless scrap of a painting I spoke of at the beginning of this story. Consider the joy of a willingness to be drenched with his pure mercy, bending to his will and not your own understanding. You are fastening the awareness of your weakness on that old wooden cross. Until the end of time, he still waits for those who willingly, obediently seek him. Christ desires only a joyful, abundant, beautiful life for you.

Be encouraged! The initial pivotal turnaround

doesn't have to take long! You'll be renewed by all the true colors of his love.

If you are honest with yourself, I am guessing there is an unspoken area where you would like to make changes for the better. Ideas include losing the extra 30 pounds, decluttering that storage room, or exploring methods to improve a relationship. I am confident in my thoughts because we are all the same. We are human, most times striving to do our best. But it is not God's Will that we Strive, meaning spending our energy worrying, fretting, and being anxious. Rather, he wants us to Thrive! Using the fantastic brain and spirit he gave us, we learn, trust, and follow. What area in your life can you give a second glance, a second chance? Is there someone you love who might need assistance in their struggle?

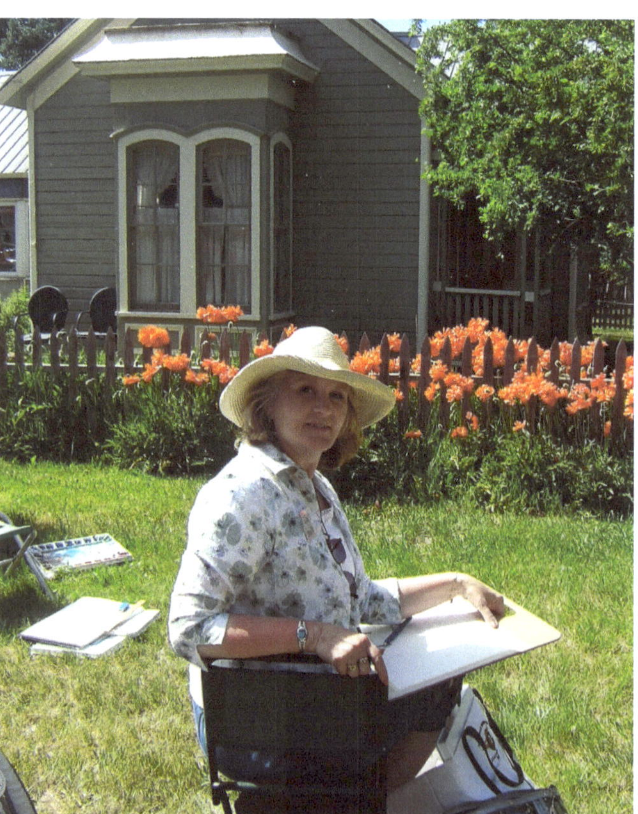

Dare to consider the possibilities of the "What ifs." Think about the wouldashouldacouldas. Lift even the smallest detail in prayer. Gather and consult a trustworthy friend or pastor, perhaps a qualified individual within the medical community or a mental health counselor. Take a second glance and consider a second chance. Make a plan and do the hard work of cutting out the concern and placing it where it belongs. You are the only one with the authority to make those changes in your life, and you decide who is on your decision-making committee.

Is there even a little slip of a sad painted memory hidden away in the deepest chamber of your heart? Consider pulling it out in the open. Please give it a second glance, a second chance. The Creator of the Universe has some ideas for you!

YaGottaKnowYaWannaCan

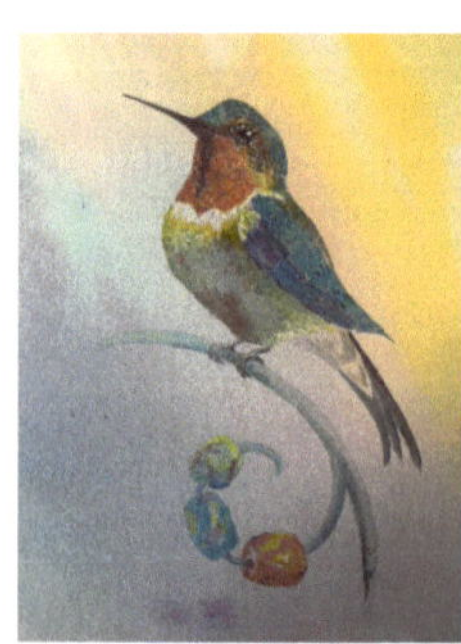

Conviction — I Do Need You to Help Me

Winding Curves Ahead

Point A ______________Point B

Point A 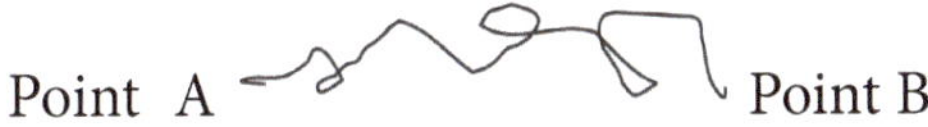 Point B

My analytical husband described our different thought processes to a friend as this: he finds the shortest route from Point A to Point B, whereas my strategy might resemble a twisty, curvy path seeking out new adventures, intriguing places, and interesting people along the way. I do admire Terry's focused discipline; however, looking back, I wouldn't change my journey one step. He even mentioned this in his talk. He recognized my joy in the journey and admitted it was a nice balance to his structured methodology.

You've read my childhood stories of being creative. In the teen years, my pivotal moments begin, then college, then marriage. (Can you relate?) There were some road sign warnings of a hairpin turn or a detour ahead. Sometimes, we merely strapped in, gripped the wheel, and kept in our lane. Two active children, mortgages, church activities, a live-in father-in-law, a full-throttle thirty-year banking career, and sharing this all with a law enforcement lieutenant were, at times, blurred memories as we raced down our highway of building our lives together.

Most of the time, I frankly was too tired to paint. However, I poured over art magazines and instructional books, hoping osmosis would seep all the knowledge into my brain's creative side while I slept. This was a perfect plan up to a point while I studied these step-by-step photos of exercises.

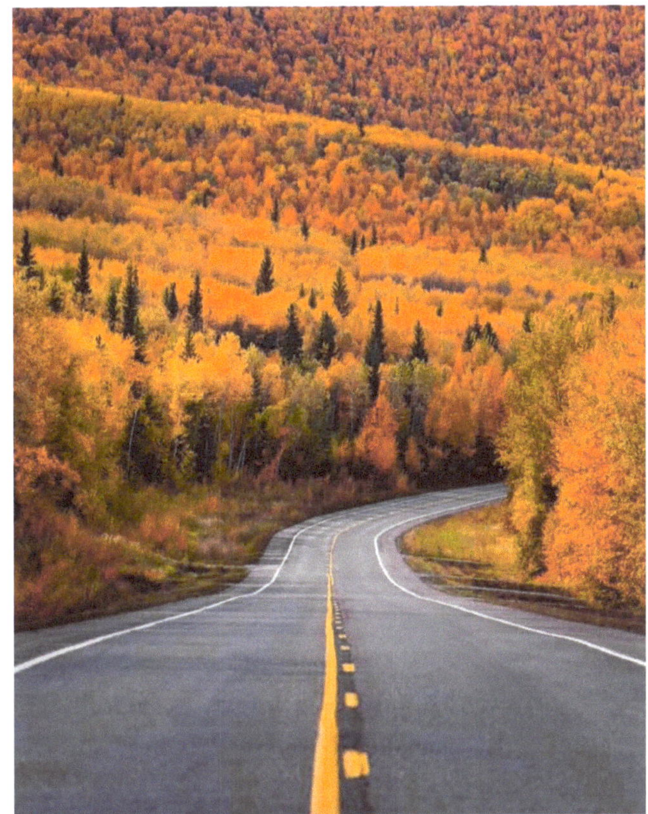

I gained head knowledge, but I was also aware there was so much more beneath the surface. I longingly hungered to grasp the concepts. I could copy anything but understood nothing. I began asking and searching for someone who could teach me, not just show me the ways.

Let there be no misunderstanding; I cherish my entire life. If you know me, you've probably heard me say, "My life is not busy; rather, my life is full. I love every part of it.

Still, my creative side was starving. I had not realized the importance of being part of a community of innovative, art-like-minded people and learning new techniques and art mediums. Anne Paris, in her book Standing at Waters Edge, helped me through. There is an ebb and flow to the process. We should have others in our lives who act as mirrors, twins, and heroes.

Additionally, I had no dedicated creative place or, for that matter, very little personal space of my own. (With a teenage daughter in the house, even my underwear drawer was not off-limits!) I shared my thoughts with Terry, although I knew I was the only one who could find a solution. I remember thinking, "Lord, I just need a little creative sanctuary, preferably a hiding place with a lock from the inside." Longing for this heart's desire seemed to take forever. Then suddenly, the answer appeared one afternoon. The unfinished storage room under the basement stairs only holds accumulated boxes of clutter. One single little light, no drywall, and a concrete floor. A door with a lock from the inside. Was this perhaps a prayer answered? Maybe? I hopped up the stairs two steps at a time and shared my findings with Terry. No questions asked; he and his brother graciously finished my little art studio with vents, lighting, walls, and flooring. My creative soul overflowed—a hiding place with a lock from the inside out.

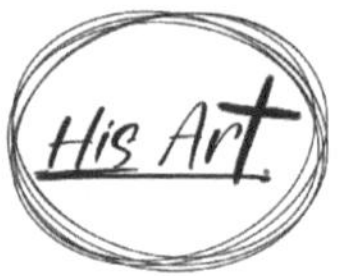

Searching for answers

"And the angel of the Lord spake unto Philip, saying, Arise, and go toward the south unto the way that goeth down from Jerusalem unto Gaza, which is desert. And he arose and went: and behold a man of Ethiopia, an eunuch of great authority under Candace queen of the Ethiopians, who had the charge of all her treasure, and had come to Jerusalem for to worship, Was returning, and sitting in his chariot read Esaias the prophet. Then the Spirit said unto Philip, Go near, and join thyself to this chariot. And Philip ran thither to him, and heard him read the prophet Esaias and said, Understandest thou what thou readest? he said unto him, how can I except some man should guide me? "And he desired Philip that he would come up and sit with him. "The place of the scripture which he read was this, he was led as a sheep to the slaughter; and like a lamb dumb before his shearer, so opened he not his mouth: In his humiliation his judgement was taken away; and who shall declare his generation? For his life is taken from the earth. [Author's note: This is a prophesied passage from Isaiah 53:7 found in the Old Testament and written over 700 years before Christ!]

"And the eunuch answered Philip, and said, I pray thee, of whom speaketh the prophet this? Of himself, or of some other man? Then Philip opened his mouth and began at the same scripture, and preached unto him Jesus. And as they went on their way, they came unto a certain water; and the eunuch said, See, here is water; what doth hinder me to be baptized? And Philip said, if thou believest with all thine heart, thou mayest. And he answered and said, I believe that Jesus Christ is the Son of God. And he commanded the chariot to stand still: and they went down both into the water, both Philip and eunuch; and he baptized him. And when they were come up out of the water, the Spirit of the Lord caught away Philip, that the eunuch saw him no more; and he went on his way rejoicing" (Acts 8:26–39).

My life is not busy; rather, my life is full. I love every part of it.

Kaleidoscope Click

Is there an unfulfilled dream you hunger for, like the hope of my little hiding place where I could create? Think outside the box (for there is no box) and consider ways to make it happen. Remember to ask for help from others, too. Most importantly, I recommend making your request known before the Holy Creator himself—even the little things. He already knows, anyway. He is just waiting for you to partner with the plan he has in store for you! Then hop two steps at a time toward it!

"I waited patiently for the Lord; and he inclined unto me, and heard my cry. Psalm 40:1 Thou art my hiding place and my shield: I hope in thy word" (Psalm 119:11).

Conviction — I Do Need You to Help Me

Then Why Take a Workshop?

As I've mentioned, my joy is in teaching and witnessing my students grasp a concept in art. Before the project is presented to my students, hours of preparation and thought go into a workshop. The workshop description, featured techniques, materials, supplies needed, costs, date, time, and location are decided upon.

The day of the workshop is always so exciting. I have in my heart what I want to share, and my students are anticipating learning something new. The What, How, When, and the Where has been discussed. I want to hear their "Why". Why are they here? What is their expectation, and what do they want to take away with them? They chose to spend money, time, and effort when so many other choices were available! This simple yet complex question surprises some, I think, because they may not have really examined the reasons "why." I ask this simple question for two reasons. 1). So, all of us can climb on board the creative train and settle into a participating mindset. 2). It clues me into what they seek and need from me personally. Otherwise, everyone begins with a slightly different version of a plan. Discussion establishes a kinship and a united energy; we are all in this together. As the instructor, I know I'll learn as much from the students as they

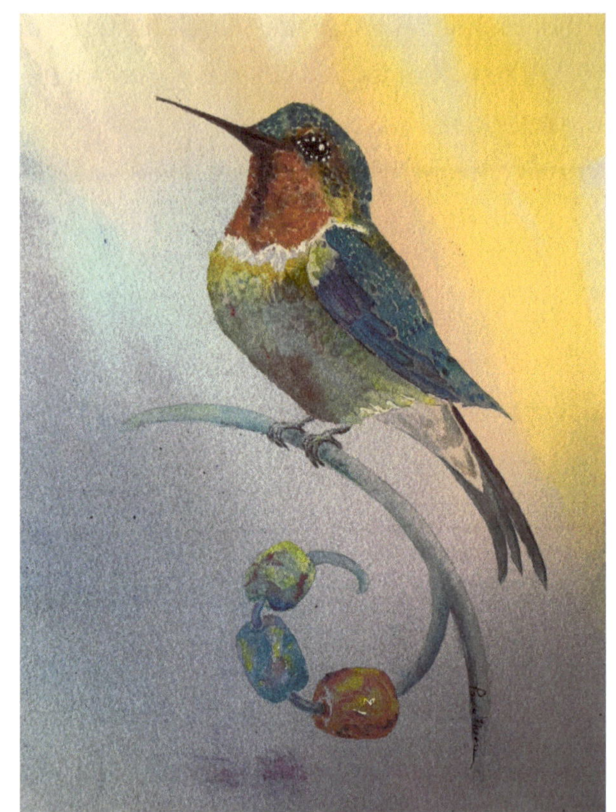

do from me! I also tell them that I will ask at the end of the workshop for one or two takeaways to share with the group. Most of the time, we are all in one accord with eager, willing hearts, wanting to learn, listen, and ask questions.

I've learned to take command early on because occasionally, I sense from the beginning that one or two may have their own agenda. The personalities can also be found in families, churches, and workplaces. Read along to see if you recognize any of these traits. I hope, hope, hope you're not seeing a reflection of yourself.

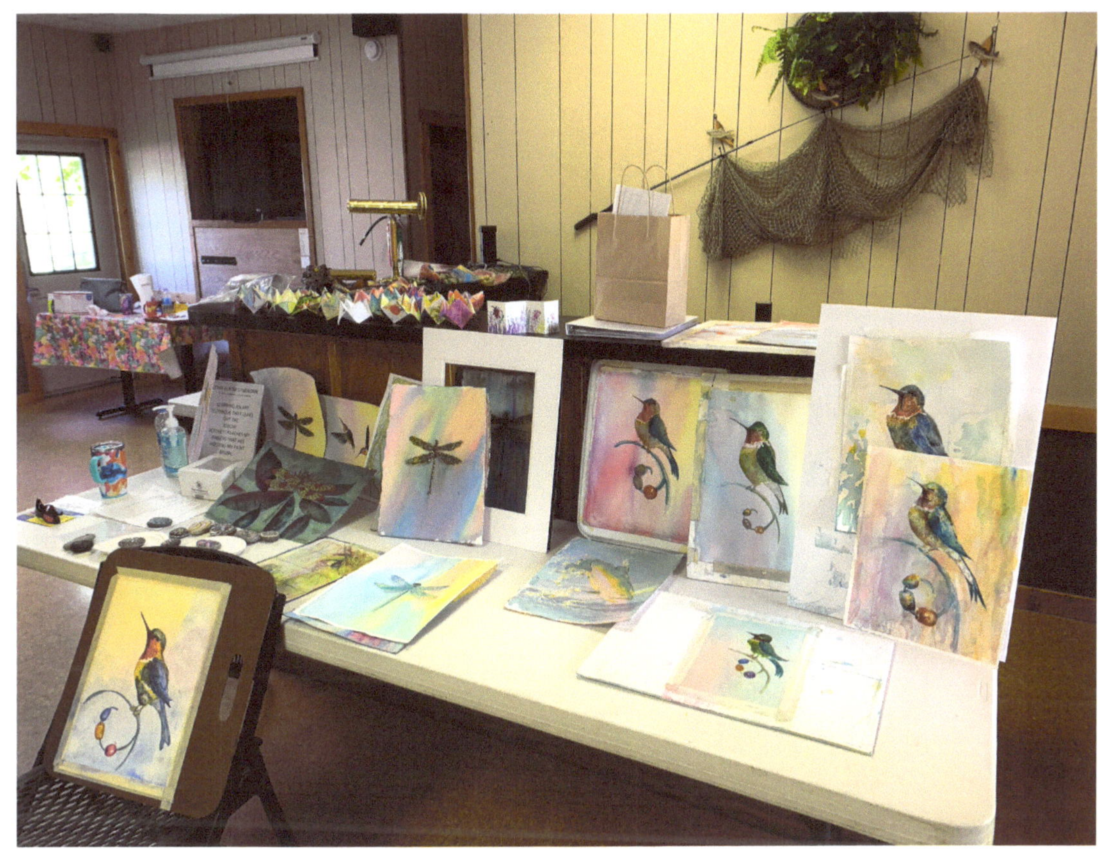

Hardened—Nope, not me…not even going to try these newfangled ideas of doing this. I know how to do it.

The Takeover—The one who feels he or she has the authority interrupts my teaching and adds unsolicited suggestions and comments, making it difficult for anyone to follow.

The Maverick—This painter is a runaway train, not even listening and way ahead of me and everyone else. (I will add that this participant usually does it wrong and then gets frustrated that their project isn't working!) I remember one lady wielding her brush, wildly splashing paint, doing her own thing before I had even started the class! Frankly, her painting was a mess; it showed, and she was embarrassed and disappointed.

Which group do you think is more enjoyable to spend the day with?

I prepare written instructional guides, actual paintings and demonstrations. The process can be compared to trying a new recipe. You look at the cookbook's appealing food photo, read the instructions, gather the ingredients, and start the project. I follow a similar format for my workshop. We read the synopsis together: Here's what we will do. Here's where we'll stop and take a break to review our paintings with friendly critiques and address any questions before proceeding again. Here's where I'll paint a demonstration. Here's when you can do the work.

Here's where you should be and what it should look like. When we're finished, we'll review our accomplishments!

So why take the workshop in the first place if you believe it is not required to pursue your goal of becoming a more successful painter?

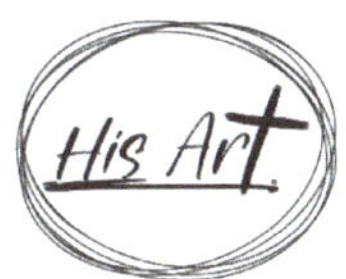

This teaching strategy is nothing I've created on my own. God leads and guides the same! Through Moses, he commanded the Israelites to follow his plan for a fulfilled journey into the Promised Land. He instructed the people to do something entirely out of the regular day-to-day routine, which was to paint the blood of an innocent lamb over the door of their household. Gather the few belongings you need and WAIT on me. I'll supply the rest. Trust the process, step into the waters because this new way will work, he promised. Just keep following. Indeed, they were scared and unsure. Most grumbled and complained. There were signs along the way that there was a change happening. TEN commandments were written in stone by God himself! Manna provided daily, Smoke by day and fire by night pointing the way. And yet, still more whining and more unbelief. Did you know the Israelites could have been to the Promised Land in less than two weeks? Instead, they marched in circles around the same mountain for forty (4-0) years. Except for very few, an entire generation was lost because of their unbelief and unwillingness to follow the leadership of God.

"And he said, Go forth, and stand upon the mount before the Lord. And, behold, the Lord passed by, and a great and strong wind rent the mountains, and brake in pieces the rocks before the Lord; but the Lord was not in the wind: and after the wind an earthquake; but the Lord was not in the earthquake: And after the earthquake a fire; but the Lord was not in the fire: and after the fire a still small voice" (1 Kings 19:11–12).

Read what God says to Job. In today's vocabulary, it would be, so, who do you think you are? "Where wast thou when I laid the foundations of the earth? Declare, if thou hast understanding. Who hath laid the measures thereof, if thou knowest? Or who hath stretched the line upon it? Where upon are the foundations thereof fastened? Or who laid the corner stone thereof; When the morning stars sang together, and all the sons of God shouted for joy?" (Job:38:4–7).

Kaleidoscope Click

I'll pose the questions to you now. Tell me your Why? Share your deepest hope, your heart's dream. Why the hesitation?

Is there a mountain or a problem in your life that you keep marching around in circles and never arriving at a resting place? If you always come back to the same conclusion, I recommend you search for new information. An example might be attempting to make your way to the West Coast by following a map of Missouri. You're not going to get there. I recommend considering laying your paint-brushed burden down. Quiet yourself from life's stormy troubles, breathe and listen for that still small voice. Follow the Holy Leader's instructions every step of the way. You will be thrilled with your BeautiFULL Life results! Here are some scriptures to claim for your own!

"Come unto me, all ye that labour and are heavy laden, and I will give you rest" (Matthew 11:28).

"Ye ask, and receive not, because ye ask amiss, that ye may consume it upon your lusts. Peace I leave with you, my peace I give unto you: not as the world giveth, give I unto you. Let not your heart be troubled, neither let it be afraid" (John 4:2–3).

What is your Why?

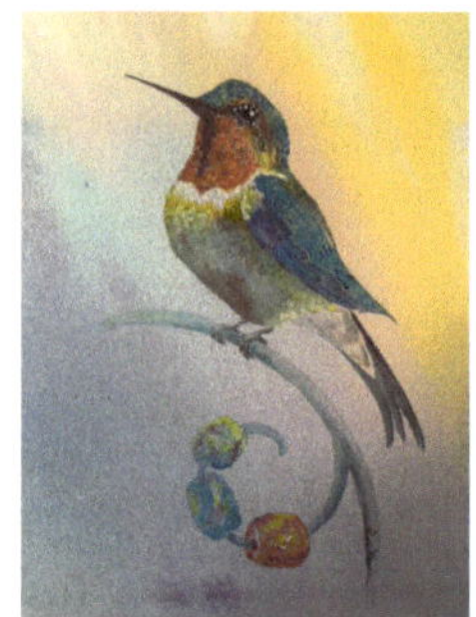

Repentance — Let Me Depend Upon You

Portrait of a Gracious Woman

My aunt Ruthie and I both enjoyed the arts, especially painting. Our visits would always include a discussion of our latest projects. She told me once, with a smile, that she didn't do portraits… "just too difficult." Yet, with the daily brush strokes of her own life, she painted an exquisite portrait painting to be cherished.

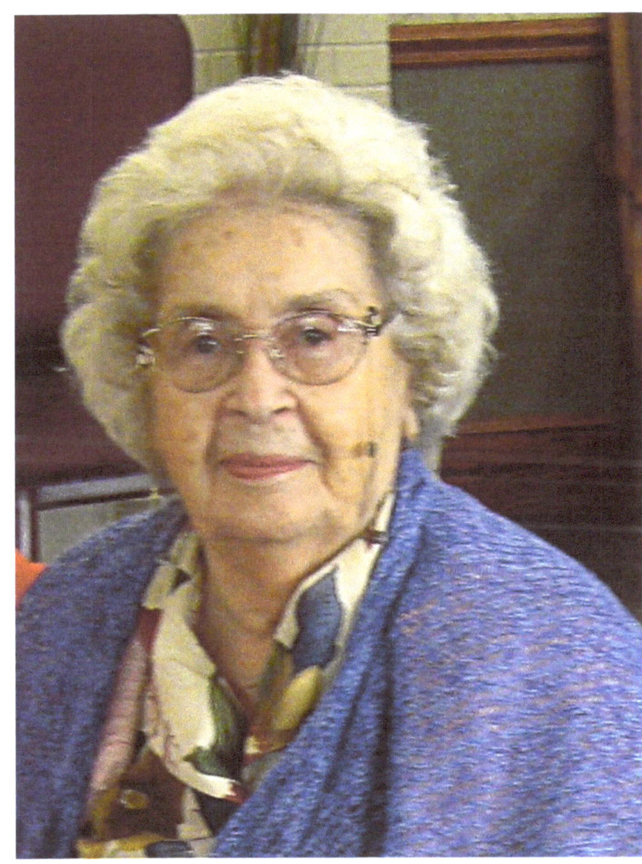

Her very best work was worthy to be purchased by the King of all Kings. It is her self-portrait of a gracious woman.

Look closely at this painting, for within is the essence of who Ruthie will always be to me.

These are the characteristics of being gracious:

Continually finds the good in others

Forgives quickly

Seeks opportunities to comfort

Desires to say and do what is appropriate

Attentive to her family and friends

Always appreciative of others

Never seeks to embarrass another

Slow to take credit and quick to lavish praise

So here is my tribute to my dear aunt Ruthie. As the verse tells us, a gracious woman retaineth honor.

All your gracious ways and the lovely memory of you will be kept close to my heart.

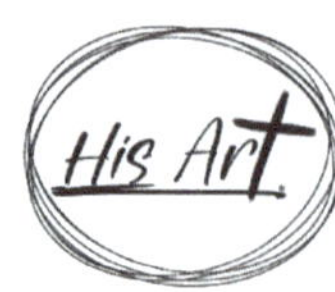

One of my favorite verses is Luke 2:19, "But Mary kept all these things, and pondered them in her heart." I am pondering this thought of which I share with you. My aunt Ruthie was a picture of grace well lived. And Grace begins in the very heart of God.

"A gracious woman retaineth
honor" (Proverbs 11:15a).

Kaleidoscope Click

Does this story remind you of a remarkable woman in your life?

Is your life portrait displayed prominently in someone's hall of remembrance?

Her very best work was worthy of being purchased by the King of Kings.

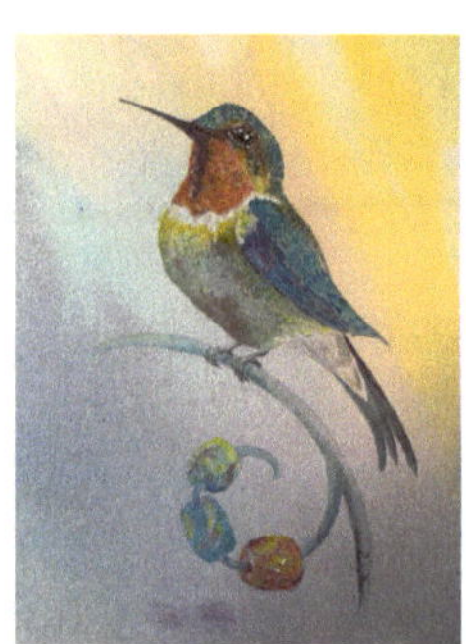

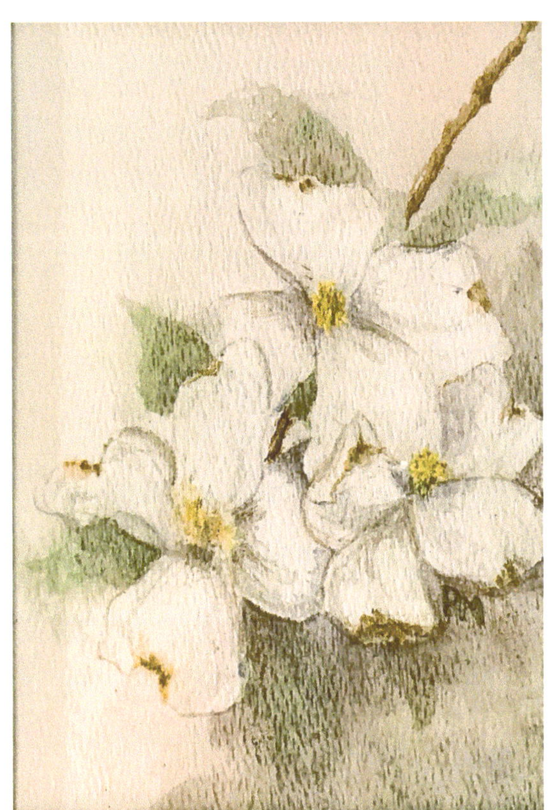

Repentance — Let Me Depend Upon You

The Gift of the Giver

Each spring, I bring out this small painting of a dogwood sprig, a token gift from my dad.

My dad was a giver. Some of my treasured memories from him remain: an oddly shaped rock riddled with holes, another flat rock which had originally been a part of the foundation of his grandfather's 1800s home place, a battered coffee grinder missing the tray that he had found in the old barn (He knew I would love it.), a beloved pinto pony named Rusty, large bouquets of multihued zinnias from his garden, whittled wood carvings, his quiet gentleness, his love of hymns and all sorts of music (except the loud rock and roll.)

One Sunday afternoon in April, my little family was headed back to north Missouri, where my husband was stationed with the Missouri State Highway Patrol. It wasn't quite the end of the world; however, you could see it from there. We were all longing for the day we could move back to southern Missouri to be closer to family and friends.

That afternoon, as we were loading up the car, my dad presented me with yet another gift from his giving heart. It was a little floral sprig of the dogwood tree he and my mother had planted in the front yard of our childhood home. The sprig had already been tenderly wrapped with wet paper towels and sealed in a plastic bag for the long journey back home.

I remember enjoying that sweet-smelling dogwood sprig for several days as it rested in a little vase of water on my kitchen counter. Then, I realized it wouldn't last forever, so I was compelled to pull out my watercolors and capture the happy moment it represented.

Decades later, this little painting still takes me back to that sunny spring afternoon. My dad, in his quiet way, offered his gift, and I gladly accepted the treasure from the giver.

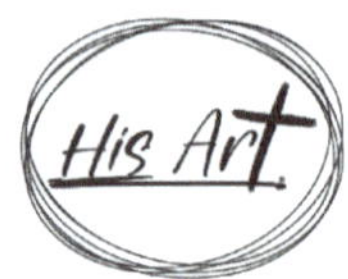

The most memorable gifts are little gestures such as a smile, a hug, and a sincere word of encouragement. You can always, always be kind.

> "Every man according as he purposeth in his heart, so let him give; not grudgingly, or of necessity: for God loveth a cheerful giver" (2 Corinthians 9:7).

Kaleidoscope Click

I have a second hobby that is so enjoyable. It cost pennies or actually nothing! It takes no skills; even a child can learn the concept. The idea translates to any language around the world. It takes just a moment, or you can practice it all day long if you're like me. It's merely a search for ways to be kind. For example, I carry little stickers in my wallet that are awarded to a little boy or girl for being so good in a store. Of course, I first catch the parent's eye and share my intention. I've never been turned down. Watching the child be praised as they choose their sparkling sticker is a delight. When I compliment the Mamma for her efforts as well, the child then gets to choose a sticker for her, too! The kindness has taken 30 seconds or less, but I know there are at least three happier people in the world.

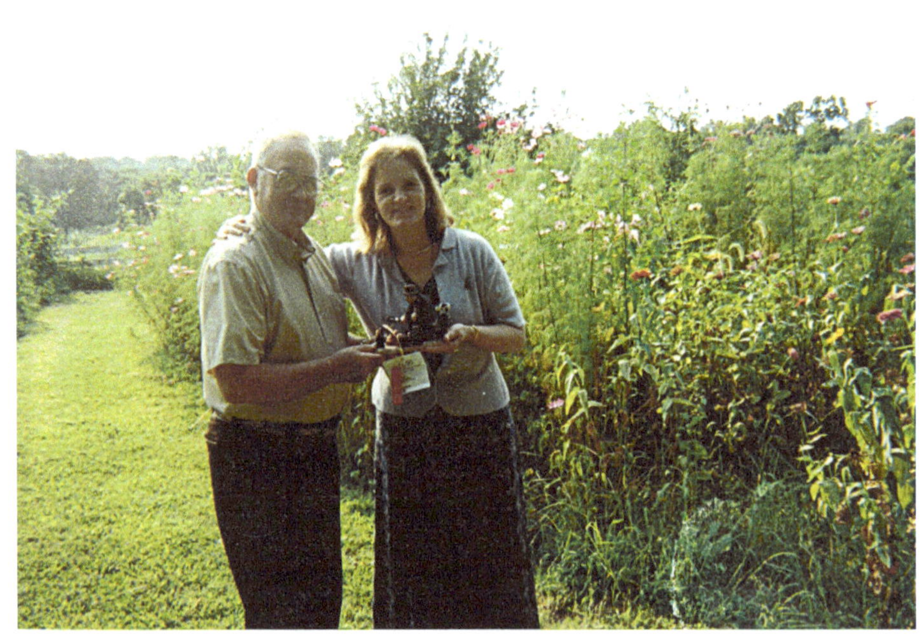

Search out ways to be kind. Even the gift of a dogwood tree sprig will evoke a lasting memory.

Always, always be kind.

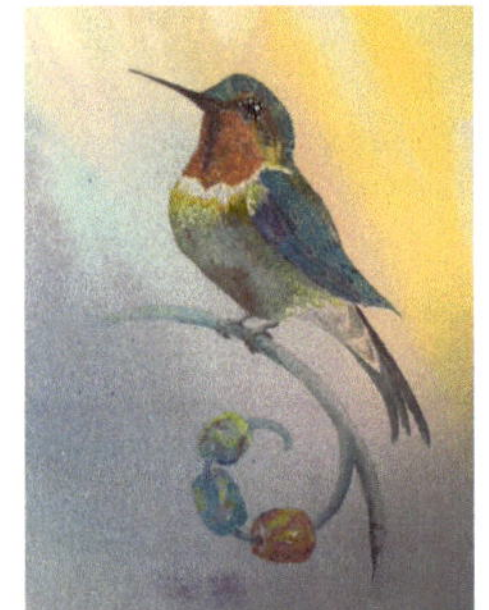

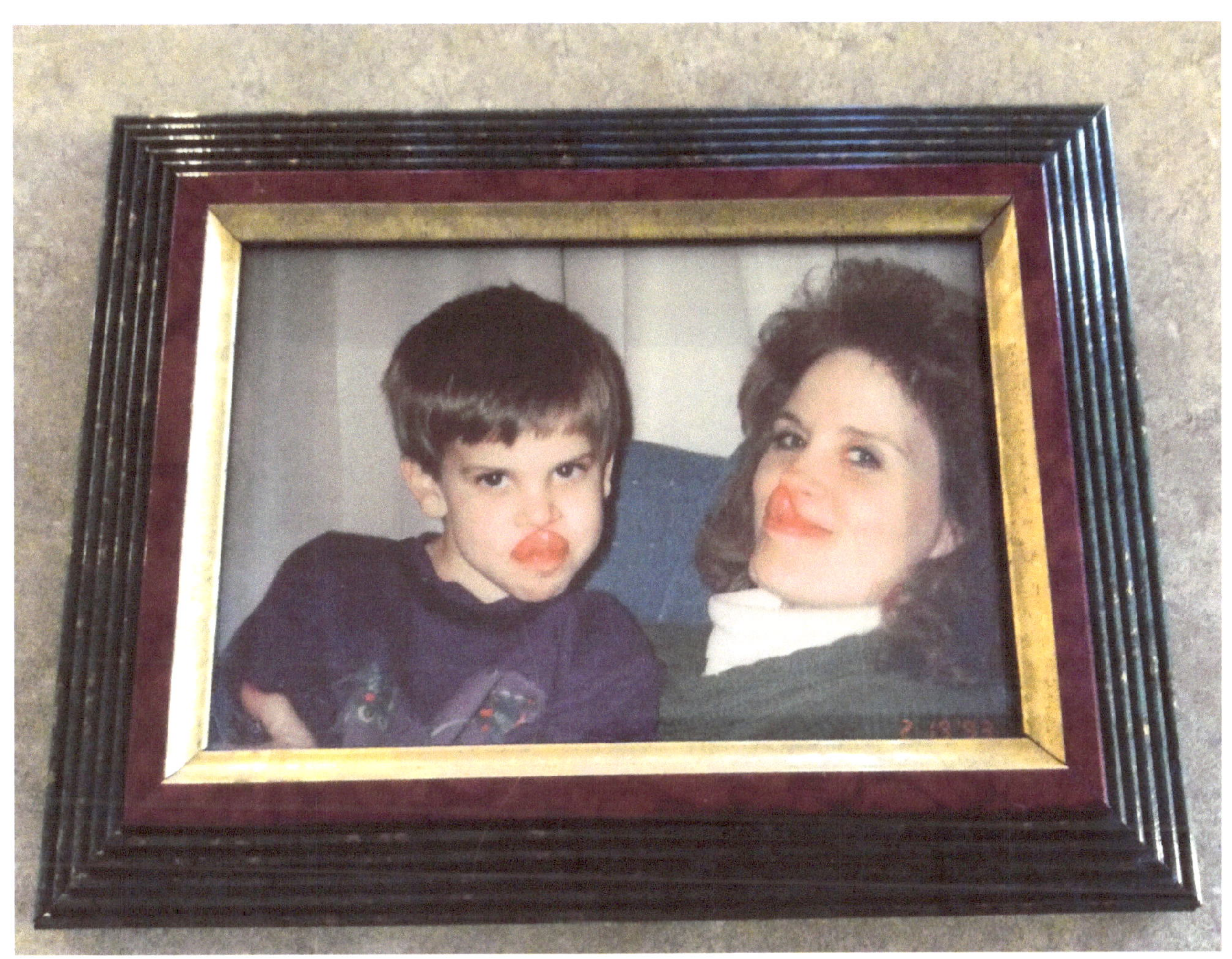

Repentance — Let Me Depend Upon You

New Winkle in Owl Bah-wain!

Years ago, our four-year-old returned home from pre-school, announcing a new fact that his teacher had told them that day. "When we learn something new, we get a new winkle in owl bah-wayn!" (and yes, this is the same fellow who, in his teen years, came up with YaGottaKnowYaWannaCan.)

A new winkle in owl b'wayn is another favorite saying at our house when we've come across a new thought or idea. After decades of observing this phenomenon, I surmise that this is an accurate conclusion for myself and the population at large. Apparently, I've learned so much that those brain wrinkles are now oozing out around my eyes and forehead!

When I prepare a fresh white canvas upon which to paint an inspiration I want to share with my viewers, it is prudent to take a few minutes to plan. There is quite a process that takes place before a drop of paint ever touches the paper. Inside an artist's mind, questions should be answered, such as:

- What do I want this painting to say to the viewer?
- What color scheme should I choose?
- What's my composition?
- Where should the light, middle, and dark tonal values be placed?

During one of my recent basic technique classes, my students were eager to jump into the fun part of touching paint to paper. They were unconsciously following my lesson plans for developing the painting assignment. In this class, I offered a new approach by teaching my students the step-by-step process of recognizing what inspired them to create and how to conjure their own questions and answers about what they wanted to paint. My students were so excited by taking the time to develop their thinking skills for themselves! Rather than copying my painting exactly, each of them came away with a successful, original painting in their own signature style.

In comparison, as we consider our own lives, there have been times when we merely jump right in without forethought to the outcome—perhaps living a fairly good rendition yet still leaving room for improvement.

Other times, we meditate, consider guidance from trusted sources, and apply faithful principles to our efforts. Are not these times, more often than not, the most satisfying accomplishments created?

I hope you will always come away from my writings with new insights, new information, and new wrinkles in your brain!

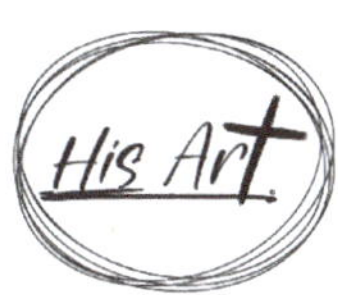

"Study to shew thyself approved unto God, a workman that needeth not to be ashamed, rightly dividing the word of truth" (2 Timothy 2:15).

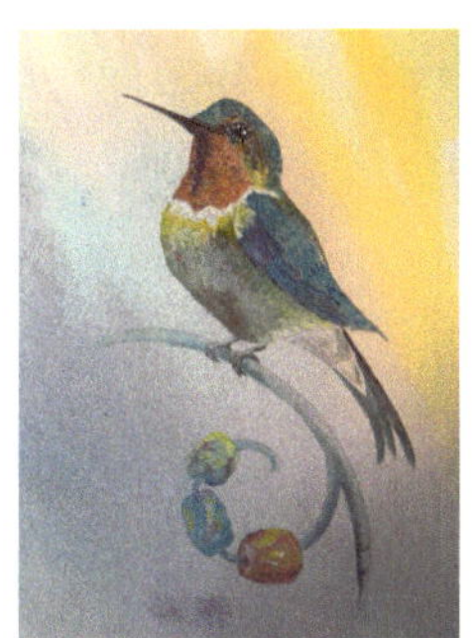

When we learn something new, we get a new winkle in owl bah-wayn.

Repentance — Let Me Depend Upon You

Like Riding a Bike

I knew the promise my parents had told us. On our eighth birthday, our gift would be a new bicycle.

Being the oldest of my siblings, we had not seen the fruition of that prize…we could only hope and trust it would happen. Sure enough, on that cold day in late January, I was presented with my shiny new sky-blue bike, featuring rainbow streamers dangling from the handlebars, a little rearview mirror, and a wire basket attached to the front. Mother only had one rule before I could pedal down the sidewalks of our neighborhood. I must learn to ride it in our small front yard without training wheels. That sounds easy enough.

Not so, especially at eight years old. Remembering the lay of the land, there was a slight grassy slope on one side, and there was no sidewalk except the bumpy concrete squares leading to the house. Obstacles included giant maple trees, shrubs and

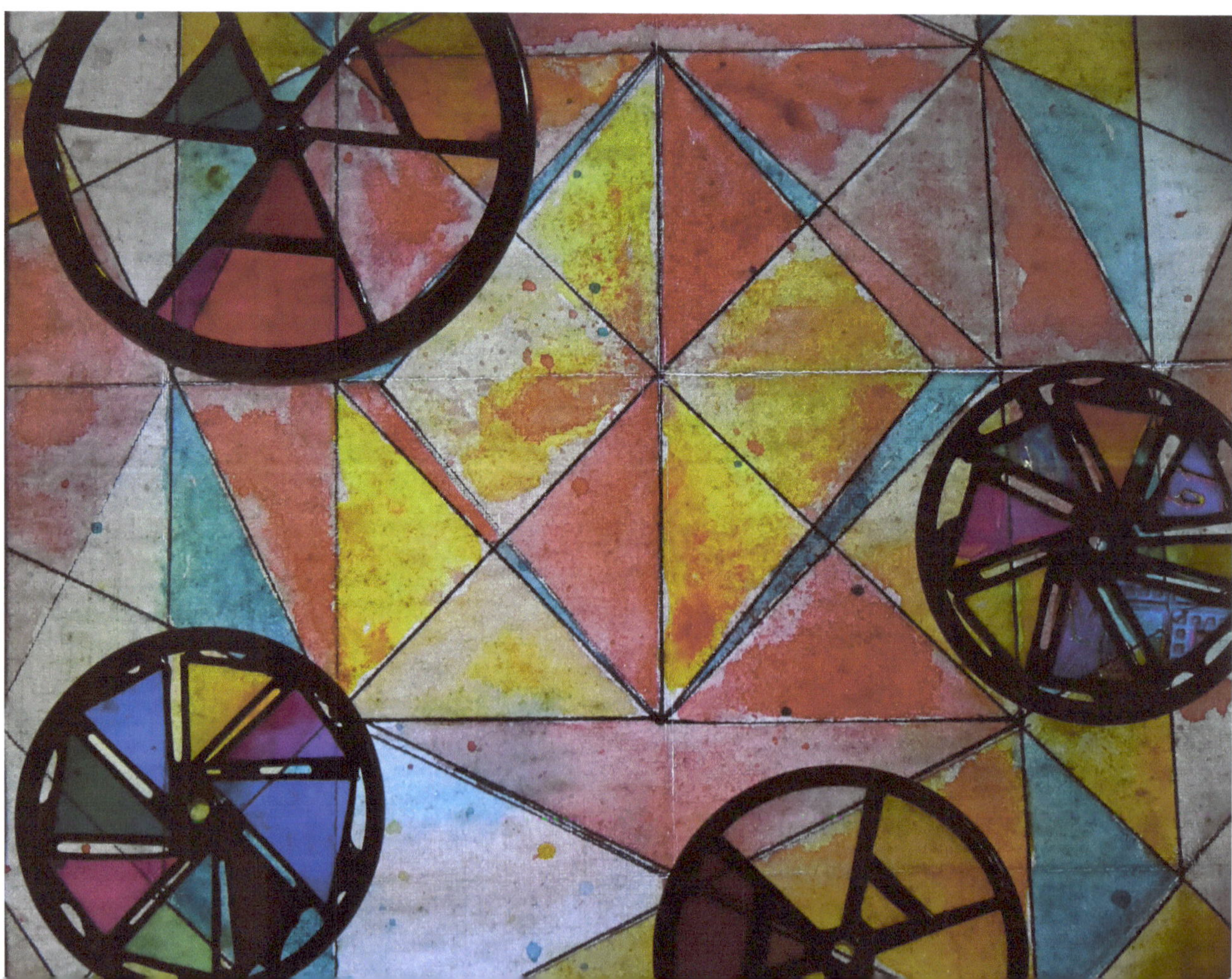

dormant, thorny rose bushes. The frigid Midwest temperatures make the grass frozen and crunchy. I had not foreseen the additional skills I would need to dodge happy dogs, a little six-year-old sister and three-year-old brother cheering me on in my unsure path. I wore a woolen coat, hat, and gloves too! Did that dampen my desire to master that blue chariot of freedom? No! I was focused on a goal. So, concentrate, I did. There was so much to learn: the balancing, pedaling, making the turns, learning how to signal your intent – left, right, stop. I focused on how to slow down, speed up, look ahead, be aware of the perils behind me, breathe, learn the safest way to fall, untangle myself, and try again. Noting where the red mercurochrome and Band-Aids were stored, mastering this bike was my dream, and I was determined to do it. I was obsessed with practicing. Before I knew it, all those skills had come into focus, and suddenly, I was riding that bike without even thinking about it. I had mastered riding my new blue bike, passing my wise mother's test. I understand now she was also teaching my siblings as they watched me go through the trials and tribulations of learning and then the thrill of hearing my mother's praise, "Wonderful! You've done it!" I remember feeling accomplished knowing my whole family watched me pedal off by myself, navigating the bumps of Lillian Avenue's sidewalks.

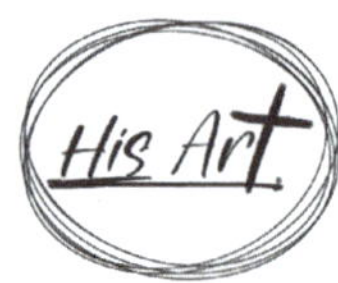

"Ponder the path of your feet,
and let all your ways be established. Do not
turn to the right or the left. Remove your
foot from evil" (Proverbs 4:26–27 NKJV).

Kaleidoscope Click

I believed in my parent's blue bike promise, knowing they would keep their end of the bargain if I kept mine of learning how to ride. It was worth their investment to teach me and my siblings the benefits of working towards a goal.

Scriptures provide many examples of perseverance and winning the reward. Partner with God, share your dreams and goals, and align your will with his. You'll soon enjoy the freedom to move down your chosen path.

Is there a dream you have that seems so impossible even to fathom? That is one of the enemy's favorite evil games, planting negative thoughts and obstacles in your way and stealing your joy. Write it down, meditate, and pray. The Lord already knows your talents…he gave them to you! He may have an even greater plan for your life than you can ever imagine. I can personally testify to this truth! The first quiet whisper and my Dream Purpose has become more than I have ever thought possible!

Before I knew it, all those skills came into focus, and suddenly, I was riding that bike without even thinking about it.

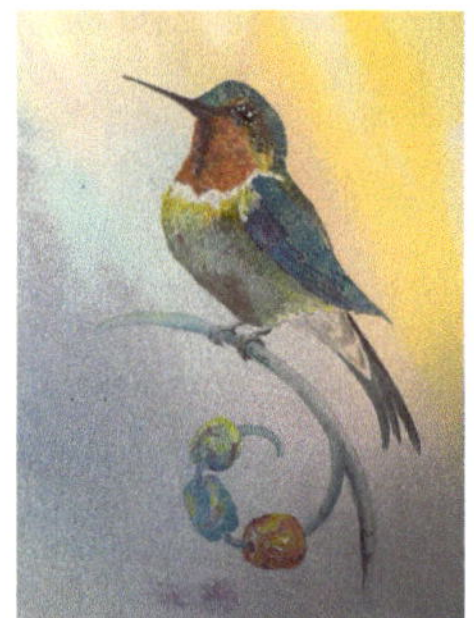

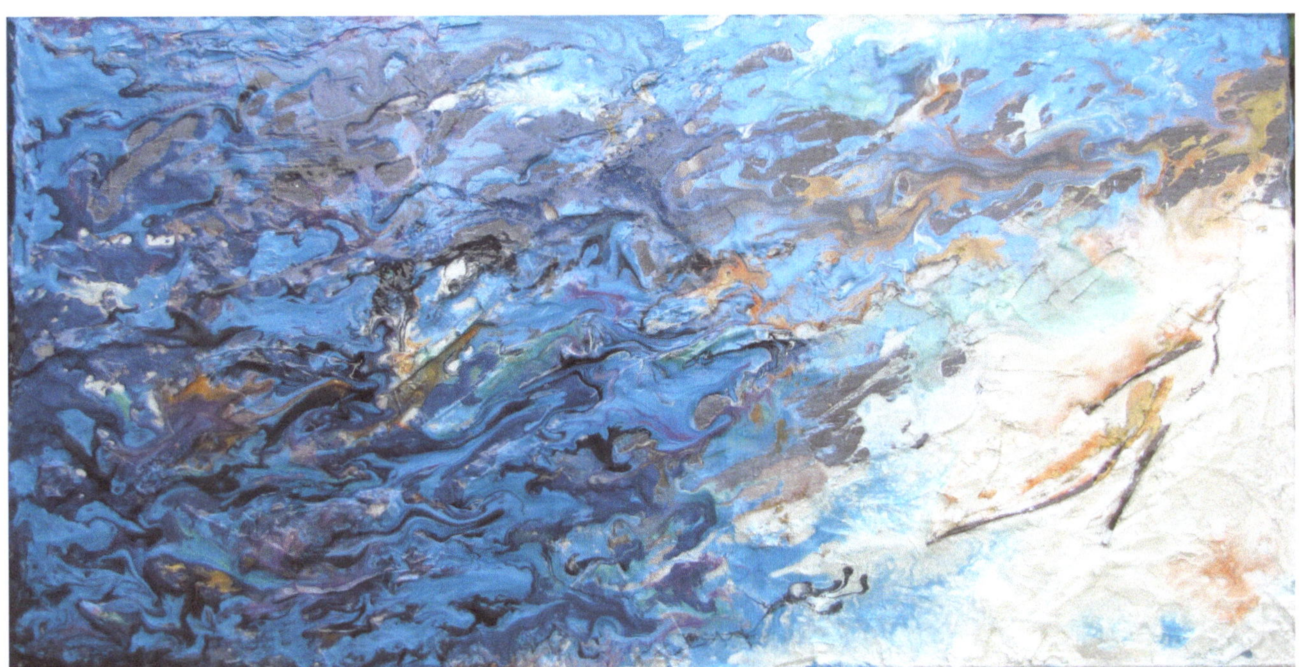

Repentance — Let Me Depend Upon You

Having a Conversation—Talking and Listening

Merriam-Webster Dictionary defines the word conversation as an oral exchange of sentiments, observations, opinions, or ideas. I would also add that it is a two-part process of speaking and genuinely listening to what the other person is saying. More often than not, when the other person is talking, we are conjuring up our response and not intently listening. We may be easily distracted by other things going on around us. We all have different talking styles, too. I remember my four-year-old son trying to tell me something so important to him. He had a slight stutter then, and my impatient tendency was to rush him and put the words in his mouth. I remember sharing my concern with my wise sister, who had been in the teaching field for many years. She gently suggested that I just be patient. His young brain was thinking much faster than his developing communication skills could form words. I became a more empathetic listener and tuned into what he wanted to share with me. (Today, that son is a passionate high school instructor within an alternative school setting. Those young adults have some essential things to communicate to those who care to listen.)

"Likewise the Sprit also helpeth our infirmities: for we know not what we should pray for as we ought: but the Spirit itself maketh intercession for us with groanings which cannot be uttered" (Romans 8:26).

I cannot think of a time when I did not have

an interest in art. The scent of a new box of crayons is still one of my favorites. (I wonder if there is a candle scent available?)

It all started with a desire in my heart to create. Each of us has deep within us a pull towards a unique purpose, an exceptional talent, a gift. Clues to those callings lie in areas that interest you. Whether it be in business, sports, or teaching, you were called to create. A wonderful book entitled Called to Create by Jordan Raynor speaks more of this subject. Step out in faith and follow the nudge, exploring where it takes you. Ask God to lead and guide you.

"A man's [or woman or boy or girl] heart deviseth his way: but the LORD directeth his steps" (Proverbs 16:9).

When those two actions collide, your desire aligns with God's messages of truth…well, get out of the way and see where it takes you!

Having a conversation with your painting

I touched on this idea earlier in this book that your artwork communicates to you if you make the effort to observe and listen. Your piece of artwork can show you where it might be strengthened. When you listen and seek, you will discern the infallible wisdom of the elements and principles of design. When you heed this art wisdom, you can take your painting to a higher level, making it as successful as possible. That knowledge and confidence can then be applied to your next artistic endeavor. Listen and test the principles of design. All the pieces align just as those little bits roll around in a kaleidoscope, perfectly finding their place in the design with each slight twist.

This book was birthed from my desire to learn more and more about the language of design. I will share my epiphany of seeing art coming together, exploding like a kaleidoscope. In Part 7 of this book, which lists resources for your review, my Elements & Principles of Design Comparisons to a Kaleidoscope Reference Guide is my gift to you. I hope it brings you a greater understanding. Please study My Self Critique Kaleidoscope slowly and mindfully. Listen to your painting as you view it through this guide. I am confident that if you have the desire to gain more understanding and are also willing to take the time and effort to learn this art language, you will surely capture the concept. Most importantly, you will have it forever, and it will continue to be an ever-sweeter part of your artist journey.

Again, I am so grateful you have walked with me on this art and faith journey. Please follow this link for a free full-color PDF version of the guide on my website: https://www.paulamooreart.com/thank-you-gift

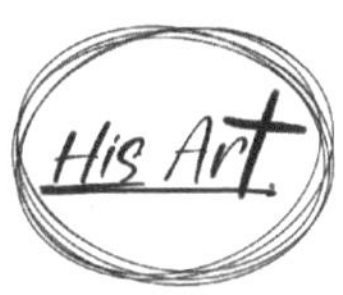

Having a Conversation with Satan – Yes, Satan.

What about the concept of the enemy, Satan? Is he real? Does he have power over us? He has power; however, he has no authority unless it is given to him. Adam and Eve gave away their rights and privileges to Satan to rule over them the moment they doubted and disobeyed God's sovereign authority. Each human born into this world since then has inherited this trait of sin disobedience.

Since the beginning of time, Satan offers a mirror image of God's love for us. It appears to be honest; however, it is the total opposite of truth and merely an illusion. The enemy's favorite playground is our mind's thoughts. Joyce Meyer's *Battlefield of the Mind* addresses how Satan sneaks his evil theories into our lives. The world is so weary of spending millions of dollars toward remedies to ease our negative thoughts, yet misses the mark as to the source. Satan is our true enemy in this world. He is the father of lies.

"For we wrestle not against flesh and blood, but against principalities, against powers, against the rulers of the darkness of this world, against spiritual wickedness in high places" (Ephesians 6:12).

These are the words of Jesus speaking about Satan as a thief:

"The thief cometh not, but for to steal, and to kill, and to destroy: I am come that they might have life and that they might have it more abundantly" (John 10:10).

Having a Conversation with God, the Creator of the Universe

What are your thoughts on God, the Creator of the Universe? Is he a far away, white-haired, angry, authoritative ancient man sitting on a throne high in the heavens? Is he unreachable and uncaring?

Are you fearful of his power? Do you even believe in a Higher Power, or perhaps are you ambivalent one way or another? One of the enemy's false lies is the philosophy that merely being a kind; good person will be their golden ticket out of this life and into paradise. Not so, my friend. Please don't fall for it. I recommend studying and searching the truth out for yourself. I may be wrong; however, what If I'm not?

In the first century, apostle Paul was allowed to preach on Mars Hill in Greece to those who worshipped idols they had made with their own hands. He said, "For as I passed by, and beheld your devotions, I found an altar with this inscription. TO THE UNKNOWN GOD. Whom therefore ye ignorantly worship, him declare I unto you" (Acts 17:23).

"Not everyone that saith unto me, Lord, Lord, shall enter into the kingdom of heaven; but he that doeth the will of my Father which is in heaven. Many will say to me in that day, Lord, Lord, have we not prophesied in thy name? and in thy name have cast out devils? and in thy name done many wonderful works? And then will I profess unto them, I never knew you: depart from me, ye that work iniquity" (Matt 7:21–23).

That unknown God is above all others. He is LOVE. He cherishes all of us as his creation; however, pause and consider this thought: We are not all God's children.

When we choose to sincerely believe, we gain the title of being an adopted child of God, purchased and paid in full by the sacrifice of his Son, Jesus. It is a close, personal relationship God desires with us. He longs to collaborate and partner with us so that we may enjoy this life more abundantly. From the very beginning, God designed each one of us to possess the free will to do and think as he chooses. He also created a masterful plan, knowing that the human race would not be able to resist the ways of Satan. Therefore, the plan for redemption was devised from the beginning, a blood sacrifice for atonement. The original masterpiece painting of Jesus the Son was the symbolic blood sacrifice providing the skins to cover the sins of nakedness of Adam and Eve. Jesus the Son is the ultimate sacrifice ever needed. He died, came back to life, was resurrected, and now sits on the right hand of God

This holy conversation I'm sharing with you is spoken from the utter depths of the individual's heart. It is a prayer not uttered from your intellectual being. You won't be able to figure out the concept of faith by logic. Rather, it is a sincere conversation of your inner self – your soul - with the Creator of the Moon and Stars and Sun and Universe, the same Creator who also thought this old world needed your intricate uniqueness! Can I give you the exact words to say? No. This is not "a repeat after me" methodology.

(Recall the mirror imagery that Satan offers us.) I will only offer these words written by King David, a man of war, an imperfect man continually after God's heart. He understood that the yearly blood sacrifice for atonement symbolized the hope of believing in a coming ultimate sacrifice. Theologians suggest that these words were written in the year 1034 BC, 1,067 years before Jesus died in 33 AD. Now, even after another 2,000 years have gone by, this passage speaks the ageless truth.

"To the Chief Musician. A Psalm of David. I waited patiently and expectantly for the Lord; And He inclined to me and heard my cry. He brought me up out of a horrible pit [of tumult and of destruction], out of the miry clay, And He set my feet upon a rock, steadying my footsteps and establishing my path" (Psalm 40:1–2 AMP).

Pray that kind of heartfelt prayer.

For those adopted into this family of God, there is a written sealed certificate of holy adoption. Our name is written in the Lamb's Book of Life.

We are saved back forever, bought and paid for by trusting that Jesus was the final blood sacrifice, the portal to reconciliation with God.

From that moment on, you are a child of God.

There begins a two-way talking and listening eternal dialog, communing between God the Father and you, his child. Those petitions are carried by God, the Holy Spirit, to God, the Father, through God, the Son. Jesus Christ is our Redeemer, Advocate, Attorney, and Big Brother. He is our defender because we trust in his ultimate sacrifice and in all he is.

I like to imagine that we are his jeweled, broken pieces within his holy kaleidoscope, finding our place in his spinning, glorious design.

Kaleidoscope Click

God, the Creator of the entire universe, thought the world needed one of you as well. It is a mystery, and we will never comprehend how he can simultaneously be available to every soul of humanity. The Spirit of God longs for you to be reconciled with him. He's just waiting for you to start up a conversation. You talk, he'll listen. He'll talk, you listen.

More often than not, when the other person is talking; we are conjuring up our response and not intently listening.

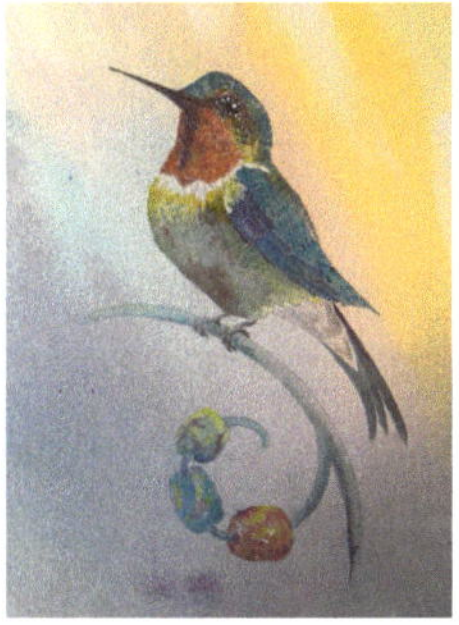

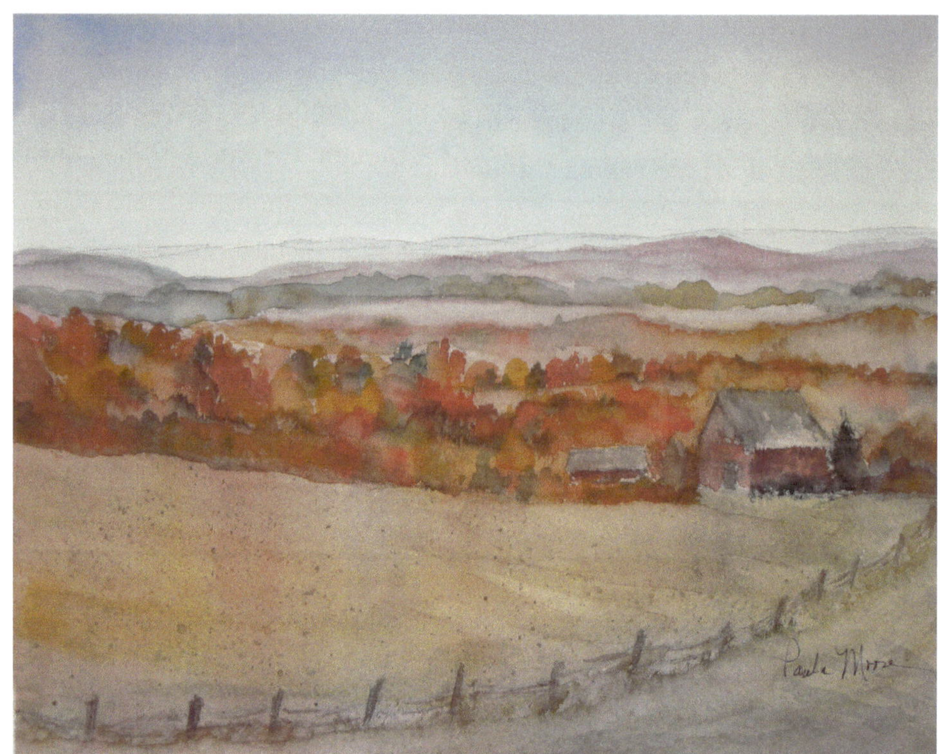

Sweet Surrender — I Trust You to Help Me

Losing an Edge

You read earlier about the importance of clear and pure pigment when painting. Have you ever wondered how the artist hones in his skill while painting the illusion of the soft edges of wispy clouds, the gradual color changing of a flower petal, or the illusion of a misty forest in the mountains? Often, in my workshops, I will gather my students around my paint station to give a demonstration where they lean in close, listen, carefully observe, and then go back to their place to practice the idea until they know the technique by heart.

Today, I am disclosing the painting technique to you in this written demonstration. The mystery is revealed: We artists know how to lose an edge. It is letting go of control and partnering with the water.

In watercolor, paint a 1" to 1 ½" brush stroke on dry paper. Before it has time to dry, quickly rinse your brush, blot the excess on a paper towel, and go to the LOWER edge of your painted section, keeping the top edge crisp. Gently wipe off a little bit of the paint in one pulling downward motion, and clean it off on your towel. Rinse your brush. Blot out the excess water and repeat gently, swiping that lower edge as the color fades into nothingness. At this point, you can paint another section beside where you've just painted and repeat the process. When painting a forest, let your first painted section dry. Then drop down a little in the misty fog you're painting and paint another line of trees. You'll soon have an entire painting of a foggy morning mountain!

This losing-an-edge technique is often used when you want the illusion of misty fog or fading into nothingness. Other times, you need a crisp, definite edge. Once you get into the easy habit of painting like this, you can paint in this manner without even thinking about it. This painting method is implemented when painting gradating color skies, skin tones, flower petals, etc.

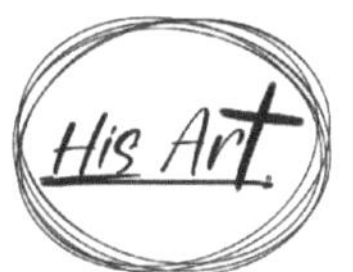

Friends, think back upon your own family, your generation, your community, our country, and our world. Additionally, consider your church family and your relationship with God. Now, compare those memories to what we see in our world today. Are we losing the crisp edges of our principles?

Is the need for God in our lives gradually being diluted from one generation to the next? It is so easy to sleep in on Sunday morning, then another Sunday morning, until it is several months or years since we have gathered in worship. Meeting together is beneficial for praying, singing songs of praise, sharing testimonies, and hearing inspired messages from the pulpit. One friend said for her, attending church acted as a "filling station for the soul," giving her the fuel to go back into life outside the church doors. I like that analogy because it is easy to run out of gas spiritually. I was invited to a women's bible study where the speaker posed the question, "What time of the day do you talk to God in prayer?" Several ladies mentioned mornings, others right before they went to sleep. My turn was coming up, and I was still trying to pigeonhole the actual time I talked to God. Memories flooded back of my childhood home; Jesus was mentioned in our everyday conversation continually. It was natural to include faith in the day-to-day activities. Christian friends, Daddy breaking out in song, Sunday afternoons after dishes were done, family gathered around the piano Mother was playing. Grandpa Pat belts out his deep, slow bass notes of a familiar hymnal chorus refrain. I am learning alto harmony, standing by Grandma BeeCee as we follow the shapes and musical notes of a tattered, orange hymnbook.

Back to the bible study…what would be my contribution to this bible study question? There was nothing until I suddenly came to the realization. I'm so very grateful I grew up in a home that kept Christ in the center. I shared with the others that I actually did not have an assigned appointed time. I have an ongoing conversation with the Holy Spirit who continues to live inside my soul since Sunday, June 30, 1963. He speaks to me anytime. I can speak to him anytime. He listens. I listen. He wakes me up in the middle of the night. He never goes to sleep. He's always there.

It is too easy to float away, drifting along with the world's glittering distraction. However, I cling to the assurance that his anchor holds and will pull me back close to him. My communion with him is a constant ribboned weaving in my life. As a mother, I have attempted to demonstrate this to my little family- now, both grown adults and families of their own—a lifetime demonstration of how reverence for God Almighty takes effort and commitment. We are to paint portraits of Christ to the next generation in living water and crystal-clear hues of truth. They are responsible for lifting up Christ's banner to the next generation. The flip side of this idea is knowing when it is best to let loose of your own understanding, a toxic relationship, or a bad idea that keeps you from knowing God personally. It is like seeing a beautiful kaleidoscope displayed on the shelf, knowing something spectacular is waiting for you to enjoy; however, not taking the opportunity to pick it up and see its beauty for yourself. Perhaps you'll consider it today.

"Hear, O Israel: The Lord our God is one Lord: And thou shalt love the Lord thy God with all thine heart, and with all thy soul, and with all thy might. And these words, which I command thee this day, shall be in thine heart: And thou shalt teach them diligently unto thy children, and shalt talk of them when thou sittest in thine house, and when thou walkest by the way, and when thou liest down, and when thou risest up" (Deuteronomy 6:4–7)

Kaleidoscope Click

My question to you and me is this: Are we losing the edge?

When facing a pivotal life-changing decision or addressing a concern before it becomes a significant issue, ask the Master to help you discern His teachings until you know them deep in your heart. It doesn't take long before you will sense results. Start small with only a few minutes a day. In this full-throttle life, carve out even five minutes to read a devotional page. You can listen to many inspiring podcasts or instrumental music. Most Bibles usually include a topical index to point you to biblical instruction. For example, the topic of fear is said to be listed 365 times, equal to one for each day of the year. There will be multiple encouraging scriptures to consider when you have questions and seek answers. When leading a Bible study, I often share an easy arthrogram for B.I.B.L.E., Basic Instructions Before Leaving Earth. You'll soon develop a calm awareness of when and when not to lose an edge. When to hold on to a situation and when to let go. Shall we ever stay vigilant so that God's messages of truth remain clear and vibrant rather than fade into insignificance?

Basic. Instructions. Before. Leaving. Earth.

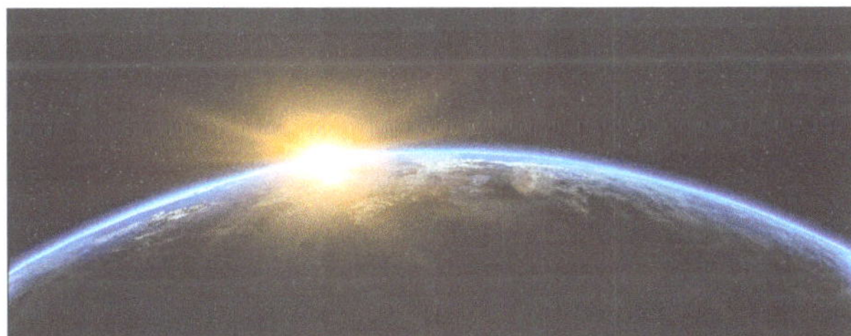

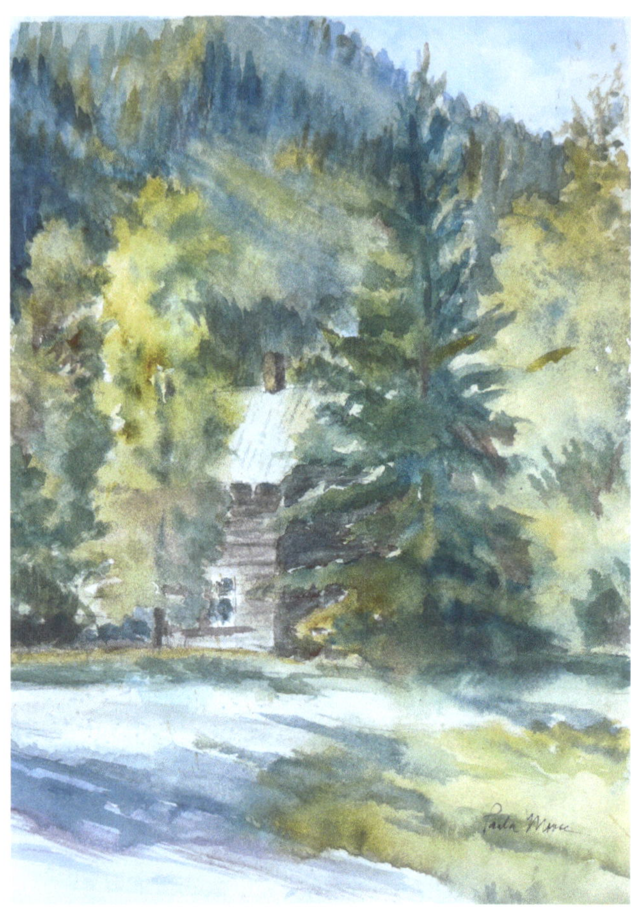

Sweet Surrender — I Trust You to Help Me

Types and Shadows versus Reality

The idea of scriptural types and shadows has always been challenging to explain, and I felt that my students were more perplexed than comprehending the meaning. I was grappling with how to add my thoughts on this topic for my readers. With eyes to see and ears to hear, the answer was given to me through my pastor's message yesterday, and I wrote it down to share with you.

The habit of taking sermon notes began when I realized I was merely going through the motions of going to church, yet where was my worship? I didn't recall any featured scripture text, main sermon points, hymns sung, and so on. With a busy toddler on my lap, I knew why I was not focused; however, it was still no excuse. The simple solution was to carry a small notebook dedicated to jotting at least the chapter, verse, and sermon topic. I then added a few notes throughout the Sunday School hour, too. This practice now is such a wealth of study through the years and has morphed into an actual history journal with other precious memories mentioned. Many of the chapters in this book came about from these recorded inspirations.

The Bible consists of sixty-six separate harmonized books divided into two divisions known as the Old Testament: the shadows, clues, and foretelling of things to come. The New Testament reveals the answers. It is similar to finding that missing puzzle piece you've been searching for. Suddenly, it fits together perfectly. The messages inspired in the thirty-nine books of the Old Testament were all written centuries before Jesus' birth. The passing of time turned a page, beginning the recording as BC, before Christ, and AD (abbreviating an ancient Latin term of anno domini), translated to the term "in the year of our Lord." The twenty-seven books listed in the New Testament provide the historical writings of the approximately thirty-three years while Jesus resided on this earth and the missionary journeys, letters to churches, specific individuals, and finally, the last book of John's Revelation, his vivid description of the mysterious visions of heaven and the end of time.

It is worth noting that the first-century people only had access to the Old Testament writings – only the types and shadows, written primarily in Hebrew and Arabic script. We are so fortunate and often take for granted that we now have the gift of the Bible in its entirety. Other historical documents and archeological relics point to the validity of God's Word. It is fascinating to read about the findings of the Dead Sea Scrolls, which were painstakingly written by scribes on parchments of grasses and dried animal skins and hidden in high desert caves. I encourage you to explore these ancient texts. Some precious original fragments are still preserved today in museums around the world.

I was inspired to add this idea from the sermon notes taken regarding types and shadows versus reality. When defining the phrase types and shadows, picture a man walking on a sunny afternoon. If you focus on the shadow the sun is creating on the sidewalk; you can discern some vague facts, not the details of his facial features or the color of his jacket. You are limited in seeing him fully. The shadow clues us to specific characteristics; however, when you see the individual in reality, you have more information and understanding. You might even recognize and know him. This is the exact manifestation when discussing types and shadows foretold in the Old Testament messages versus the fulfilled scriptures in the New Testament. The old stories are types and shadows of the new stories. All sixty-six books fit perfectly together with pictures of Christ. Can you discern this passage's sharing of the shadows mentioned by Old Testament Prophets and the life-like painting of Christ?

These are the writings from Peter, one of the original twelve apostles:

"Though you have not seen him, you love him; and even though you do not see him now, you believe in him and are filled with an inexpressible and glorious joy, for you are receiving the end result of your faith, the salvation of your souls.

Concerning this salvation, the prophets, who spoke of the grace that was to come to you, searched intently and with the greatest care, trying to find out the time and circumstances to which the Spirit of Christ in them was pointing when he predicted the sufferings of the Messiah and the glories that would follow. It was revealed to them that they were not serving themselves but you, when they spoke of the things that have now been told you by those who have preached the gospel to you by the Holy Spirit sent from heaven. Even angels long to look into these things" (1Peter 1:8–12 NIV).

For your review, consider studying the Old Testament types and shadows mentioned in the eleventh chapter of Hebrews, known as the Heroes of Faith Chapter, written by apostle Paul. What a thought to realize you are reading a translation of the original Greek language written over 2,000 years ago. It is still relevant today and forever!

"Now faith is confidence in what we hope for and assurance about what we do not see. This is what the ancients were commended for. By faith we understand that the universe was formed at God's command, so that what is seen was not made out of what was visible.

"By faith Abel brought God a better offering than Cain did. By faith he was commended as righteous, when God spoke well of his offerings. And by faith Abel still speaks, even though he is dead.

"By faith Enoch was taken from this life, so that he did not experience death: "He could not be found, because God had taken him away." For before he was taken, he was commended as one who pleased God. And without faith it is impossible to please God, because anyone who comes to him must believe that he exists and that he rewards those who earnestly seek him.

"By faith Noah, when warned about things not yet seen, in holy fear built an ark to save his family. By his faith he condemned the world and became heir of the righteousness that is in keeping with faith.

"By faith Abraham, when called to go to a place he would later receive as his inheritance, obeyed and went, even though he did not know where he was going. By faith he made his home in the promised land like a stranger in a foreign country; he lived in tents, as did Isaac and Jacob, who were heirs with him of the same promise. For he was looking forward to the city with foundations, whose architect and builder is God. And by faith even Sarah, who was past childbearing age, was enabled to bear children because she considered him faithful who had made the promise. And so from this one man, and he as good as dead, came descendants as numerous as the stars in the sky and as countless as the sand on the seashore.

"All these people were still living by faith when they died. They did not receive the things promised; they only saw them and welcomed them from a distance, admitting that they were foreigners and strangers on earth. People who say such things show that they are looking for a country of their own. If they had been thinking of the country they had left, they would have had opportunity to return. Instead, they were longing for a better country—a heavenly one. Therefore, God is not ashamed to be called their God, for he has prepared a city for them.

"By faith Abraham, when God tested him, offered Isaac as a sacrifice. He who had embraced the promises was about to sacrifice his one and only son, even though God had said to him, 'It is through Isaac that your offspring will be reckoned.' Abraham reasoned that God could even raise the dead, and so in a manner of speaking he did receive Isaac back from death.

"By faith Isaac blessed Jacob and Esau in regard to their future.

"By faith Jacob, when he was dying, blessed each of Joseph's sons, and worshiped as he leaned on the top of his staff. By faith Joseph, when his end was near, spoke about the exodus of the Israelites from Egypt and gave instructions concerning the burial of his bones.

"By faith Moses' parents hid him for three months after he was born, because they saw he was no ordinary child, and they were not afraid of the king's edict. By faith Moses, when he had grown up, refused to be known as the son of Pharaoh's daughter. He chose to be mistreated along with the people of God rather than to enjoy the fleeting pleasures of sin. He regarded disgrace for the sake of Christ as of greater value than the treasures of Egypt, because he was looking ahead to his reward. By faith he left Egypt, not fearing the king's anger; he persevered because he saw him who is invisible. By faith he kept the Passover and the application of blood, so that the destroyer of the firstborn would not touch the firstborn of Israel. By faith the people passed through the Red Sea as on dry land; but when the Egyptians tried to do so, they were drowned. By faith the walls of Jericho fell, after the army had marched around them for seven days.

"By faith the prostitute Rahab, because she welcomed the spies, was not killed with those who were disobedient.

"And what more shall I say? I do not have time to tell about Gideon, Barak, Samson and Jephthah, about David and Samuel and the prophets, who through faith conquered kingdoms, administered justice, and gained what was promised; who shut the mouths of lions, quenched the fury of the flames, and escaped the edge of the sword; whose weakness was turned to strength; and who became powerful in battle and routed foreign armies. Women received back their dead, raised to life again. There were others who were tortured, refusing to be released so that they might gain an even better resurrection. Some faced jeers and flogging, and even chains and imprisonment. They were put to death by stoning; they were sawed in two; they were killed by the sword. They went about in sheepskins and goatskins, destitute, persecuted and mistreated— the world was not worthy of them. They wandered in deserts and mountains, living in caves and in holes in the ground. These were all commended for their faith, yet none of them received what had been promised, since God had planned something better for us so that only together with us would they be made perfect" (Hebrews: 11:1–39 NIV)

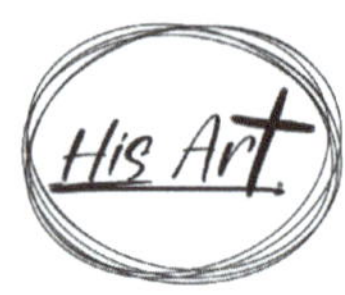

From the first book of Genesis, we are told that God divinely devised a plan to restore the relationship between him and mankind. The Creator would keep his promises; however, because he purposefully fashioned his magnificent creation, designed in his own image, to have free will over his thoughts and actions, a perfect plan was required for restoration of fully acknowledging God's authority. God knew ahead of time that man and woman could not keep this obedience and would go against his Laws. It was faith in believing God would send a Redeemer in the Old Testament. It was faith in believing who Jesus claimed he was as the Son. It is that same faith we seek even two thousand years later, until the end of time. Trusting and receiving faith in the ultimate sacrifice of Jesus the Son, what he did, faith in believing who he is, the fact that he died and was resurrected and now sits on the right hand of God. Jesus' willingness to die for each of mankind's sins continues to satisfy the requirement of atonement.

The prophecies are fulfilled in the New Testament, the scriptures after Jesus came to earth, as all man and all God. J. Barton Payne's *Encyclopedia of Biblical Prophecy* lists 1,239 prophecies in the Old Testament and 578 prophecies in the New Testament, for a total of 1,817. These encompass 8,352 verses. In the Resources Section of this book, I have listed a few of these scriptures and I challenge you to study them for yourself. I hope you can catch a glimpse of God's magnificent kaleidoscope of scriptures and how they divinely fit perfectly together.

Kaleidoscope Click

Keep an open mind and open heart when embarking on this kaleidoscope click view. It may be the most important of all. I suggest locating the passage in a few biblical sources for clarity and, most certainly, relying upon the Holy Spirit to help with your understanding. In the Resource Section of this book, select one of the prophecy verses from the Old Testament listing and read it carefully. I suggest reading the entire chapter mindfully as you search for the clues hidden in plain sight. Then, research the fulfillment of scripture from the New Testament. Consider how they align together!

Focusing on the shadows only gives you clues. Focusing on reality will provide more information and understanding.

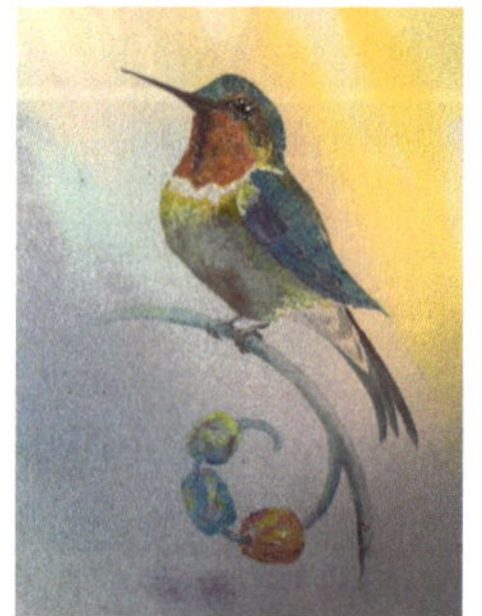

Sweet Surrender — I Trust You to Help Me

Reflections of His Love

Over twenty years ago, we experienced a tragedy in our family. You will recall my sharing some stories of my younger sister, Krista, who is very dear to me. Her husband, Rick, was a quiet, gentle giant at a height of 6'8". His expertise was in the computer field, which earned him the title of chief informational officer at a local college. Rick was a talented photographer, played with a weekly basketball league, and collected unique stained-glass kaleidoscopes. He and my husband were close friends, and in the fall of 2002, they had thoroughly enjoyed a memorable motorcycle ride through the West. A few weeks later, on one of those rare warm Indian summer late Saturday mornings, I answered the door to find Rick standing on my front porch in full motorcycle gear, looking for Terry. Rick said, "I just want to see something beautiful today, so I'm going on a ride to see the autumn colors." Terry came walking up just then, saying he couldn't join him this time since he was going on duty that afternoon. We talked about our upcoming plans for Thanksgiving, the giclee painting he had found in Santa Fe, New Mexico, for Krista, which, ironically, was the same that Terry had given to me when he returned home. Rick stepped into the living room to see mine hung on the wall. Rick was saving it to give her for Christmas. "She's going to love it," he said with his bearded grin and walked out to find something beautiful.

That was the last time this side of eternity we spoke with Rick. Just a few hours later, my husband, Terry, a Missouri Highway Patrol trooper, received word that Rick, only forty-nine years old, had lost

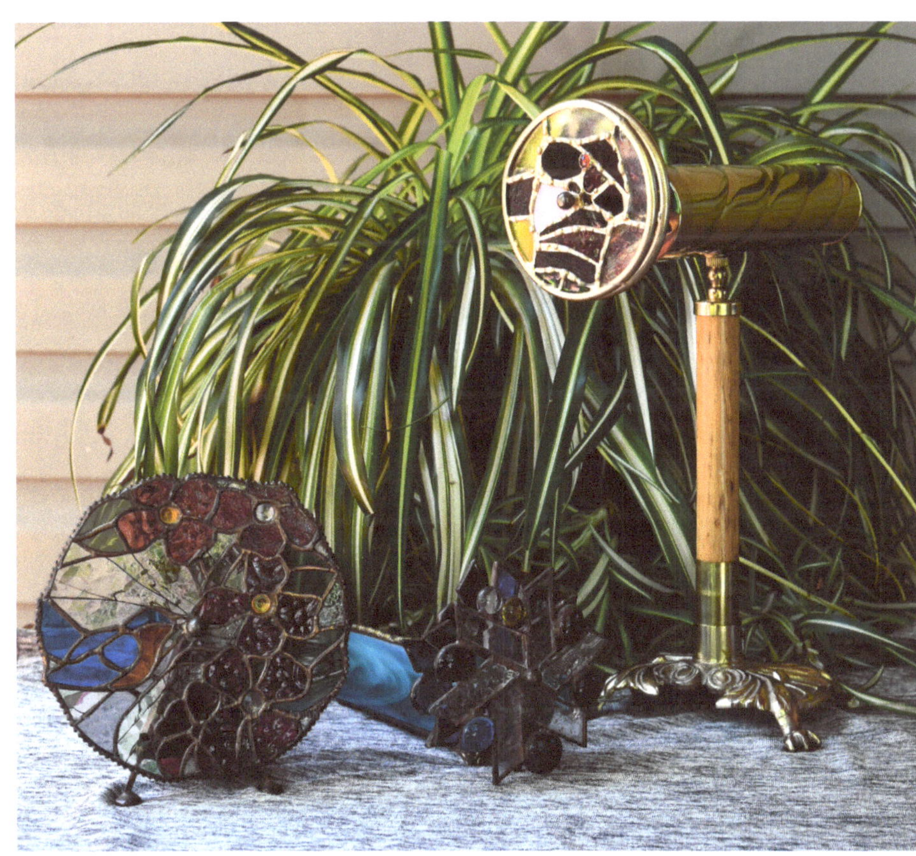

his life due to injuries from a motorcycle accident. What a surreal anguish dealing with his loss. A man who had no idea that sunny day would be his last. He had future plans, a career, friends, and family. He was a devoted husband and father of four.

Thankfully, years earlier, in preparation for this very moment, Rick had trusted, and his name was recorded in heaven's promise book, reserving his deed in God's eternal home. We also have the blessed assurance of knowing that Rick's last conversation rang true. "I just want to see something beautiful today." That very afternoon, Rick's eyes of faith opened to survey heaven's glorious colors. (I will add that at our annual Christmas gathering only a few weeks after losing Rick, Terry lovingly told Krista the story of the painting and presented Rick's last gift to her.)

All our hearts were broken like those bits of stained glass from Rick's kaleidoscopes. The day we lost Rick, my sister and her nine- and twelve-year-old children would begin a new normal. She would start preparing for funeral arrangements, and I stepped in to be available for her. The following poem poured out of my heart during the hour's drive to her home at sunrise the next day. I literally pulled over to write the words down as a tribute to my friend and brother-in-law, Richard F. Nebel, II.

Reflections of His Love
Paula L. Moore

"Here, Lord," I cried, "take these, please.
Here are bits of shattered, colored dreams,
They have no purpose for me now."

The reds, my broken heart.
These…are all my hopes dashed small.
Here is a true-blue piece of love.
It's all that's left of a near-perfect life."

My Lord lovingly reached down, accepting
My broken shards and said,
"All things work for good. I have a glorious plan."

I marveled as he dusted crystal promises, weaving
golden rays so bright.

He offered the jeweled treasure back to me
which once had been my broken life.
Whispering, "Now, look through with eyes of faith
to see…hold it up into MY light."

As I trusted and believed,
I lifted up my eyes to see
All my shattered hopes and dreams.

Beautifully patterned together, encircled by the
reflections of his love.

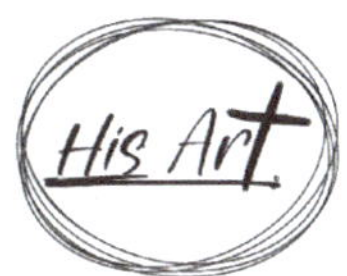

"And we know that all things work together for good to them that love God, to them who are the called according to His purpose" (Romans 8:28).

Kaleidoscope Click

Re-read the poem again, only this time, imagine it is YOU giving the broken bits and chards back to the Lord.

Ponder the scenario for a few moments and write down your thoughts.

He offered the jeweled treasure back to me, which had once been my broken life. Whispering, "Now, look through with eyes of faith to see....hold it up into MY light."

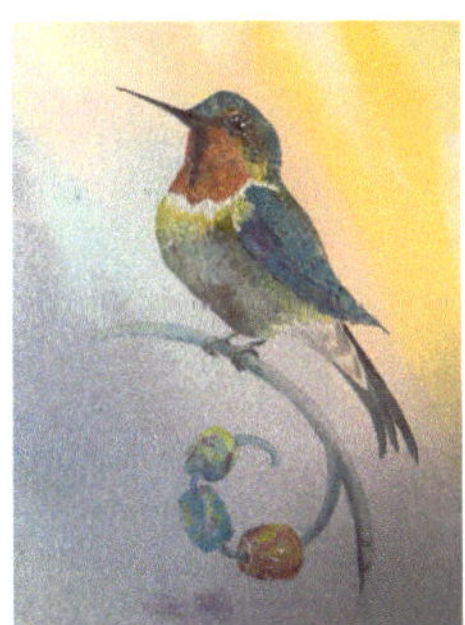

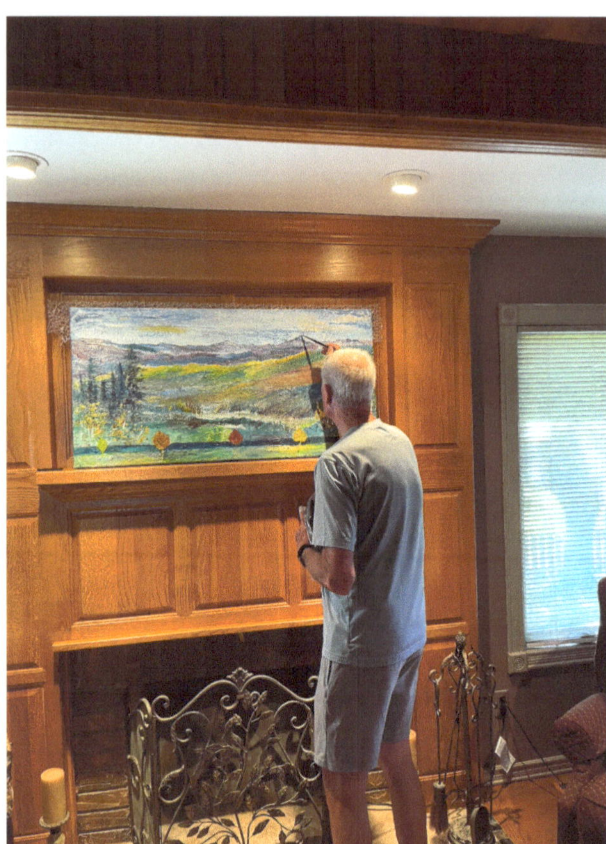

Sweet Surrender — I Trust You to Help Me

The Last Finishing Touch

As an artist, there is a knowing when a painting is nearing completion. I remember Jane saying something to the effect that most artists only paint about 85 percent of the painting, then stop calling it done when, in reality, there may be only a few finishing strokes needed to make it the best it can be. At that moment when you've done all you know how to do, it is the signal to slow down, step away from the painting, and take time to consider. This is the moment when I need to earnestly reflect on my effort in a self-critique. I make myself a cup of tea, take it to my quiet living room, and lean the work up high on the fireplace mantle. Then I sit across the room, methodically searching each inch, taking notes where it might be strengthened. Turning the paper, a quarter-turn at a time helps locate evidence of every single element and principle of design. This entire writing has compared the intricacies of the seven elements—the bits in the kaleidoscope—within the eight principles, the structured mirrored boundaries. I would encourage you to review those again.

As I examine my painting, I ask myself if each element is evident: line, shape, size, direction, value, color, texture? Then I go around a second time looking for each of the eight principles within each separate element. Do I have unity, dominance, repetition, harmony, balance, gradation, alternation and conflict? This testing will identify any areas that need a tweak, even when it's upside down! Even in this position, the design qualities will still be organized successfully!

Another method to see your painting in a new way is to hold it up to a mirror. The reflection will show the truths of your endeavor. A problem area will stick out like a sore thumb. I first observed this technique when I watched a street pastel chalk artist silently and efficiently painting an individual's portrait as she sat motionless before him. Occasionally, he would pull out a little pocket mirror and glance at the reversed mirrored reflection, confirming he had captured the stranger's facial feature likeness as she posed quietly in front of him. Sometimes, he would make a slight adjustment; other times, he would continue drawing. To watch his talented, confident strokes was fascinating.

Continuing with my painting critique, I carried my painting, hot tea mug in tow, with those few jotted notes back to my quiet studio. Referring to my notes, I spent a few minutes applying a light brush stroke here and defining a crossover line there. Softening an area so it sinks back into the background, successfully making it less prominent. Was the story I wanted to tell quite apparent? Would the design lead the viewer where I hoped he would stop to observe and ponder? Early in my painting career, my problem was that my dark, middle and light values needed to be strengthened; however, now, I see those more clearly. I'm not as afraid of the dark anymore.

There is also a tendency for the artist to overwork a painting, diving in with an attitude of "I'll fix just this one thing!" which, as you can suspect, completely changes the cohesiveness with other areas. This is why understanding the foundational concept of design from the beginning to the end creates a more successful work of art. Personally, I became a more confident artist when I finally grasped that vision - it all works together as one. For me, the conceptualization was gradual. However, I was willing and determined with my heart's desire to understand the language of design. The diligent pursuit of this hope suddenly came into clear focus. I understood. The language of design fits perfectly together like a 2,000-piece jigsaw puzzle. Nothing amiss and nothing to be added. While you are observing and waiting, the painting in a still, small voice will let you know when it's all it can be. It's a matter of trusting the process of understanding the design language.

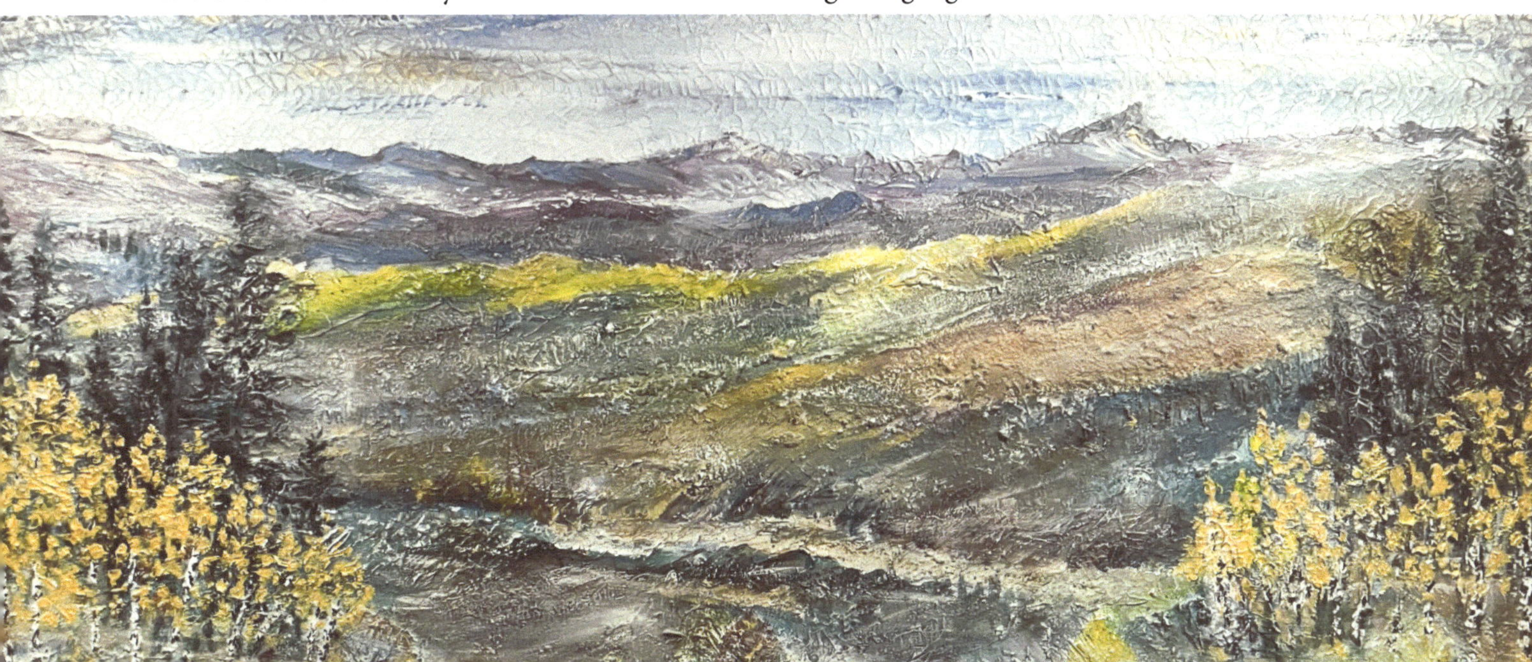

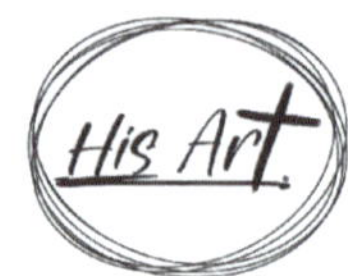

I have recently come to an awareness that perhaps comes with age. Although art has been such a constant in my life since an early age, the writing and teaching of its importance shared with others could not have manifested itself until now. Life experiences include misty memories of youth, my time and place when I became a follower of Christ, faded friendships, and love. The love and friendships that took root and continue to bloom. The mistakes I made along the way. It is all this and more while a noisy and turbulent world continues its daily twists and turns. Then, there are elements of grace, forgiveness, maturity and trust. Perhaps I knew a little about each. I see now how this imperfect painting of a life can move toward the very best it can be. It can go without saying we all will experience difficult times. A life can be marred by wrong decisions, circumstances beyond their control, and regrets. Hard struggles do not have to define a person. Might I suggest stopping cleaning yourself up before sharing your needs with Jesus? He wants you just the way you are now – mess and all. That is when he works the best. With much prayer, effort, and dedication, that struggle can be turned into something beautiful to help someone else in their journey. A happy existence is not a guaranteed gift you can buy. Even though many try to do so or create a resemblance of a great life, there will be something missing—a missing piece: his peace. Additionally, God's messages of truth are not forced upon you. Instead, his peace is a gift offered freely to anyone who will ask with their whole being with a willingness of heart, mind, and spirit. The dominance of the Almighty Creator will work through you and in you for a well-lived life, regardless of the circumstance.

> "For God is not the author of confusion, but of peace, as in all churches of the saints" (1 Corinthian 14:3).

Kaleidoscope Click

In your mind's eye, I hope you will align your heart, mind, and soul with the principles of God. I cannot give you the words to say because it is your journey to discover a deeper relationship with the Creator himself. I recommend simply asking him to show you those areas needing revision and strengthening. Then, commit to listening as you align your efforts with his plan. Allow the Master Artist to restore your soul with a mere touch of his holy brush.

Allow the Master Artist to restore your soul with one final touch of his holy brush.

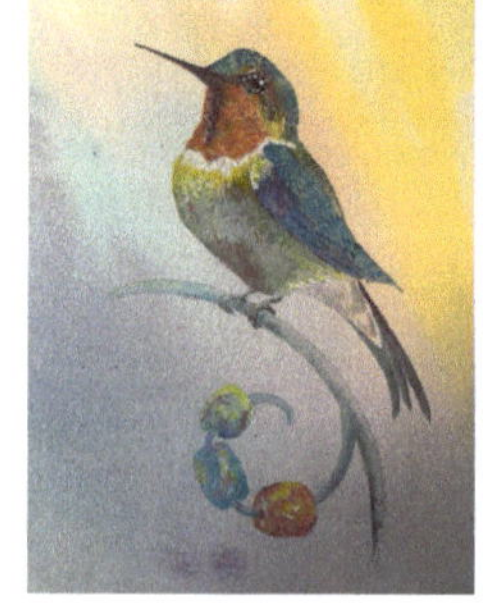

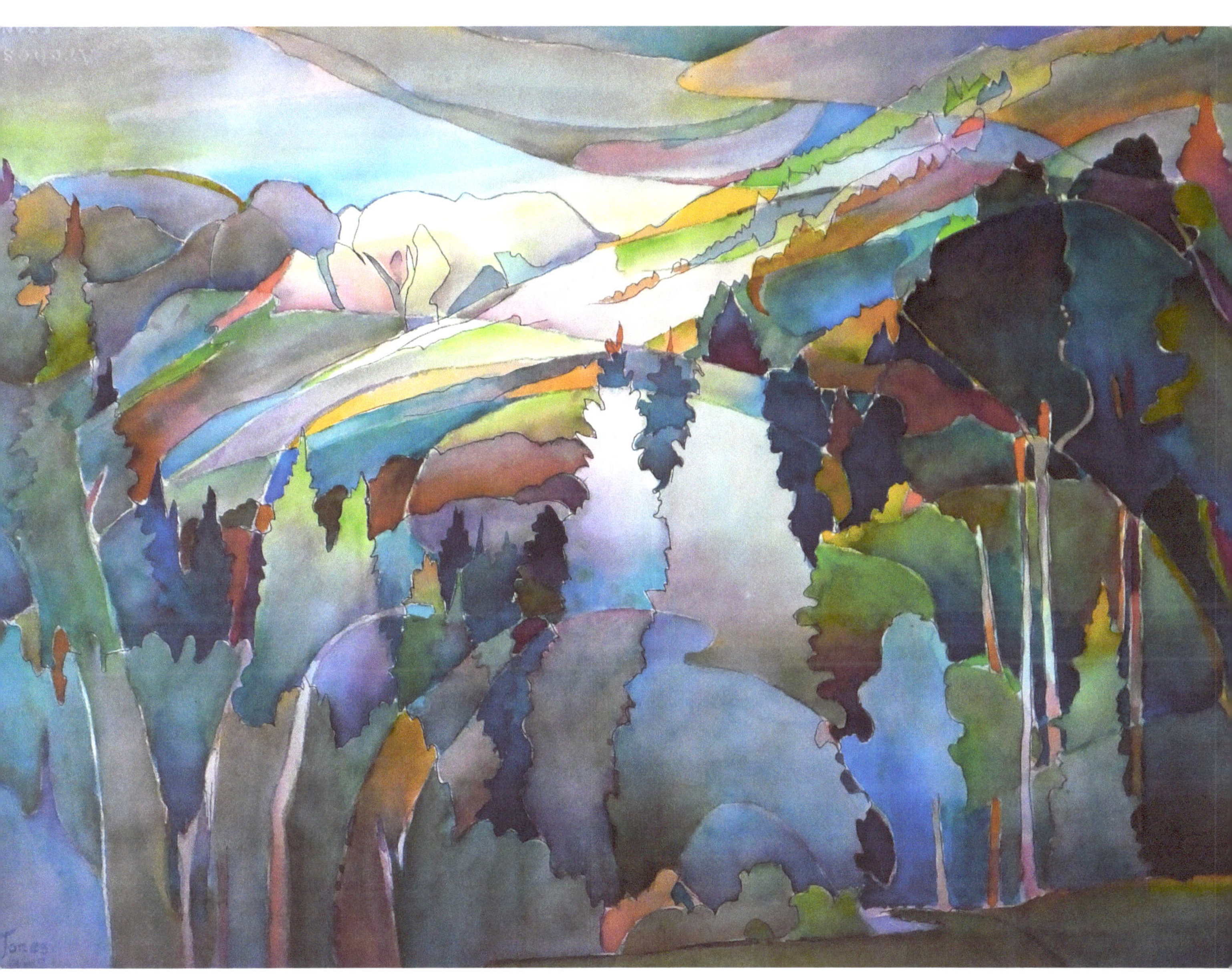

Stormy, author's private collection, painted by Jane E. Jones

Sweet Surrender — I Trust You to Help Me

The Final Critique: Is It Wow Worthy?

Late in the final afternoon of Jane's week-long workshop, I jokingly quipped that I must be getting close to the end because I was running out of paper! After a few chuckles as I reviewed my efforts, I wondered if the painting was as successful as possible. We all listened intently, trying to remember everything we had learned. I found myself early on comparing my techniques and style to those of the others. I recalled Jane instructing us to mindfully consider areas where we might improve our painting and that the purpose of a workshop is to have a "takeaway or two" to strengthen our understanding.

Your focus should be that you can successfully identify all the Elements and Principles of

Design in your piece. Then, learn and apply that wealth of knowledge to the next painting. At the end of that last day, we lined up all our efforts, each surrounded by its white mat, separating it from all other distractions. Jane sat in the back of the room, perched on her three-legged high throne, where she had the best vantage point. The room grew quiet as a courtroom.

With authority and kindness in her voice, the Critiques Session began. Our work was brought before her separately, displayed alone. We all watched respectfully, gleaning more knowledge as we listened to each critique. Taking a deep breath, my painted offering was next up. Silence dripped from the room as Jane judged my efforts and searched for evidence of all the elements and principles. There was more silence. Thinking back now on this scene, I'm sure it was only moments for others; however, I stood there with bated breath.

…And then, as only Jane can sound it: WOW! Sign it!!!

My friends all clapped and cheered for joy and a flood of relief and gratitude overflowed in me. The art language of Jane's teachings had taken hold.

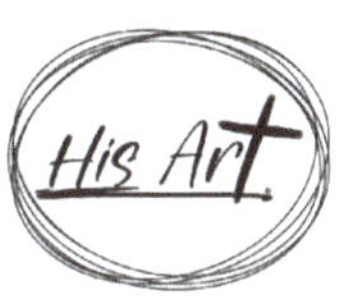

Is it Wow-Worthy?

While on this side of eternity, each of us has the same twenty-four-hour day opportunity to practice, study, strengthen, and apply his principles. Indeed, we are imperfect human beings, each striving to paint our lives so that when held up before the Almighty Creator of the Universe, he will recognize the evidence of his teachings. It is not anything that I have done. Instead, it is all that he has done. That 10-year-old little broken soul signed up for his lifetime workshop and continues to paint her heart out for him all these years later. If you're there watching that glorious day when my life's painting comes up front and center before him, I'm confident you'll witness a shout of happiness and thunderous clapping. I don't know if he will actually say "WOW" like Jane! Assuredly, he will proclaim, "Well done, good and faithful servant; thou hast been faithful over a few things, I will make thee ruler over many things: enter thou into the joy of thy lord" (Matthew 25:23).

I like to imagine that my little life's painting will be surrounded by a gleaming white mat framed in gold and displayed in his heavenly gallery of art. Wow!

> "Let not your heart be troubled: ye believe in God, believe also in me. In my Father's house are many mansions: if it were not so, I would have told you. I go to prepare a place for you. And if I go and prepare a place for you, I will come again, and receive you unto myself; that where I am, there ye may be also" (John 14:1–3).

Kaleidoscope Click

Did you know the call for entries into heaven's art gallery is open 24/7? It is! And I have good news to tell you: the entry fee has already been paid for you. Look at the prospectus and see for yourself. All you have to do is come willingly and believe it with your whole being, mind, body, and soul.

I hope to see you at His Art Grand Opening!

When our life painting is held before the Almighty Creator of the Universe, he will recognize the evidence of his teachings.

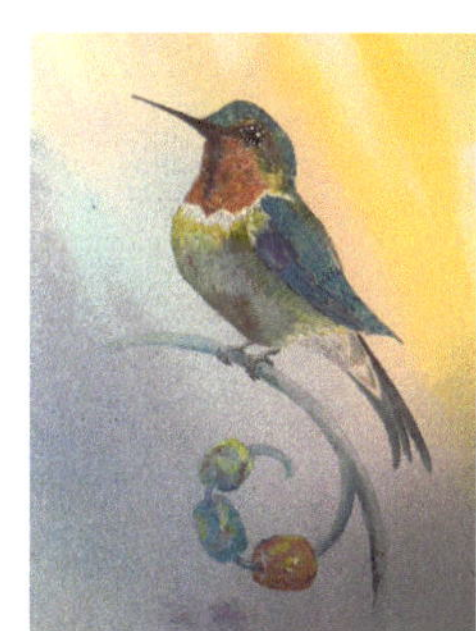

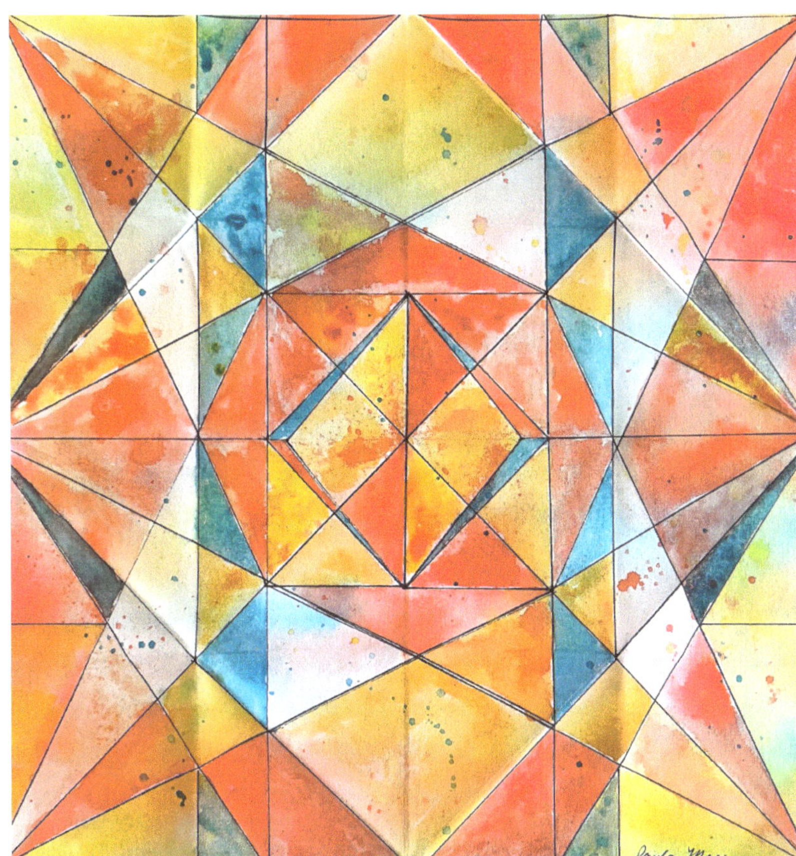

Are you beginning to see the world differently?

As I stated earlier, my writing has a two-fold parallel purpose. First, to point to the need for greater awareness of how the language of art perfectly fits together. There is nothing to be added or taken away. Secondly, you, too, will see through the eyes of faith the many-faceted layers of God's messages of truth for you. There is nothing to be added or taken away. I envision it as ever-changing, broken, jeweled pieces and bits in a kaleidoscope. I desire that you, the reader, will catch a glimpse of how art and God's truth move in alignment with the elements and principles of design. More importantly, it is a consciousness of how God's truth moves in perfect rhythm with the very essence of your inner being when you believe fully in mind, body, and soul. Before the beginning of time, he made a way for us to restore the close relationship. It is nothing of our own device that we have done. Instead, it is what he has done for us. His perfect plan is through the ultimate sacrifice of his Son, Jesus Christ. Man will never find the words to tell you how to find him. Man has never logically figured out the way to God because there is no formula to do so. It is a matter of faith believing. It is an intimate conversation between your soul and the Creator.

The Final Turn of His Art Kaleidoscope

You may be on the last page of my book, but I pray that you are just beginning your journey to finding God in a way you've never experienced before… through his art.

Gently twist the holy kaleidoscope and discover a fresh new view all your own.

Thank you from the depth of my heart for your curiosity and willingness to participate as I painted my Dream Purpose for you.

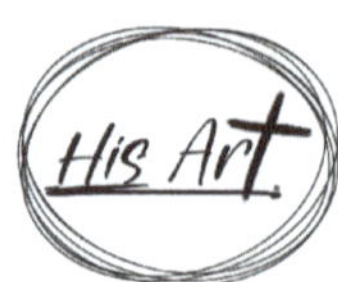

I am offering the key to where and how to search for this personal relationship between your spirit and God's spirit. The mysteries will only unlock when your willing heart and eyes of faith turn towards him. You'll have to experience this peace on your own regardless of how much I want to share the knowledge with you. King David in the Old Testament penned these words.

"For thou desirest not sacrifice; else would I give it; thou delightest not in burnt offering. The sacrifices of God are a broken spirit; a broken and a contrite heart, O God, thou wilt not despise" (Psalm 51:17)

Kaleidoscope Click

You, my friend, are one of the most beautiful crystals within his Kaleidoscope.

Does your life reflect his love?

Gently twist the Holy Kaleidoscope and discover a fresh new view all your own.

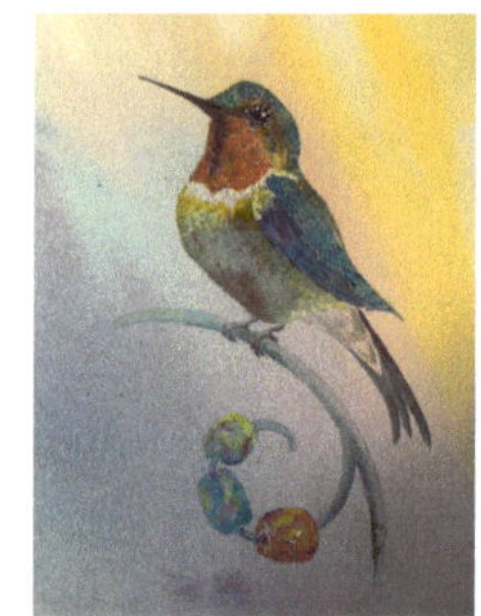

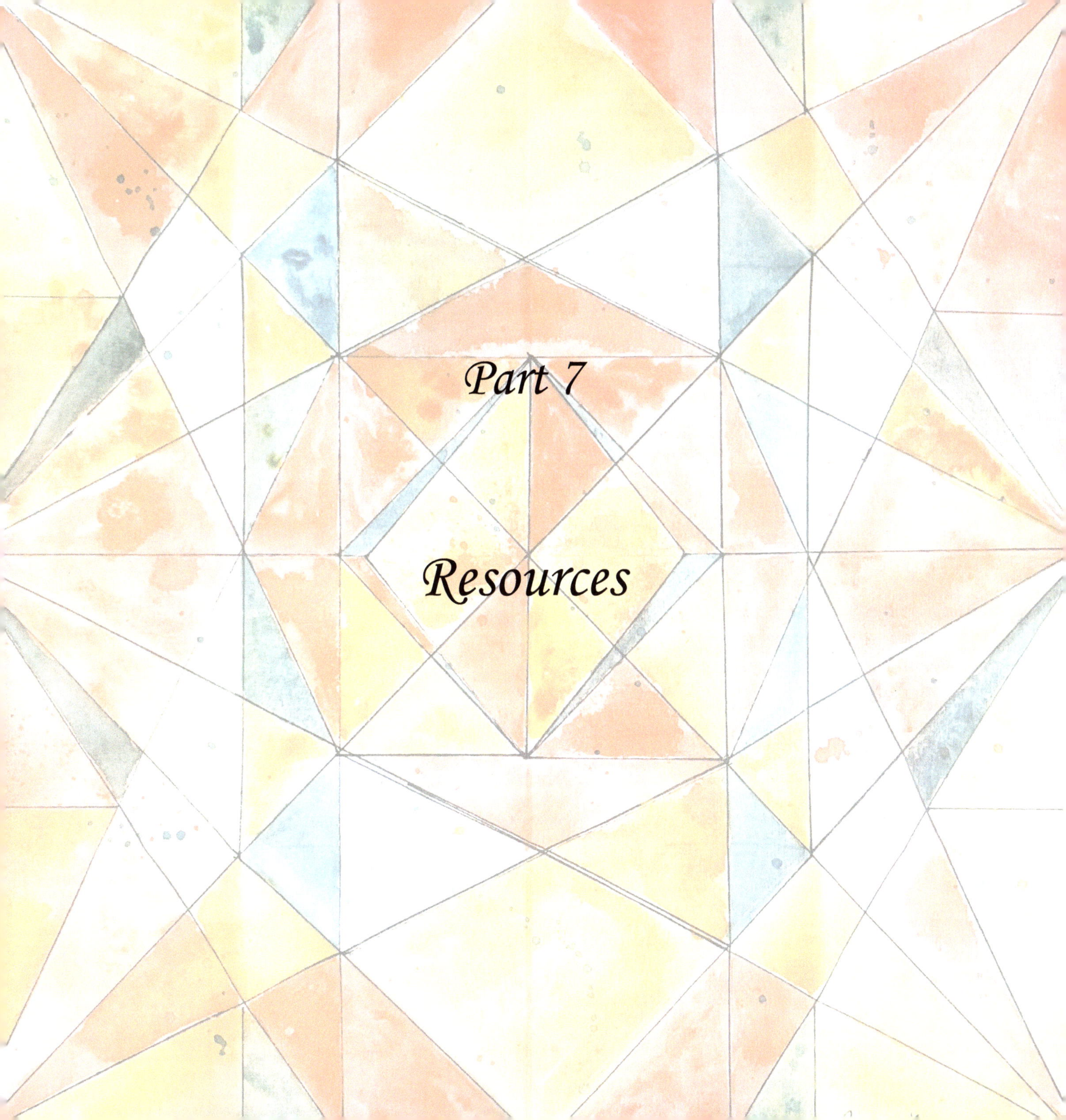

Part 7

Resources

Elements & Principles of Design Comparisons to a Kaleidoscope Reference Guide

When considering the mechanics of a kaleidoscope, there are at least three lengths of mirrors that when connected together, create optical illusions of the items displayed within its borders. These wedged shapes act as boundaries wherein the bits and pieces can bounce at will and create thrilling and everchanging designs. These wedged mirrored walls are similar to the principles of design and remain constant and dependable

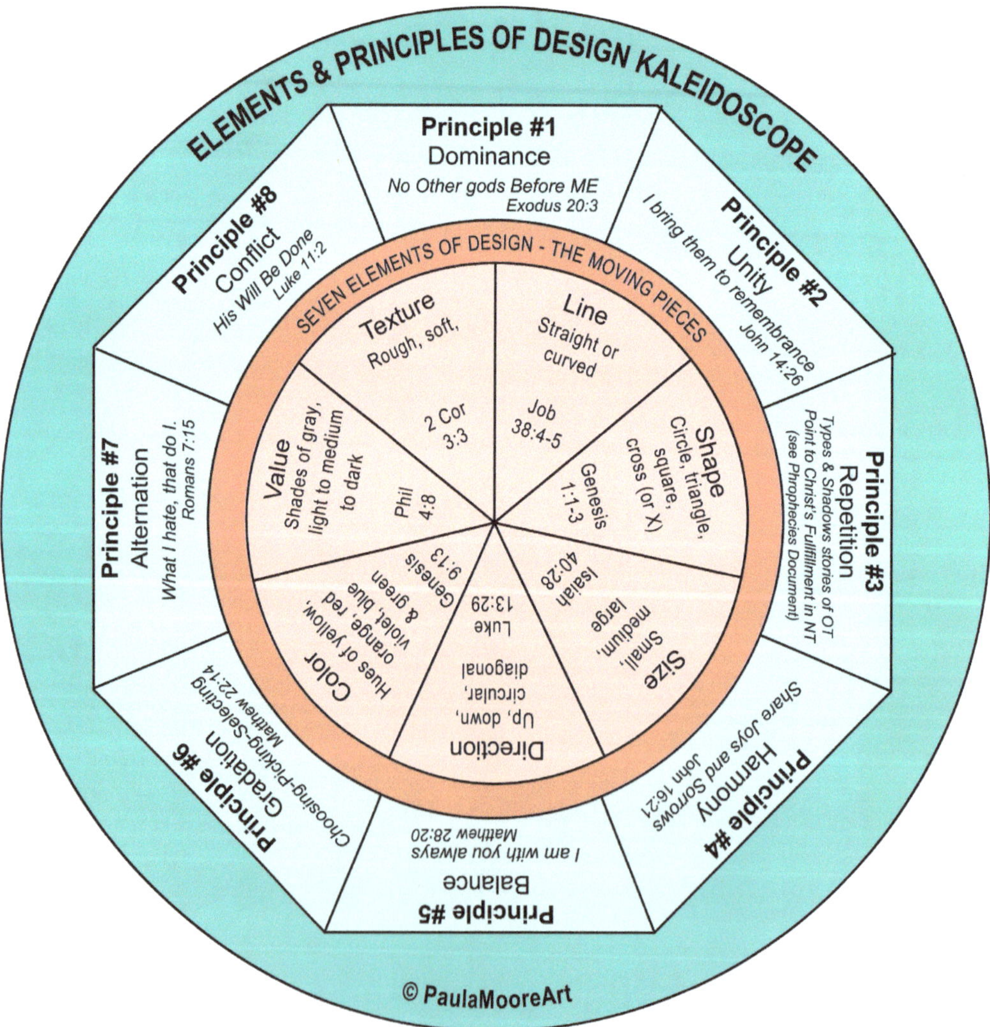

The eight principles of design are: Dominance, Unity, Repetition, Harmony, Balance, Gradation, Alternation, Conflict.

There are volumes of art theory books with detailed definitions and descriptions and I encourage you to continue learning more about the design language. (I recommend Jane E. Jones "Creativity Through Design" co-authored by Jane E. Jones and Linda Franklin, available on Amazon.) For my reference guide sheet, I am giving simplistic explanations of each individual principle. By associating each principle with a known familiar concept, you will begin to comprehend the language of design.

Consider the following examples:

Dominance – A prevailing wind, an influential individual, a prominent facial feature

Unity – Everyone is getting along. Think ingredients in a blender thoroughly mixed together.

Repetition – A rhythm, a repeat pattern is evident such as footprints in the sand or clouds in the sky.

Harmony – A pleasing melody made up of a variety of musical notes.

Balance – Think of a flamingo confidently standing on one foot. Weighted scales moving up when fruit is placed on the other side.

Gradation – A gradual transition of a beautiful sunrise moving seamlessly from one color to the next.

Alternation Think braiding a little girl's long braid or weaving a basket over and under. A bird singing out a few notes over and over again.

Conflict – Everyone agrees except for a few individuals. Two appointments scheduled at the same time.

The seven elements of design are: Line, Shape, Size, Direction, Color, Value, Texture

Continuing with my vision of a spinning kaleidoscope, consider these seven elements as the bits and pieces of colors and shapes contained within the enclosed compartment of one end of the cylinder. The miniscule bits by themselves may seem to represent nothing as they float randomly within their confines. However, when spinning together, the spectacular bursts of designs are mesmerizing! It is a simple yet complex invention that can be enjoyed by adults and children alike.

Consider the following examples:

(The first three elements are used when drawing.)

Line – Straight or curved.

Shape – The five basic shapes include circle, triangle, square, cross (or X), and spiral

Size – Small, medium, large

Direction – Up, down, circular, diagonal

Color – Hues of yellow, orange, red, violet, blue and green

Value – Shades of gray, light to medium to dark

Texture – Rough, soft, smooth

Methodically considering each element, what does your painting "say" to you. Are there adjustments that can be made to strengthen your painting?

In this beginning phase of my painting, I had chosen Red Orange, Blue and Yellow as my color theme, Red Orange being the dominant (more) color in my painting. Of course, what is going to naturally happen is that I will also see shades of light greens (blue+yellows), light yellow orange (yellow+red orange). I am working only with light values of my colors and avoiding making grey, dull values at this point. (i.e. blue+orange).

Although I'm obviously not finished with my work, I stop here and look at my painting against the kaleidoscope guide. (Much like we would take a look at the road map to make sure we were on the right road.)

Note: This process will take longer in the beginning as you are training your artist's mind eye to "see". Soon, it will be more automatic where improvements can be made!

Spin around the kaleidoscope guide with me!

For each element ask yourself do I have the design principle? The painting answers back.

Let's look at the design element of Line on the next page.

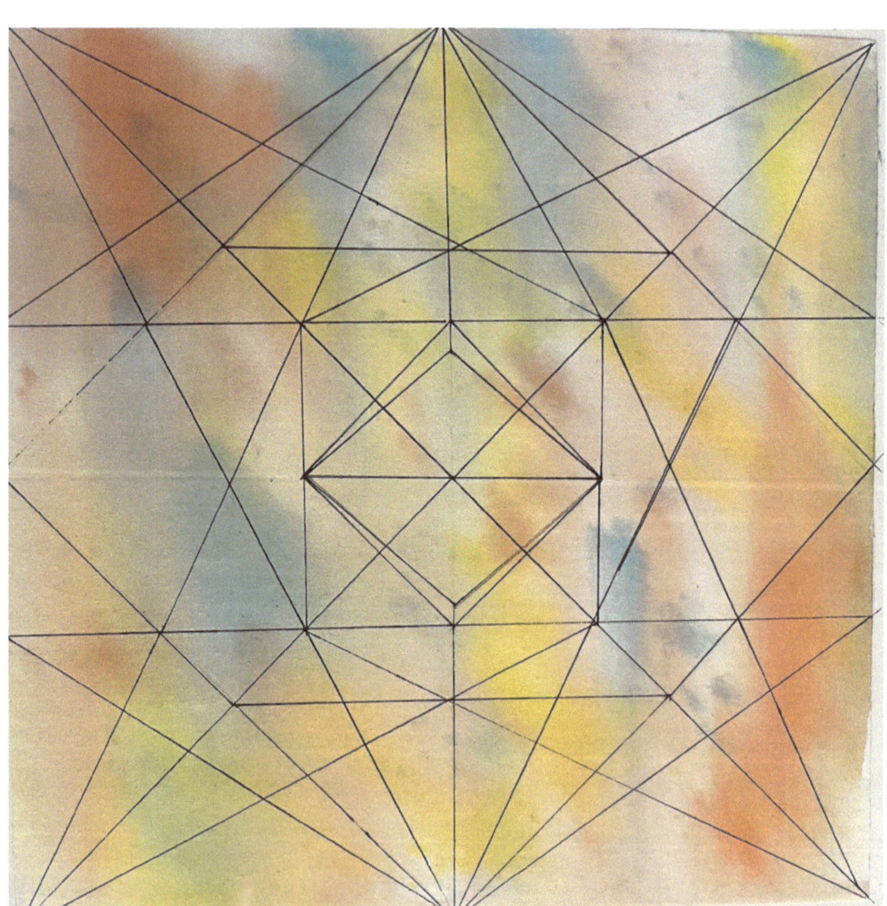

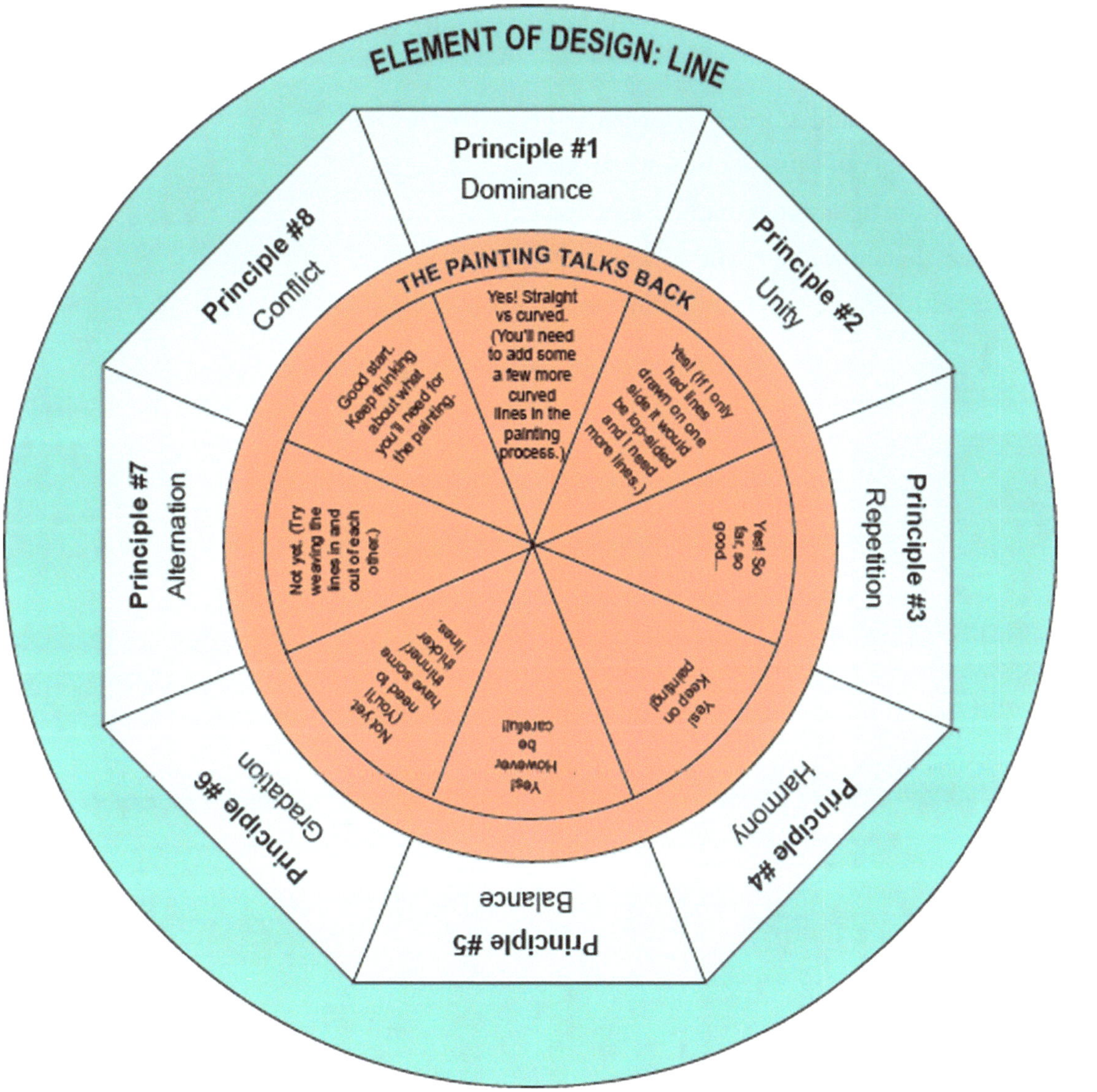

ELEMENT OF DESIGN: LINE

Principle #1
Dominance

Principle #2
Unity

Principle #3
Repetition

Principle #4
Harmony

Principle #5
Balance

Principle #6
Gradation

Principle #7
Alternation

Principle #8
Conflict

THE PAINTING TALKS BACK

Yes! Straight vs curved. (You'll need to add some a few more curved lines in the painting process.)

Yes! (If I only had lines drawn on one side it would be lop-sided and I need more lines.)

Yes! So far, so good...

Yes! Keep on painting!

Yes! However be careful!

Not yet (You'll need to have some thinner/ thicker lines.

Not yet. (Try weaving the lines in and out of each other.)

Good start. Keep thinking about what you'll need for the painting.

I make notes that I need to still work on Gradation, Alternation and Conflict. The other principles are set in place and will be strengthened as I paint.

At this juncture, I would do the same exercise with the other elements. Color, Shape, Size, Value, Direction and Texture.

I continue to paint and stop again anytime I want to check the progress. I usually stop when my values are moving from light values to middle values.

Can you see that how the painting has progressed? I have added more color and some spattering to it. Also, more lines to creating an interesting pattern. I still don't know the final outcome. I'm trusting the process.

Let's do the self-critique Kaleidoscope exercise with the Element of Color on the next page.

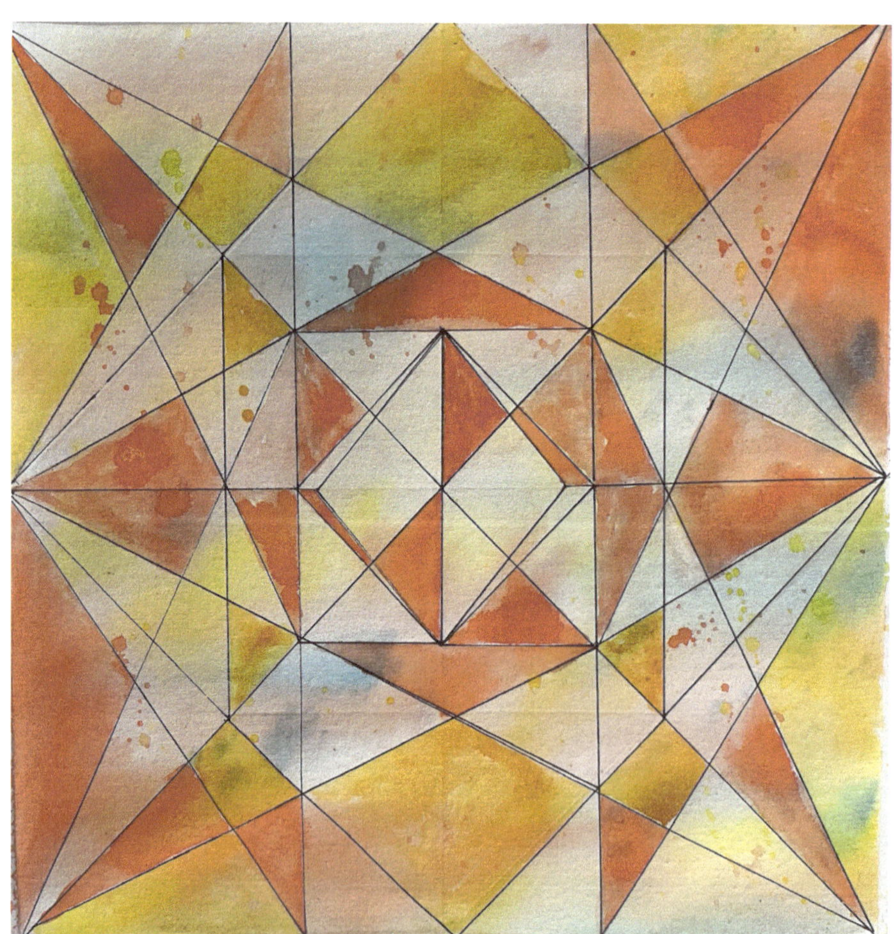

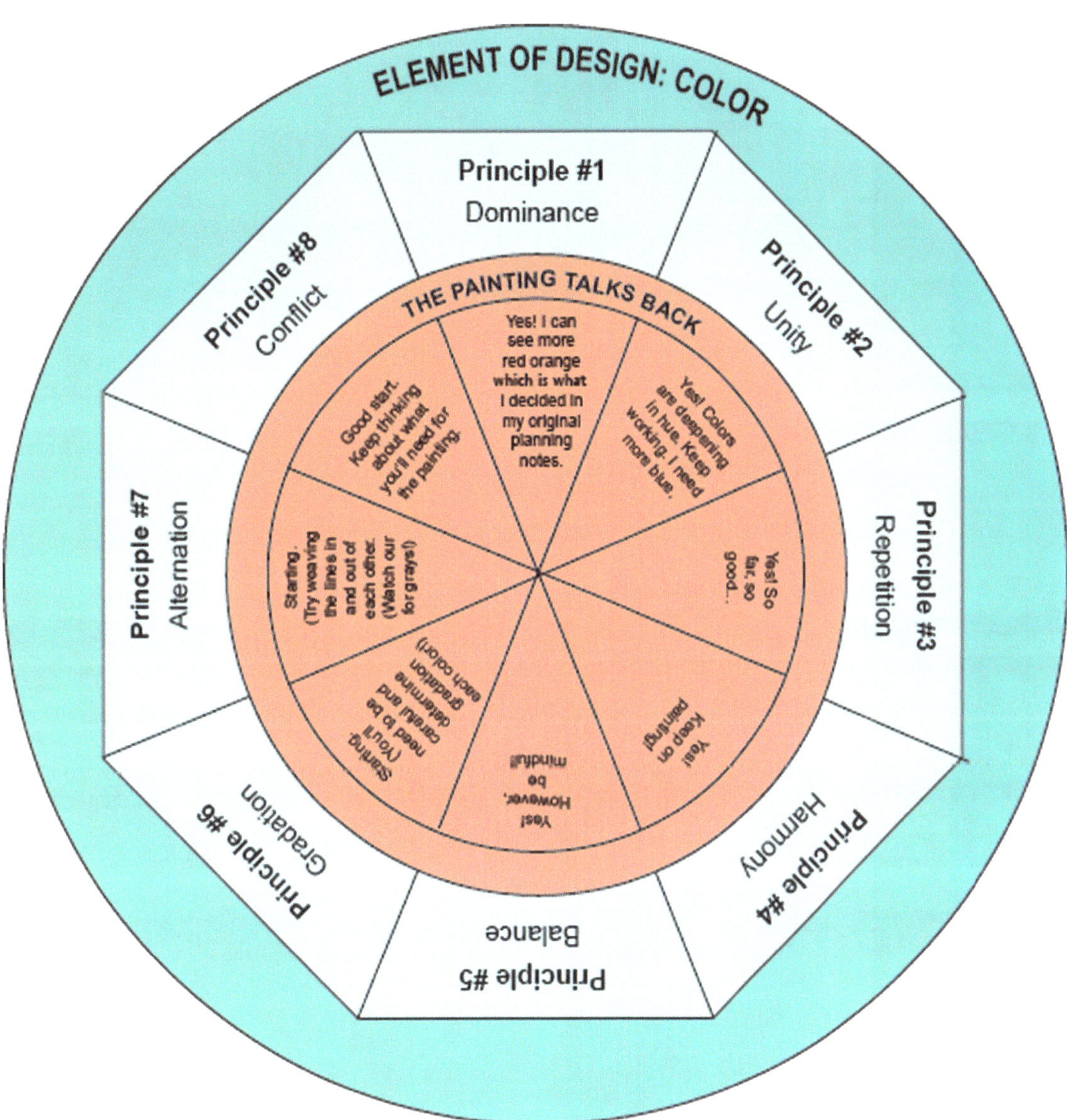
ELEMENT OF DESIGN: COLOR
Principle #1
Dominance
Principle #2
Unity
Principle #3
Repetition
Principle #4
Harmony
Principle #5
Balance
Principle #6
Gradation
Principle #7
Alternation
Principle #8
Conflict
THE PAINTING TALKS BACK
Yes! I can see more red orange which is what I decided in my original planning notes.
Yes! Colors are deepening in hue. Keep working. I need more blue.
Yes! So far, so good...
Yes! Keep on painting!
Yes! However, be mindful!
Starting. (You'll need to be careful and determine gradation each color.)
Starting. (Try weaving the lines in and out of each other. (Watch our for grays!)
Good start. Keep thinking about what you'll need for the painting.

Here is my final kaleidoscope painting! I invite you to take each seven element tools of design around the eight principle of design self-critique kaleidoscope.

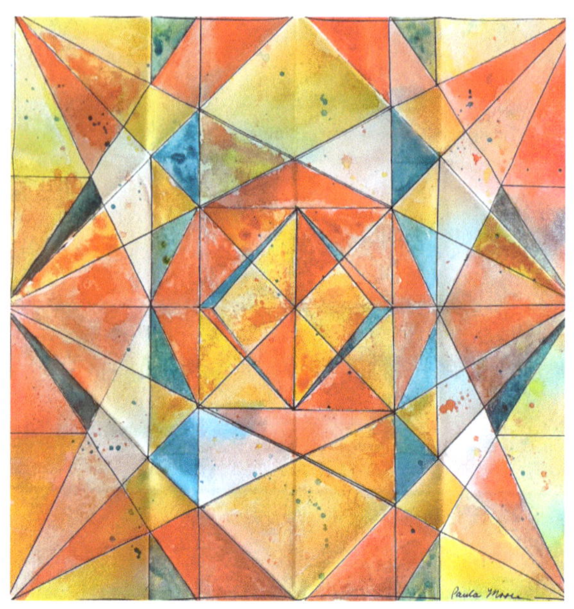

Here are a few photos of my kaleidoscope folded in several different ways. The language of design continues to shine through these folded kaleidoscope variations.

Can you find each of these elements of design? Line – Shape – Size – Direction - Value – Color and Texture

Can you determine the eight principles of design? Unity – Dominance – Repetition – Harmony – Balance –Gradation – Alternation - Conflict

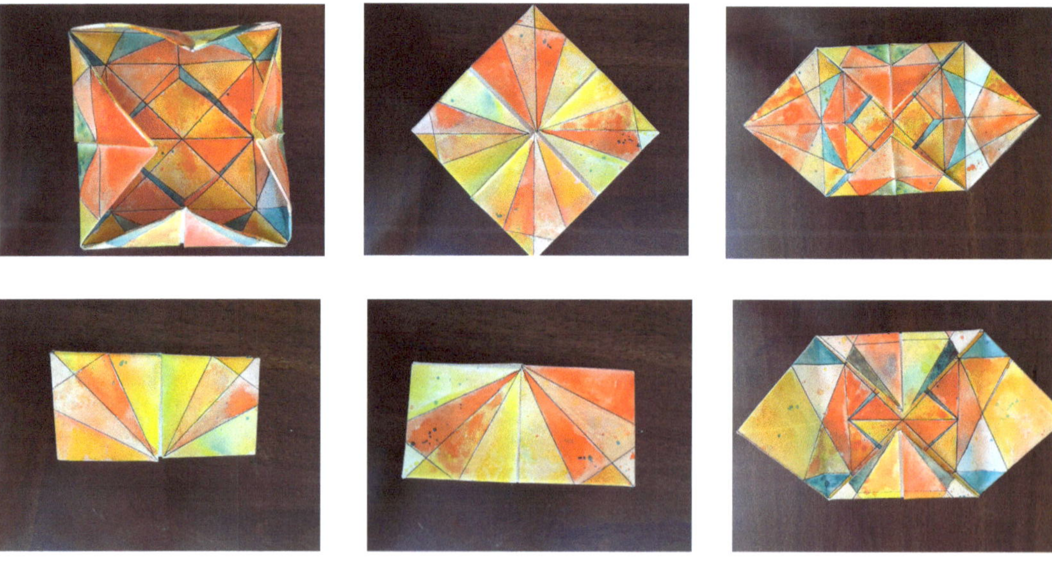

Self-Critique Kaleidoscope Guide

When you take the time to test your efforts through the elements and principles of design, you will experience the satisfaction of creating a successful work of art. The design language remains true no matter which direction your painting is turned.

I so hope you find this Kaleidoscope Reference Guide useful in your own creative endeavors. I suggest making seven blank copies of this guide so that you can analyze each of the seven elements within your painting. Search for them individually to determine where they might be strengthened. Follow this link, https://www.paulamooreart.com/thank-you-gift, for a free full-color pdf version of the guide on my website. Please let me hear from you by commenting on my website, PaulaMooreArt.com. Also, follow me on Facebook.

Keep discovering!

- *Paula L. Moore*

And ye shall seek me and find me when ye shall search for me with all your heart. Jeremiah 29:13

Ask and it shall be given you; seek, and ye shall find. Knock, and it shall be opened unto you. Matthew 7:7

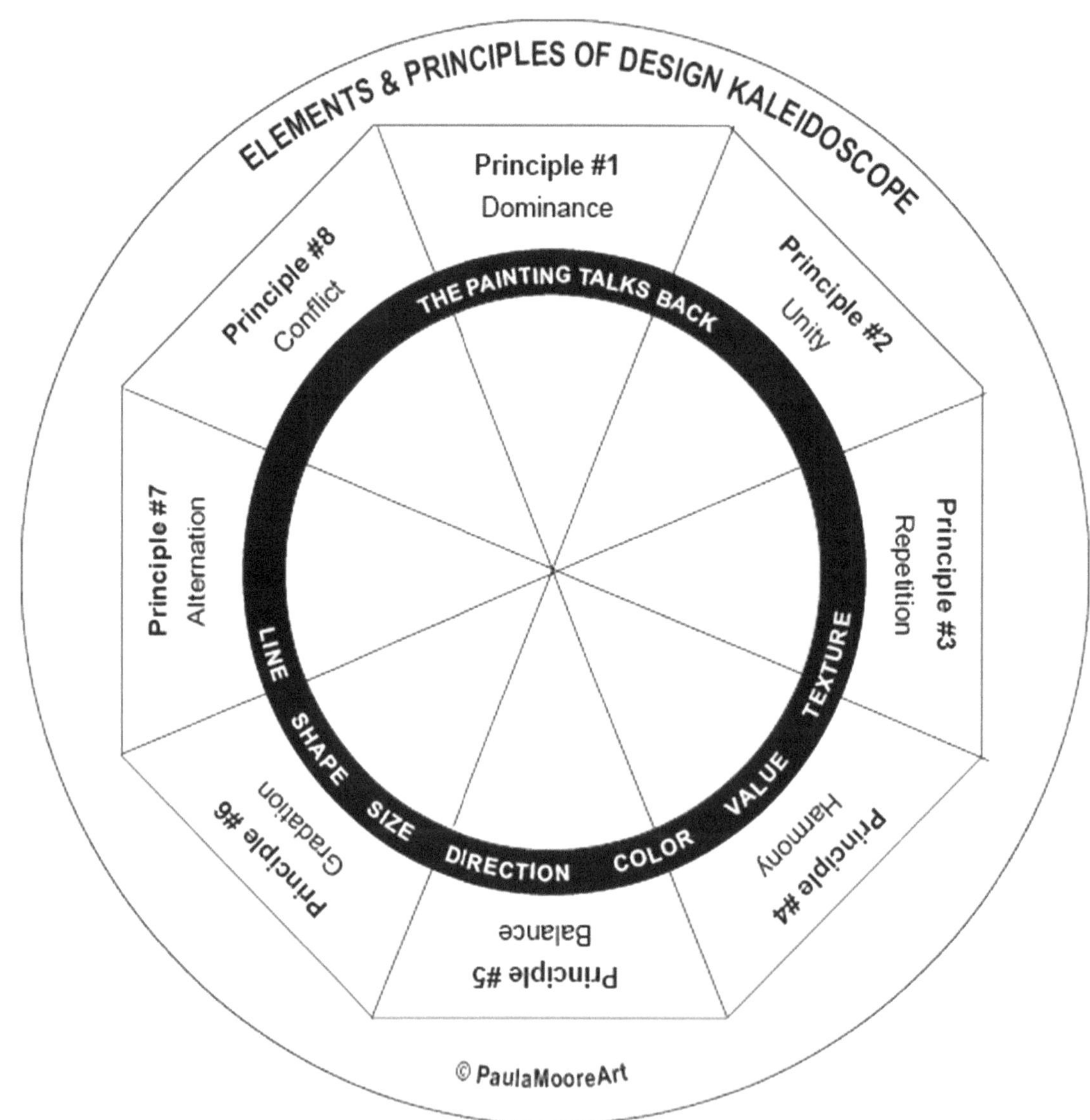
ELEMENTS & PRINCIPLES OF DESIGN KALEIDOSCOPE
Principle #1
Dominance
Principle #2
Unity
Principle #3
Repetition
Principle #4
Harmony
Principle #5
Balance
Principle #6
Gradation
Principle #7
Alternation
Principle #8
Conflict
THE PAINTING TALKS BACK
LINE
SHAPE
SIZE
DIRECTION
COLOR
VALUE
TEXTURE
© PaulaMooreArt

Old Testament Prophecies fulfilled in the New Testament

There are over 1,000 prophecies listed in the Bible. Here are twenty-five of them for you.

Old Testament Prophecy	Event Foretold	New Testament Fulfilled
Genesis 3:15	Seed of a woman	Galatians 4:4
Micah 5:2	Born in Bethlehem	Luke 2:4-5, 7
Isaiah 7:14	To be born of a virgin	Luke 1:26-27, 30-31
Psalm 2:7, Proverbs 30:4	Declared the Son of God	Luke 1:3, Matthew 3:17
Psalm 69:9	The zeal of Jews for the temple instead of God	John 2:17
Isaiah 29:18, Isaiah 35:5-6	Blind, deaf, and the lame are healed by the Messiah	Luke 7:22, Matthew 11:3-5
Isaiah 61:1-2	To bind up the brokenhearted	Luke 4:18-19
Isaiah 53:12, Isaiah 59:16	To intercede for the people	Romans 8:34, Hebrews 7:25
Isaiah 53:1	Not believed	John 12:37-38
Psalm 41:9, Psalm 55:12-13,	Betrayed by a close friend	Luke 22:47-48,
Zechariah 11:12	Betrayed for thirty pieces of silver	Matthew 26:14-15
Isaiah 53:5	Scourged (whipped)	Matthew 27:26

Old Testament Prophecy	Event Foretold	New Testament Fulfilled
Zechariah 12:10, Psalm 22:16	Pierced through hands and feet	John 20:25-27
Psalm 69:21	Given vinegar for his thirst	John 19:28-29
Psalm 22:17-18	Soldiers gambled for his clothing	Matthew 27:35-36
Psalm 22:1	Forsaken by God	Matthew 27:46
Psalm 31:5	Committed his Spirit to God	Luke 23:46
Psalm 38:11	Friends stood afar off	Luke 23:49
Psalm 34:20	No bones broken	John 19:32, 33,36
Amos 8:9	Darkness over the land	Matthew 27:45
Psalm 16:10, Psalm 30:3, Psalm 49:15, Psalm 118:17	To be resurrected	Mark 16:6-7
Isaiah 44:3, Joel 2:2	Sent the Holy Spirit	John 20:22, Acts 2:16-17
Isaiah 55:3-4, Jeremiah 31:31	Establishes a new covenant	Matthew 26:28, Luke 22:20, Hebrews 8:6-10
Psalm 68:18, Psalm 110:1	His ascension and seated by God's right hand	Mark 16:191, 1 Corinthians 15:4, Ephesians 4:8
Zechariah 14:3	Jesus Returning	Revelation 16:18-21

Acknowledgments

These pages could not have been written without the loving support of the following people.

My loving husband, Terry, who honored that this calling was of great importance to me, I am grateful for your patience and serving all those wonderful suppers, allowing me the time to complete this book.

Mike Rowan, our adult Sunday school instructor, planted the seed of possibility that the language of art design was evident in every facet of God, the Great Creator's message to us!

My sister, Krista Nebel, for her patience in reading my writings repeatedly. (Thank you for not using the red butcher pen for the many corrections.)

The following dear friends cheered me on to write my heart out. Kay Johnson, Suzi Agee, Mary Parks, Lynnette Horn, LaDonna Greiner, Linda Franklin, Alicia Farris, and Emily Russell, one of my original His Art for Youth students. It was Emily who validated my inkling of an idea to launch His Art Youth Ministry. I was humbled when she asked me if she could read my manuscript.

Thanks go to LaDonna Greiner, https://barnsbackroads.com, for her photography of the stain-glassed kaleidoscopes. I so appreciate my webmaster and friend, Melissa Winebrenner, with Winebrenner Designs, https://winebrennerdesigns.com for her assistance.

To Bethany Stephenson, owner of Designs by Bethany, https://designsbybethany.com, for her creative design advice. I'm honored to have both of your sons in my His Art for Youth classes. They kept me on my spiritual toes!

To Debra Butterfield for her design work, knowing which button to push first during my publishing endeavor, https://themotivationaleditor.com.

My wonderful daughter, Mackenzie, for her unique insight. My daughter-in-love, Amy, for graciously reading my manuscript.

My mother, Helen Roberts, bought box after box of crayons, baskets of coloring books, and my first kaleidoscope. She continues to cheer me on.

To the precious memories of my dad, Paul H. Roberts: his loving gentleness continues to inspire us. I know he would enjoy looking at this book.

My heartfelt gratitude goes to my dear friend and art mentor, Jane E. Jones. My love and devotion to you are written throughout this book.

Thank you to my church family for your prayers and encouragement.

A special thanks goes to my original His Art Youth Group. I learned so much from you all. As you continue through life, may the His Art messages you learned be ever etched on the pages of your soul.

Most importantly, I thank God, the Creator of the Universe, for the gift of creativity. For Jesus Christ, for thinking of me on the cross as you willingly died for me, knowing I would someday be a tiny jeweled crystal fitted in your plan. To the Holy Spirit for the gentle whispers, encouraging nudges, and patience, and for placing these people in my path. You guided me through this journey of writing my soul's dream purpose. As I offer back my *Kaleidoscope of God's Messages of Truth to Us through the Elements and Principles of Design*, may my heart's pourings be placed into service to further his art in the kingdom.

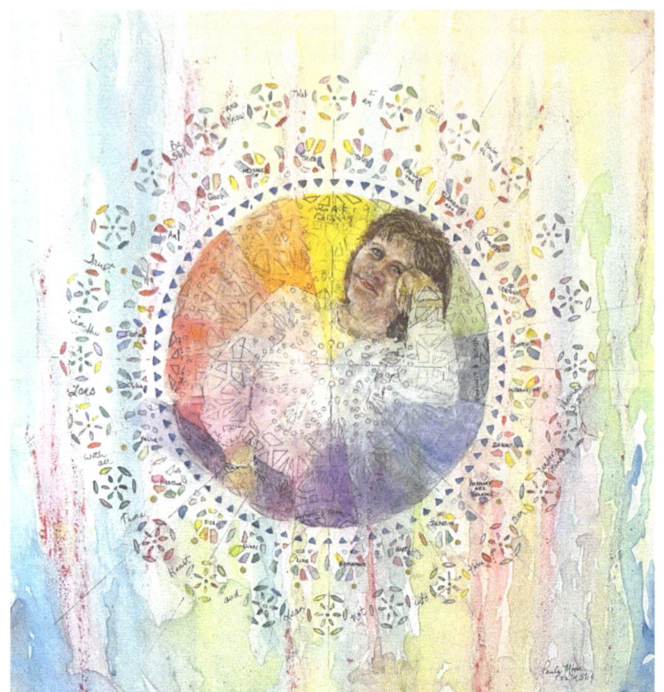

References

Color Wheel and Value Finder: Permission was granted to use images. The Color Wheel Company, PO Box 130, Philomath, OR 97370 https://colorwheelco.com

Boggs, Robert "The Great Artist" poem

"Perspective." Definition Merriam-Webster Dictionary.com 2011. https://www.merrian-webster.com

"Kaleidoscope." Definition Merriam-Webster Dictionary.com 2011. https://www.merrian-webster.com

"Ponder." Definition Merriam-Webster Dictionary.com 2011. https://www.merrian-webster.com

Photography – Permission obtained: Kitty's Starfish, Kitty Kissel; Tiffany's Progression and Final Kaleidoscope, Tiffany L. Collins; Reference photo for Balancing Act, Jo Dooley; Winding Curves Ahead photo, Terry Moore; Stormy, Jane E. Jones; Black-eyed Susan painting, Debra Gill. All other images are those of the author. Stained-Glass Panel Watercolor Painting by His Art Youth, Canaan Church; Narrow Escape, Roberta Sponseller. Permission granted for use of original stained-glass design by Ron and Lin Shawgo, Ozark Mountain Stain Glass.

Kaleidoscope Photography, contracted through LaDonna Greiner, https://www.barnsbackroads.com

Permission granted by Krista Nebel to photograph glass kaleidoscopes collection.

For Further Reading and Research

Graves, M, *The Art of Color and Design*, McGraw-Hill Book Company, Inc. https://mheducation.com

Jones, J.E., Franklin, L.B. (2023) *Creativity through Design*.

Paris, A., (2008) *Standing at Water's Edge*, New World Library, https://newworldlibrary.com

Raynor, Jordan, (2017) *Called to Create*, Baker Books

Meyer, Joyce, (2002) *The Battlefield of the Mind*, Warren Faith, https://faithwords.com

City of Springfield Art Museum, Watercolor USA Exhibit https://www.sgfmuseum.org

CJ and Shelley Hitz, Kingdom Writers, www.christianbookacademy.com

About the Author

Paula L. Moore, a Missouri award-winning watercolorist, has enjoyed a unique artist journey. After retiring from a banking career, she now enjoys teaching painting workshops locally and in other states. She is grateful for the opportunity to travel the world with her husband, Terry. From an early age, Paula loved creating and taking an occasional class; however, she was a self-taught artist. Her dedication and passion led her to pursue how to improve through searching, asking, listening, and studying how to unlock the door to understanding the intriguing mystery of art! There were a few wonderful mentors along the way who guided Paula until there was a breakthrough. The sudden knowing and envisioning that all art is like a spinning kaleidoscope. All these creative moving pieces, Line, Color, Value, Size, Shape, Direction, and Texture, when held in alignment with the proven design principles of Dominance, Unity, Repetition Harmony, Balance, Gradation, Alternation, and Conflict, fit perfectly together—Every Time.

Paula's most recent calling took a life of its own when the rich parallels of faith and art poured out into a calling to share this concept with others. Since then, Paula recently launched her His Art teaching program for youth, thought-provoking women's Gather and Create Bible studies, retreats, and foreign mission field opportunities.

This is Paula's first nondenominational book. It is an art instruction book and a faith gallery of essays, each providing a unique perspective on how art and faith are one and the same. Plans for faith-based journals, workbooks for His Art Youth ministries, and other exciting ideas are being developed. Paula is an inspirational teacher and speaker and is available for your gathering. Please get in touch with her through her website, https://paulamooreart.com.